THE VIOLENCE OF PETRO-DOLLAR REGIMES

COMPARATIVE POLITICS AND INTERNATIONAL STUDIES SERIES

Series editor, Christophe Jaffrelot

This series consists of translations of noteworthy manuscripts and publications in the social sciences emanating from the foremost French researchers, from Sciences Po, Paris.

The focus of the series is the transformation of politics and society by transnational and domestic factors—globalisation, migration, and the post bipolar balance of power on the one hand, and ethnicity and religion on the other. States are more permeable to external influence than ever before and this phenomenon is accelerating processes of social and political change the world over. In seeking to understand and interpret these transformations, this series gives priority to social trends from below as much as to the interventions of state and non-state actors.

LUIS MARTINEZ

The Violence of Petro-Dollar Regimes

Algeria, Iraq and Libya

Translated by
Cynthia Schoch

HURST & COMPANY, LONDON
*In Association with the Centre d'Etudes et de Recherches
Internationales (CERI), Paris*

First published in the United Kingdom in 2012 by
C. Hurst & Co. (Publishers) Ltd.,
41 Great Russell Street, London, WC1B 3PL
© Luis Martinez, 2012
Translated by Cynthia Schoch
All rights reserved.
Printed in India

A Cataloguing-in-Publication data record for this book
is available from the British Library.

ISBN: 978-1-84904-174-4

This book is printed using paper from registered sustainable
and managed sources.

References to Internet Web sites (URLs) were accurate at the time of
writing. Neither the author nor [Hurst] is responsible for URLs that
may have expired or changed since the manuscript was prepared.

www.hurstpub.co.uk

CONTENTS

v

PREFACE

REVOLUTION AND INSURRECTION: WILL THE DEMOCRATIC WAVE COME UP AGAINST THE OIL RENT?

Revolution in Tunisia and Egypt

In the wake of the unanticipated fall of Tunisia's President, Ben Ali, followed by that of Hosni Mubarak in Egypt, after the outbreak of a surprise protest movement, a fresh look at the stability and future of political regimes in North Africa and the Middle East is required, especially the Tunisian paradox. How can an educated society composed of a middle class and employed in a diversified economy cohabit over time with a brutal and corrupt police regime? The various techniques devised by the Tunisian regime to bring all of the country's political, economic and societal resources under its control provide part of the answer. How did the riots triggered by the immolation of Mohamed Bouazizi, dramatically highlighting the despair of the youth, day labourers, educated and uneducated unemployed, and many others manage to provoke a nationwide frenzy leading to the fall of Ben Ali? Tunisia specialists point to the density of virtual and informal social networks, which helped to politicise the initial social demands expressed in small, inland towns, as well as the role of intellectuals in translating grievances and complaints into a political idiom and then spreading them over a symbolic geographic space—such as the capital—while making the Trabelsi clan into an expiatory victim. The ability to bring socio-economic demands into convergence with political demands in record time—less than a month—was an incredible feat for the Tunisian opposition, which brought the revolt to a political outcome rather than winding up as an umpteenth hunger riot, such as those sparked at the same time in Algeria by the sharp rise in the price of wheat on the international market. Furthermore, although the dynamics of the uprising appeared to be linked to the successful politicisation of social riots based in the capital, the success of the uprising nevertheless hinged on one condition: the army's refusal to fire on the demonstrators.

The Tunisian and Egyptian revolutions offer the opportunity to challenge a certain number of preconceived notions about the region. First of all, that concerning the Islamist threat: for the past two decades the area has been analysed in terms of an Islamist threat to regime stability embodied by movements that are poorly understood as moderates and partisans of Al-Qaeda are often deliberately confused. The risk of Islamists intruding as actors in political institutions served to justify the deprivation of political freedoms and the repression of opponents. The fear of seeing post-colonial regimes set up Islamic states meant that democracies allied themselves with the region's police and authoritarian regimes. Adopting this concern as its own, the EU has sought to promote stability and security in the framework of various accords with countries in the region, rather than promote respect for human rights and encourage the establishment of democratic regimes. Its disinclination to open a dialogue with civil society reveals its strategy of furthering the region's political development at the level of its political leaders only, even though they are rarely elected democratically. Against all expectations, these movements, far from been spurred by Islamist organisations, have risen in flagrant contradiction to the presumptions of the security obsession. Having disregarded social evolutions and lent too much credence in the theories of an Islamist threat, the EU and the United States are discovering that a dynamic and courageous civil society is taking the risk to defy a regime considered as solid, not with an aim to establish an Islamic state, but a democratic regime. Will the Tunisian and Egyptian experiences manage to generate a domino effect in the region? Are the conditions favourable for the emergence of a demand for democracy in the Arab world? In the name of democracy, the revolts in Tunis and Cairo ended up running out two discredited chiefs of state. What seemed unimaginable and unthinkable not long ago has happened.

Insurrection in Libya

The Iraqi experience under Saddam Hussein shows that domestic pressure and intimidation from the outside have little effect on an authoritarian oil regime, convinced that it has no other choice than to destroy its adversaries in order to survive. The revolutions in the Arab world provide an opportunity to test the hypothesis of the specificity of authoritarian oil regimes. Indeed, Tunisia and Egypt have shown that regimes cannot resort to mass violence to remain in place: their economies, highly dependent on the tourist industry, foreign investment and international aid, would have been wiped out. Sacrificing the head of state and his political party seems to be an exit route that will help restore the degree of stability needed for the economy to pick up again. In both Libya and Algeria, 95 per cent of the regimes' external revenues come from hydrocarbon sales; imposing an embargo on oil sales would amount to fostering speculation on fears related to the oil supply, leading to a rise in oil prices. Revolts and riots have only limited impact on this type of regime, international press campaigns are ignored and international sanctions easily circumvented. The overthrow of the Qadhafi regime reinforces the hypothesis that outside help is necessary to the successful pursuit of political change in authoritarian oil regimes.

The Libyan uprising demonstrates that the fear the regime inspired in its opponents has been overcome, particularly in the area of Cyrenaica; in Tripolitania, fierce repression was used to spread terror and to inhibit protest attempts. The Jamahiriyya deprived the population of political freedom. Aware of the difficulty of maintaining such archaic structures of domination, Seif el-Islam had experimented with relative liberalisation between 2007 and 2009. The regime's hardliners, however, put an end to these attempts. The uprising began in the east and pushed the regime to the verge of collapse, prompting it to use force against the rebels in an attempt to survive. Cut in two, the east of Libya came under the control of the interim National Council for Libya (NCL) while the west remained under the domination of Muammar Qadhafi's forces until August 2011.

Today's Libya was fashioned by Italian colonial rule (1912–1943), which unified the three regions of Cyrenaica, Tripolitania and Fezzan. From 1951 to 1969, the country was administered by a monarchy. King Idriss, from the Senussiyya tribal confederation, made El Bayda in Cyrenaica his capital. With the coup led by Muammar Qadhafi in 1969, a small tribe from the Sirte region, the Qadhafa, managed to take control of the state's resources. Sirte became the capital, and Tripoli provided administrative and political support. Benghazi reverted to the state. The new regime considered Cyrenaica as the cradle of the monarchy and counterrevolutionaries. This regional antagonism has remained strong. Hence, when the city of Benghazi fell into rebel hands on 20 February, the former flag of the monarchy reappeared. Ensured of the population's support in Cyrenaica, the rebels, from Nasserian, monarchist, Islamist and democratic movements, were united in their determination to bring down one of the oldest dictatorships in the region.

On 1 September 2011, Moustapha Abdeljallil announced the end of the revolutionary interlude in Libya and the start of the transition to democracy. Less than a month later, doubt persisted about the ability of insurgents to overcome a system that, despite the NATO bombing, was able to maintain its position. Unable to move the front lines, the fear of stagnation dominated the general perception. The assassination of General Abdel Fatah Younes, head of the rebel army, on 28 July only increased this sense of anxiety. When, on 17 August, the CNT indicated its roadmap in Tripoli, Seif el Islam and the government spokesman mocked those who planned to overthrow them, even though they had not been able to move for months. At the same time in Djerba, Tunisia, mysterious negotiations took place between government members, representatives of the CNT, and emissaries of Venezuela, all denied by the parties involved, yet a few days later, Operation Sirene was launched. In less than 48 hours, the rebels entered and took Tripoli Green Square. Cleary much of the discussion in Djerba must have focused on the defection of some of the regime's security forces, leaving the way to Green Square open. Muammar Qadhafi's bodyguards lay down their arms, suggesting that Muammar Qadhafi was no longer in the capital. Coincidentally, this is when the Libyan regime's former second in command (in the 1980s), Commander Jallud, managed to escape to Rome. From there he called on members of the tribe of Qadhafi that same evening to dissociate themselves from their leader, trying to preserve their future in the new Libya. So against all odds, the conflict that had seemed to freeze and threaten a useless stalemate turned into an attack on the capital. Foreign military instructors can savour this victory, where a ragtag group of inexperienced fighters with no strategy became a military force capable, with the help of NATO, of overcoming loyalists and mercenaries. During the six months of the war, the CNT and the rebels have shown that despite many differences, they remained united in their desire to hunt down Muammar Qadhafi and his sons. But will they maintain this unity during the transition phase? Will Islamist fighters continue to obey the authority of the CNT? The challenges of post-Qadhafi Libya are numerous: to "de-Qadhafi-sise" Libya without falling into the excesses of post-Saddam Hussein Iraq; to reconcile Libya; to demilitarize the militias; and to build relationships of trust with the Algerian army, who must feel uneasy in the new situation. However, Libya has many assets to help with these goals: a society eager to show that Libya is not the caricature painted by Muammar Qadhafi, and the considerable financial resources of frozen assets and oil, which were miraculously spared during this war.

Like the Qadhafi regime, Bouteflika's Algeria has the means to resist the wave of democratic protest. Considered to be ailing, weakened and vulnerable, Abdelaziz Bouteflika looks like an easy victim, but this is only because the regime he represents has assets it can use to resist a democratic tidal wave. First, the Interior Ministry has considerable experience in handling demonstrations, riots and revolts. Since the 1980s, Algeria has been rocked by revolts. Police ranks now number 200,000, they are well equipped and amply funded. At the international level, unlike Tunisia and Egypt, Algeria has an oil rent that makes it immune to any pressure that the international community might exert: 10 per cent of the EU's natural gas supplies come from Algeria. The country does not depend on the tourist industry or rent from the Suez Canal for its resources; it does not receive the type of aid that the United States army supplies to the Egyptian army. Moreover, to avoid the fate of its neighbours, since January 2011 the Algerian government has been redistributing a portion of the oil rent through salary increases for all its civil servants in order to ensure their loyalty.

The surfacing of civil society in the fight for recognition of political rights comes as a salutary surprise for democratic forces. Since the 1980s, only Islamist organisations (associations, movements and parties) have expressed a protest discourse. Although their radicalism found resonance among the masses, it deprived them of support from democratic movements, which worried that popular protest would serve as a springboard for the establishment of an Islamic state. The failure of the Algerian transition was full of lessons for all: the collapse of the FLN-state brought in tow not the success of political forces bearing a democratic project but the Front Islamique du Salut (Islamic Salvation Front) and its plan to set up an Islamic state. By placing their support behind the army to "save the nation" from the "Islamist peril," democratic parties at the time were considerably discredited in the eyes of the population and went through a long period in the wilderness. Unable to convey a credible discourse, often due to their connivance with the authoritarian regimes, the democratic forces became prisoners of the security paradigm. After 11 September 2001, the "War on Terror" lent the region's authoritarian regimes legitimacy on the international scene: Libya, Algeria, Egypt and Tunisia offered their services to allay the threat posed by Al-Qaeda. During the first decade of 2000, only human rights organisations managed to resist the security rationale and denounce the flagrant human rights violations perpetrated in the name of the "War on Terror". For many of them, this remained a combat in vain, as the major democratic nations were so overcome by the fear of terrorism that they accepted regressions in respect for human rights in exchange for increased investment in security. Blinded by their fear of terrorism, democracies put a damper on their values.

The peaceful protests calling for democracy offer a compelling counterweight to these preconceptions. Nevertheless, the hardest task for societies in the Arab world is yet to come. The regional and international context is changing. Islamist organisations are no longer the only ones to voice denunciation of authoritarian regimes. A convergence of views is looming: the revelations on Wikileaks highlight awareness and recognition of criticisms levelled at the regimes. Their weakening is not a guarantee of a successful democratic transition. Thus, in Tunisia, the challenge now is to turn the revolution into a democratic regime, in other words set up institutions that guarantee that the new system will endure, despite sabotage by the former regime's hatchet men and regional pressure. In Egypt, the army opened doors to dialogue with the opposition; it has made slight concessions on the constitutional level and made a few commitments as regards its democratic agenda. Army dignitaries know that even if in the short run abandoning Mubarak immediately alleviated the pressure on the domestic level, they also know that a democratic post-Mubarak era could be shaped in opposition to the political system they have made their fortune from. The army in both Tunisia and Egypt have become the de facto guarantors and guardians of the transition, but it is unclear if they are prepared to protect political transactions that are meant to lead to a democratic agenda. Several conditions must be met so that both armies play by the rules of democratic transition. First, the degree of incertitude that integration of new political actors on the scene will inspire must be reduced (such as the Muslim Brotherhood in Egypt and the Renaissance Party in Tunisia). Second, the spokespersons of the revolt must make the protestors realise that compromises will have to be made with members of the former regime to guarantee the army's impunity; the army will accept the sacrifice of the presidents and the discredit of the presidential parties, provided they do not become the scapegoats of a nascent political system. Furthermore, negotiations cannot go on forever because of economic and financial contingencies; Egypt and Tunisia both depend on the tourist industry, and the confidence of foreign investors. For the armies, the transition is a frightening process because they are not in control: they want guarantees because if the process derails, they will have to confront the ensuing chaos. The unexpected fall of Ben Ali and Hosni Mubarak inspired a wave of enthusiasm in the area, bringing the hope of seeing other regimes rapidly collapse.

For the West, the democratic revolution in the Arab world amounts to a strategic surprise on a par with the fall of the Berlin Wall. After considerable hemming and hawing, the EU seems to have changed its operating system: fear of Islamism can no longer justify the impossibility of democratizing the region. Regimes faced with the democratic tidal wave will now be encouraged to change in order to take on board legitimate demands. From this standpoint, Tunisia's experience will prove fundamental: if Tunisia manages to make the necessary compromises to set up democratic institutions, it will demonstrate that political radicalism in the region belongs to the past and will serve as a model. If it happens to fail due to intransigence on any or all sides, it will awaken the old demons of discord and join the long list of failed political transitions. Similarly, will the Libyan insurgency lead to the beginning of a transition to democracy or the start of a violent cycle? The example of Iraq under Saddam Hussein, as well as Algeria after the failed political transition in the 1990s, does not augur well for a peaceful outcome. This book shows how the oil rent in the context of an authoritarian regime has been conducive to the use of violence against its society, and the tragedies in Libya unfortunately show the violent nature of oil regimes.

11 December 2011

INTRODUCTION

OIL CAN'T BUY HAPPINESS

Between 1970 and 2000, Algeria, Libya and Iraq, all endowed with considerable hydrocarbon resources,[1] despite the best of intentions, wasted most of their revenues on commercial and military projects, the consequences of which have been disastrous. Exhausted and ruined after thirty years of random experimenting, these three countries rediscovered the advantages of their past wealth with the third oil crisis (2003–08).[2] Oddly enough, though, this renewed wealth did not inspire the enthusiasm one might have expected, unlike the two prior oil crises (1973, 1979). A few decades ago, black gold was viewed as the weapon of mass destruction that would make it possible to overcome underdevelopment, imperialism and Zionism. But in 2008, reactions were extremely lukewarm, even as the price of oil approached $150 per barrel in July 2008. What happened? Has the magic of petroleum disappeared?

Algeria, Libya and Iraq have demonstrated unusual caution in the face of this beneficial financial tidal wave that within the space of five years enabled them to accumulate substantial dollar reserves again (in 2008, Algeria held $140 billion, Libya $100 billion and Iraq $40 billion).[3] In fact, since the very beginning of the decade, these countries' populations had already come to believe that oil is a curse. From 1970 to 2000, the oil rent had produced wealth but no true economic development. Many people thus view the return of financial abundance with circumspection. The rise in per-barrel oil prices since 2003 has no doubt enabled the Algerian, Iraqi and Libyan regimes to shed the opprobrium heaped upon them since

1

the 1990s and made them attractive markets again. However, this new financial windfall did not awaken among the people a belief in the oil illusion. For the "people", oil does not buy happiness. Although these countries have enjoyed an oil rent since the early 1970s, it has not particularly improved the welfare of their inhabitants, at least not any more than was achieved by non-oil authoritarian regimes. The human development indicators for Algeria, Iraq and Libya are not especially different from those for Tunisia, Morocco or Syria. In 1992, Syria ranked 79th whereas Iraq was 100th, Libya 26th when Tunisia was 27th, Algeria 109th just ahead of Morocco in 111th place. In 2000, Morocco devoted 4.8 per cent of its GDP to health expenditure whereas Algeria's health spending was 3.5 per cent, and Tunisia's was 5.6 per cent compared to 3.5 per cent in Libya.[4] As A. Mebtoul points out, this ranking would make a country like Algeria drop back by 20 points if hydrocarbons were excluded in calculating GDP (this is also true of Iraq and Libya).[5] Algeria, ranked 102nd (out of 177) in 2005–06, would thus fall back to 153rd place.

Moreover, between 1974 and 2004, the annual growth rates of Morocco (1.4 per cent), Tunisia (2.3 per cent) and Syria (1.1 per cent) were higher than those for Algeria (0.1 per cent), Iraq and Libya.[6] Thus, in 2004, Libya's GDP ($29.1 billion) was scarcely higher than Tunisia's ($28.2 billion); Syria's GDP ($24 billion) was greater than Iraq's ($21.1 billion).[7] Only Algeria's GDP ($80 billion in 2004) was greater than Morocco's ($50 billion). However, in 2000, a National Economic and Social Council report[8] highlighted the fact that 19 per cent of the population, or nearly 6 million people, lived in poverty. It also pointed to the serious threat represented by an unemployment rate varying between 22 per cent and 28 per cent, which could pose a serious threat to stability. In Iraq, the final years of Saddam Hussein's rule were characterised by a tragic humanitarian situation and the disintegration of society while the severity of the sanctions placed the state in danger.[9] In Libya, the social situation constantly deteriorated throughout the 1990s. The government estimated the unemployment rate to be 11 per cent in 2000, but many observers evaluated it at closer to 30 per cent. In such a context, characterised by a total lack of future prospects, most young people wanted nothing better than to emigrate.

In addition, on the eve of the third oil crisis, the governments' room for financial manoeuvre was limited because of the debt. In Algeria, debt servicing absorbed the equivalent of 47.5 per cent of foreign resources in 2000. In Iraq, the debt hovered around $100 billion. In Libya, it was the inflation rate, not the debt, that was the largest concern, being in the neighbourhood of 200 per cent during the 1990s.[10] Such an assessment prompted Muammar Qadhafi to ask whether it had been "worth making forty years of sacrifice... Unfortunately, those who carried out the Revolution were neither scholars nor experts. They were mere revolutionaries. Some of us did not even know how to read and write! Others did not even have a secondary school degree. We were nothing but illiterate noncommissioned officers!"[11]

Certainly, thanks to oil prices, between 1973 and 1985, the high growth rates these countries showed sometimes doubled their GDP. But over time, this wealth did not materialise as an improvement in the general population's overall welfare. What factors can explain this paradox? Does the resource curse theory help to understand the trajectory these three countries have followed? If it does, how is it that oil and gas sales are not detrimental to Norway, for instance?[12] By the same token, why has Indonesia managed to escape this curse[13] and join the club of "oil democracies"[14] whereas Algeria, Iraq and Libya have failed?

In search of the resource curse

The abundant literature on the oil curse seeks to explain the paradox between bountiful natural resources and weak economic performance. The theory was formulated in the 1970s taking the Netherlands as an example. Dutch manufacturing industries in fact collapsed in the wake of natural gas exports, which raised the cost of labour as well as the value of the guilder. The theory has spawned a host of analyses of "the rentier state", which has become a commonly used explanation for weak or absent democracy.[15] A more sophisticated model has shown how the exploitation of bountiful resources in a state with weak democratic institutions is likely to produce irreversible perverse outcomes.[16] Oil, natural resources and raw materials more generally also emerged as the primary cause of violence and civil war.[17] In reaction to these studies, perceived to be analytical oversimplifications, a body of critical literature has emphasized that it is impossible to boil down phenomena as complex as violence, civil war and the lack of democracy to a single causal variable.[18]

Like other OPEC members, between 1970 and 2000 Algeria, Libya and Iraq experienced lower than world average economic growth, thereby confirming the inefficiency of rentier economies. These countries, depending almost exclusively on hydrocarbon exports, would not only suffer from fluctuations on the world energy market, but also see their domestic market reduced to a warehouse filled with imported goods and products. On the political level, these three countries (Iraq until 2003) were confronted with the "authoritarian syndrome" seen in all the Arab countries, whether they produce oil or not.[19] They therefore do not differ from the other countries in the region. On the other hand, they differ from them in their relationship to violence, in particular in the development of conflicts, even civil wars. Research carried out by Collier and Hoeffler, for instance, reveals that between 1960 and 1999, out of a 161-country sample, 79 civil wars took place in countries endowed with abundant natural resources: "The effect of primary commodity exports is considerable: at the risk-maximizing value of the primary commodity export share (0.32), the risk of civil war is about 22 per cent, while a country with no natural resource exports only has a probability of a war-start of one percent".[20] The theory of a correlation between natural resources and civil war is also supported by other research. This economistic approach, which views resource abundance as the primary risk factor in countries that experienced conflicts in the 1990s, is the one that would hold the attention of international institutions in search of solutions. This approach offered a simple explanation for the causes of conflicts and their duration. However, the arguments are less than convincing.[21]

The resource curse theory has raised a number of criticisms. Not only does it overly simplify phenomena as complex as armed conflict and civil wars, but it reduces historical and political factors to a marginal explanatory role with regard to economic determinants,[22] even though such factors are fundamental. As Ross points out, "The natural resource-civil war correlation could be spurious: both civil war and resource dependence might be independently caused by some unmeasured third variable, such as the weak rule of law".[23] As a result, it is the absence of democratic mechanisms for redistributing the oil rent that becomes decisive. Nevertheless, in a study of twenty-two oil-producing countries between 1960 and 1999, Ross noted that thirteen of them had to contend with separatist movements precisely in the areas where oil reserves lay.[24] With regard to this correlation, the sociology of conflicts suggests that historically, "rebel greed" is not motivated only by profit. It holds that the violence of separatist movements is instead an instrument of regulation, even negotiation with the authorities. The case of Nigeria supports this hypothesis: during the past thirty-five years, cumulative revenue has amounted to $350 billion, but 70 per cent of the population lives on less than $1 per day, and 80 per cent of the oil income benefits only 1 per cent of the population. Thus, populations living in the delta oil fields back the separatist Movement for the Emancipation of the Niger Delta (MEND).[25]

As opposed to advocates of the resource curse theory, the work of Benjamin Smith shows that the oil rent contributes to the longevity of these regimes. He claims that "oil wealth is robustly associated with more durable regimes and significantly related to lower levels of protest and civil war".[26] He thus introduces a statistical correlation between oil wealth and political instability, the latter being the result of oil barrel price fluctuations. But this political instability, in a context of financial and economic crisis, does not necessarily lead to a collapse of authoritarian regimes: "A central tenet of democratic transition studies is that authoritarian regimes are more likely to collapse during economic crises... Yet, a close look at the authoritarian breakdowns that led to the Third Wave transition reveals a suspiciously absent but especially crisis-prone set of states: oil exporters".[27] Smith notes that the more a regime controls petroleum resources, the more it is assured of remaining in power despite the prevailing economic and social situation, an observation for which the Libyan, Iraqi and Algerian examples provide ample proof. This ability to survive economic and political crises enables organisations and institutions created during the oil

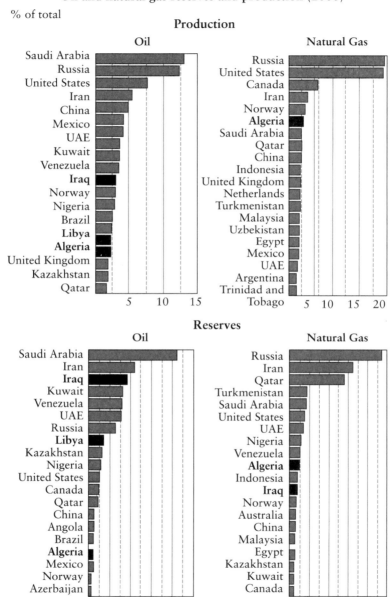

Oil and natural gas reserves and production (2008)

% of total

Source: BP Statistical Review of World Energy, June 2009.
Atelier de cartographie de Sciences Po, April 2010.

boom to overcome "hard times": "One of oil's most important effects seems to be the simple fact that it gives political regimes more money with which to pursue their various strategies for staying in power".[28] That said, the many means of survival deployed by authoritarian regimes, from North Korea to Zimbabwe, disprove the hypothesis that the oil rent alone accounts for their longevity.[29]

National revolution and oil wealth

In fact, the survival capacity of authoritarian regimes is not characteristic of authoritarian oil regimes alone.[30] What distinguishes Algeria, Iraq and Libya from other authoritarian oil and non-oil regimes, are the historical conditions that enabled revolutionary political organisations in the 1970s to capture the oil rent. Other authoritarian countries are also ruled by revolutionary organisations or parties, but do not have an oil windfall at their disposal. Their "destructive potential" can thus be deemed limited by comparison with authoritarian oil regimes.[31] In Algeria, Iraq and Libya, on the contrary, the oil rent enabled regimes that were either revolutionary or led by revolutionary parties or organisations to carry out their plans and feed their ambitions with substantial means. The present research thus puts forth the hypothesis that these regimes' violent political trajectory, as well as their economic failure, results from the conjunction of specific revolutionary dynamics and unforeseen oil wealth.

Are oil and gas, then, a poisoned chalice? The example of the countries analysed herein would seem to bear out this hypothesis: Algeria, Iraq and Libya are simply victims of the oil curse. After all, many of the symptoms inventoried by proponents of this theory can be found in these countries: violence, war, authoritarianism, poverty and economic failure.[32] Yet, this automatic correlation does not always stand up to historical and political analysis: is the oil rent the factor that explains the tragic path these countries have taken, or has it merely amplified the destructive potential of these regimes? In other words, would the FLN-state, the Iraqi Baath party and the Libyan *Jamahiriyya* have been more democratic without the oil rent? Nothing in the political structures of these organisations or in the choice of their leaders justifies an affirmative answer to this question.

By advancing the hypothesis that capturing the oil rent has made it easier for these autocracies to fulfil their destructive potential, this research also aims to contribute to the current debate on the "authoritarian syndrome" in the Arab world. The political literature on democracy and authoritarianism fortunately no longer neglects the Arab world. As M. Camau points out, "the Arab world is more than ever present in regime transformation comparisons".[33] Even better, it now poses a novel perspective on the "democratic slide" of authoritarian regimes that helps to comprehend the vulnerability of regimes in the face of political pressure.[34] Now the aim is to analyse the role of the oil rent with respect to "the issue of the conditions by which authoritarianism and more precisely autocracy is maintained through the very changes that it implements".[35]

The moment that triggered the dynamics of destruction really began with the first oil crisis in 1973, which exponentially multiplied the revenues of those in power. As a result, they suddenly had the financial means they had previously lacked, forcing them to revise their regional ambitions downward and pay greater attention to the national level. It was not until after 1973 that a dynamic typified by domestic domination by revolutionary organisations, and especially an exacerbated personalisation of power, could be observed. Thus the path taken by these countries is not a result of the rentier economy or their natural resources, but the historical meeting between the rise in oil prices after 1973 and the control of the state by political organisations characterised by a revolutionary ideology and violent methods of political domination. The financial bounty of the first oil crisis gave these regimes the means necessary to dominate their hegemony on the political scene, transform their societies and broaden their countries' influence at the regional level. The first oil crisis thus led to concentration of power in restricted circles that were increasingly cut off from their social bases, because they were blinded by a wealth that was as sudden as it was imposing. The regimes, which were fragile and vulnerable in the early 1970s, used this financial windfall to consolidate their power. The socialist and Baathist revolutions, far from "freeing the people from the chains of the past", placed their populations under authoritarian regimes that made particularly frequent use of violence. The oil rent exacerbated Algerian nationalism, multiplied the ambitions of the

Libyan *Jamahiriyya* tenfold and sounded the knell of the Iraqi Baath
by overvaluing its power. Without the oil rent, these three countries
would probably have conducted themselves like Morocco, Tunisia,
and Egypt—that is, with measured authoritarianism restrained simply by limited resources. Thus it is not the oil rent as such that is a
curse, but the way it is used. There is no curse on rentier states. On
the other hand, a nation is in danger if the authoritarian regime that
controls the rent is the product of a combination of factors that
include a colonial history not yet overcome, excessive nationalist
ideology, and a political organisation that controls society using
brutal methods. The oil rent can in that case bring about the com-
monplace use of violence and a pathological rejection of any form
of self-criticism.

By identifying state-building with the Revolution (and not with
democracy), these authoritarian regimes have linked oil wealth to
an escape from colonialism and its legacy. Endowed with sizeable
revenues, they have been able at once to implement a development
policy, thereby ensuring a social base, and grant privileges to the
"authoritarian coalitions"[36] that govern and finance their ambitious
and costly regional policy. From this perspective, it is not so much
the abundance of oil resources that explains their violent trajectory
as the use that has been made of them within a legal framework
defining specific ownership rights.[37] This aspect is indeed central:
what distinguishes the Persian Gulf oil monarchies (which hold
most of the world's oil reserves) from Arab socialist oil republics is
how the rent is captured by these revolutionary political organisations. Libya before the coup d'état of 1969 seemed to be going down
the peaceful road of an emirate,[38] Iraq before the 1958 coup d'état
shared similar characteristics to the Gulf monarchies.[39] In Algeria,
the establishment of the single party in 1963, followed by the 1965
coup d'état, was conducive to the building of a populist authoritarian regime.[40] But capture of the rent by revolutionary movements
produced a particularly toxic political alchemy between authoritarian regimes with a destructive potential and the financial abundance inherent in the nationalisation of the oil-gas sector: lavish
projects, arms purchases, regional ambition, exclusive control of the
rent, social transformation, etc. The oil counter-crisis (1986–2000), in
a context of reform (modification of ownership rights), fostered the

9

rise of mafia-like regimes characterised by an economy of plunder. For the populations, the cost of maintaining revolutionary and populist coalitions was hard to bear by comparison with neighbouring non-oil regimes such as those in Morocco and Tunisia. This was because the oil rent enabled considerable experimentation that "simple" authoritarian regimes, with limited resources and no extensive revolutionary experience, could not afford.

To sum up, the oil rent is not the sole explanatory factor for the consolidation of these regimes. Nor did it reinforce their authoritarian methods or destroy the political space for negotiation with society. However, the concentration of wealth in favour of a minority led to the fragmentation of societies into geographical, ethnic, political and religious spaces of dissidence. The revolutionary regime/oil rent combination undermined the original plans of nationalist movements, which were literally submerged by financial abundance. Lacking sufficiently consolidated political institutions—not being in a position to manage this influx of revenue— national socialist revolutions have been placed under the control of security agencies. And these agencies have become the *de facto* managers and regulators of national revolutions, a situation that has also made the question of rent distribution fundamental for the legitimacy of regimes. The question to ask is therefore not "why did the oil rent generate political violence?" but rather "through what political mechanisms have oil revenues become the exclusive property of revolutionary regimes?"

In fact, for the ordinary citizens of these countries, the mirage of oil wealth only lasted for a decade, that of the 1970s, for the early 1980s ushered in a bitter period. Saddam Hussein's Iraq embarked on a war against Iran (1980–88),[41] Muammar Qadhafi's Libya turned into a terrorist state,[42] and the FLN-state in Algeria began to crack under the pressure of the first signs of social and political unrest.[43] Hopes of development based on the oil rent vanished; the direction these regimes were taking was plain to see. Victims of the rent were many: embryonic political institutions eroded by corruption and nepotism, political opponents crushed by repression and brutality, and populations having to face the unfathomable—oil wealth impoverished them and blinded their leaders, not to mention the ecological damage caused by the oil rent, which remains to be fully assessed. Yet, in the 1970s, Algeria, Libya and Iraq were considered to be countries with strong economic potential. Algeria was presented as a "Mediterranean dragon", Libya as an "emirate", and Iraq as the rising military power of the Arab world. Politically speaking, progressive socialism suggested that deep transformations were under way: women's liberation, urbanisation, education, rising life expectancy. Owing to the oil rent, these countries seemed engaged in an accelerated modernisation process. Petroleum was perceived as a blessing. Thanks to oil, these states would be in a position to catch up economically. A few decades later, the disillusion was cruel. Indeed, the oil rent developed a feeling of wealth among the rulers—a feeling that led them to undertake political and military experiments with disastrous consequences that still trouble them today.

How can we explain the astonishing similarity among these three trajectories, as well as the regimes' choices and the course of events? Three countries, colonised by European powers—Algeria by France (1830–1962),[44] Iraq by the United Kingdom (1914–32)[45] and Libya by Italy (1911–42)[46]—captured the oil rent through national revolutions to implement policies based on a quest for economic or military power. In all three cases these policies would lead to wars (regional and civil) and embargos, destroying the hopes of a better life promised by revolutionary regimes that all transformed over time into genuine predatory enterprises. The present research in fact shows that the oil rent is neither the cause of the lack of democracy nor the explanatory factor for the descent into violence. It has simply been the resource needed to realise the destructive potential inherent in revolutionary political organisations. However, the ways that the oil rent is used in non-democratic revolutionary regimes, from nationalisation to the third oil crisis (1971–2008), make them stand apart. Oil revenues have fostered the erection of complex political and security frameworks that ensure the consolidation of broad coalitions. They have reinforced traditional practices of predation that represented a threat to be eradicated for progressive elites: "Use cunning to steal from the state", President Boumediene said, "seems to have become the rule, as if the state were a foreign state. We must erase from people's minds the archaic idea of the beylicate".[47] The massive arrival

11

of revenue in the "state" coffers would severely damage its functioning, all the more so since the merger of the rentier economy and security apparatuses spawned mafia-like regimes that are as strong as they are flexible. We can thus speculate that if it had not been for the invasion of American troops in Iraq, the Baath party would have celebrated forty years in power in 2008.

1

CAPTURING THE RENT

Revolution, nationalism and socialism

In the early 1970s, nationalisation of the hydrocarbon sector provided the socialist regime in Algeria, the Baath regime in Iraq and the Libyan revolutionary regime with the financial windfall they needed to fulfil their political ambitions. Oil was perceived as a blessing. For President Houari Boumediene it was "the people's blood",[1] for Muammar Qadhafi the "fuel of the Revolution"[2] and for Saddam Hussein the energy required to build regional power.[3] Some of the revenue from oil and gas sales was invested in civil infrastructure, thus considerably improving the population's living conditions. The abundance of revenue was such that many believed oil would enable these countries to catch up with Western economies. These regimes undertook industrialisation on an unequalled scale: the industrial sector was associated with modernity and oil was precisely what should enable them to "buy modernity". Taking control of the oil sector was thus considered to be revenge on history. It was savoured all the more since access to independence seemed incomplete in a context of hegemonic international oil companies. Their control over energy resources prevented these regimes, with their staunch nationalism and pan-Arab socialist ideology, from turning the page on their colonial past.

Imbued with Arab nationalist ideology, these regimes were also convinced that the socialist path was the only answer to economic underdevelopment and the "state of backwardness" of their societies. "Arab socialism" appeared as an instrument that could accel-

13

erate development. Agrarian revolution and industrialisation were the obvious means to combat peasant poverty and mass unemployment. The progressive nature of the regimes in matters of public health, education and gender policy illustrated their desire to lift the population out of its precarious condition. The revolution aimed to destroy the socio-economic framework of the past, considered as an obstacle to modernity. Implementation of this socialist development path soon made nationalisation of the oil sector essential. Taking control of national wealth at once showed a desire to combat a reviled colonial legacy and aimed to endow the state apparatus with the necessary means to dominate it. That said, the Libyan revolutionaries were not out to "perfect the state, but to smash it",[4] a pious hope since the state machinery developed despite the desire to destroy it being reiterated with each anniversary of the Revolution.

In the 1970s, Algeria, Iraq and Libya thus appeared as progressive regimes stirred by the firm conviction that development could only be achieved through industrialisation and agrarian reform. Marked by their colonial past, the nationalist elites in these countries were motivated by feelings of revenge. They wanted to prevent any return to the historical conditions that had made colonisation possible. Post-colonial states had to become strong in order to better protect themselves from, and if necessary combat, new forms of imperialism and colonialism. But where would they find the resources required to conduct such a policy?

Without control of the oil rent, Algeria today would resemble Morocco, Iraq Syria, and Libya Mauritania—that is, they would have been three more countries with precarious economic and financial resources precisely because they lacked means in the aftermath of independence. Taking control of energy resources—oil and natural gas—had a dual objective: to put an end to the new states' limited sovereignty, limited because foreign companies controlled oil exploitation, and to provide the countries' leaders with considerable financial resources. Following the model of Mexican oil nationalism (the Mexican government had nationalised the hydrocarbon sector in the 1930s),[5] these three countries thus engaged in a process of nationalising the oil-gas sector in the early 1970s. Saddam Hussein justified this move by explaining that "for us, nationalisation is a means to achieve total economic independence, enabling us to be the absolute masters of our wealth and do business with the countries of the world freely and on a basis of reciprocity and mutual interest. Lastly, nationalisation enables us to ensure prosperity for our people and all the peoples of the world". The Iraqi Charter for National Action moreover restated these principles word for word.[6] In 1968, three years prior to the nationalisation of the hydrocarbon sector, Algerian president Houari Boumediene had already declared, "Our policy, based on the industrialisation of the country and the building of a national economy, primarily implies recovering and exploiting its wealth for the exclusive benefit of the people".[7]

Once "recovered", oil was supposed to become a weapon of development as well as the one with which to confront the "imperialist West" via OPEC. After the war of 1973 Algeria, Iraq and Libya were considered the "hardliner clan" of OPEC, always opposed to Saudi Arabian policy.[8] This OPEC hardliner clan also formed the core of the "refusal front" after the September 1978 Camp David Accords, and those countries presented themselves before Arab public opinion as the champions of the Palestinian cause, "deserted" by Sadat's Egypt. Oil would be the powerful weapon that could undermine support for the "Zionist enemy".[9] Even more than boycotts or price increases, Saddam Hussein recommended that "the only effective means for using oil as a weapon against America and the Zionist enemy is to nationalise American oil concerns as well as those of any country backing the enemy. This is the weapon that could effectively force the United States to cease aid to the enemy".[10] Was this political radicalism the product of colonial history? The perception of a violent colonial history had certainly marked collective memories: a terrible war of conquest in Algeria ended with a dramatic war of liberation; Mussolini's plan to colonise the "fourth shore" in Libya was achieved by aerial bombings of civilians and by locking people up in "concentration camps";[11] the British expeditionary corps that wrested Iraq from the Ottoman Empire in 1917 later placed it under British supervision until the 1958 coup d'état.[12]

Prior to nationalisation of the hydrocarbon sector, control by foreign companies clearly reduced Algeria, Libya and Iraq to the rank of poor oil states. Although the regimes were paid royalties on profits, the amounts remained relatively small owing to the low price of oil.[13] Nationalisation of this sector, followed by the first oil crisis (1973), caused a substantial increase in revenues. An oil rent then began to develop and was soon to account for most of the export revenues, and this remains true today,[14] highlighting its strategic importance in domestic political balances. The regimes began by building up a petrochemical industry needed to exploit the resource and instituting "state distribution" of goods and services that would guarantee social peace and stability. This is why the 1970s are generally perceived as a bygone golden age, the time of a utopian belief in the limitless power of black gold.

Control of the rent

For these countries, the proven existence of oil reserves enabled them to foresee a radiant future as long as they exercised absolute control of the hydrocarbon sector. Capture of the oil rent was essential to the consolidation of regimes that arose out of violent capture of power and were sustained by an egalitarian revolutionary ideology. Implementation of a "socialist" allocation policy in fact required means that only the oil rent could provide, all the more so since these three countries at the time had very low per capita incomes. In the 1960s, the situation in Libya was so deprived that a United Nations mission classified the country as underdeveloped. In a study dated prior to 1958, Benjamin Higgins described Libya as a country poor in raw materials and skilled labour, with no indigenous entrepreneurship and virtually no capital accumulation. In 1958 in fact, hence just before oil was discovered, Libya received 214 per cent of the value of all its exported goods in the form of official donations. Per capita income in Libya was $100 per year.[15] In Iraq, the situation was no better: in 1969, despite its oil wealth, annual per capita income was $225, a very low amount comparable with poor developing countries.[16]

In Algeria, the discovery of oil in 1948 had the effect of reinforcing France's colonial claims and worried the nationalist campaigners for independence. Hence, during the Algerian war, the French authorities that began to consider independence only envisaged it as long as the "Southern Territories" remained under French control. The promulgation of the Sahara Oil Code in 1958 defined the conditions for exploiting oil in terms that were eminently favourable to the French companies. In the face of the independence movement's unconditional rejection of French plans, the fate of oil was turned over to a joint Franco-Algerian organisation under the Evian Accords of 1962. Once independent, Algeria governed by the FLN fully assessed the limits on its sovereignty over exploitation of its energy resources. The establishment of Sonatrach in 1963 aimed to give Algeria the oil technology that it lacked, and which remained concentrated in the hands of French oil companies. Following Algeria's request to modify the Evian Accords on hydrocarbons, the Franco-Algerian accord of July 1965 promised cooperation in this sector. Its application was however difficult owing to irreconcilable "divergences of interest".[17] For the FLN-state, ruled by Boumediene since the 1965 coup d'état, foreign company control over oil and gas could not endure. The regime had no other resource. The demands of the Iraqi Baathists and revolutionary Libya were similar. The Energy Ministers of the three countries met in Algiers in May 1970 and declared that "direct exploitation and total control of national wealth [was] their primary objective".[18] On 24 February 1971, Algeria nationalised the hydrocarbon sector.

In Libya, oil was first discovered in 1959 under the King Idris monarchy. The Oil Law introduced in 1955 allowed foreign companies to explore and exploit the resources of an underground believed to have a wealth of reserves. Between 1955 and 1965, the monarchy had set up a legal framework for exploitation made attractive by its low taxes: 137 concessions were granted to 39 oil companies.[19] Government revenue increased from $40 million in 1961 to $625 million in 1965. Libya became a major player in OPEC—which it had joined in 1962—and five years later was the world's fourth largest oil exporter. The establishment of LIPETCO (Libyan General Petroleum Company) in 1968 demonstrated the kingdom's desire to take oil exploitation into greater consideration. "Oil wealth", however, did not make Libya a prosperous country. Thus when a coup d'état brought down the monarchy in 1969, one of Muammar Qadhafi's justifications for it was the need to put "the economy in the service of the people's needs". The socialist revolution was under way, but to prosper it still had to capture the oil rent. In the aftermath of the overthrow of the regime, Libya established a new oil company, the NOC (National Oil Company), and negotiated (with OPEC support) a 30 cents per barrel increase in the price of oil. In 1971, Libya nationalised BP, and then, in 1973, all the foreign companies, thus completing its programme of nationalisations.[20] The revolution henceforth had the means to pursue its policies, and the regime could finance the instruments to consolidate it.

In Iraq, discovery of oil in the area around Kirkuk in 1927 encouraged the grip of British, American, French and German interests on black gold through the Iraqi Petroleum Company (IPC). The concessions granted to the IPC (1925, 1932, 1938) made the Iraqi government, at the time ruled by the Hashemite monarchy, highly dependent on dividends paid by that company. Even before its independence in 1930, Iraq was bound by a treaty (1925) that authorised British military presence for twenty-five years[21] and offered extraterritorial concessions to oil companies, which ended up virtually representing a state within the state. The active Iraqi population worked in agriculture, the only source of external revenue at the time being the export of dates. Imports of foodstuffs could only be financed by dividends IPC paid to the government. The nationalists believed the monarchy was sacrificing Iraq's interests to "imperialism". The overthrow of the monarchy in 1958 and the institution of a nationalist republic was to usher in a period of tension between the IPC and the new Iraqi government. Law 80 of 1961 took over oil wealth by dispossessing the IPC of its concessions. But the new Iraqi government did not have the technical and human means to nationalise the company; in fact it feared a boycott of Iraqi oil like the one levied against the Mossadeq government in Iran.[22] Overthrow of the monarchy thus did not lead quickly to the end of the IPC's reign in Iraq. The republic depended too much on the company's dividends to remain in power—that is, to pay the army that backed it.[23] Establishment of the Iraqi National Oil Company (INOC) in 1964 would however provide the Baath party, which took power in Iraq in 1968, with the instrument it needed to capture the oil rent. The Iraqi government henceforth had the means to make its voice heard in negotiations and, like

Libya, it demanded an increase in the per-barrel price of oil (from $2.24 to $3.21) in June 1971. One year later, on 1 June 1972, it nationalised the Iraqi Petroleum Company. The Baath party now had exclusive control over natural resources.

During the 1970s, these regimes set up an effective form of political authoritarianism. Coercive structures ensured relative stability for the authoritarian coalitions, though without completely immunising them against attempted coups. Charismatic leaders proceeded to develop a form of oil nationalism that conveyed the belief in a better future. Nationalisation of oil and gas strengthened and reassured the leaders as to their abilities to satisfy the people's needs. "Development without growth", to borrow A. Sid Ahmed's expression,[24] expanded rapidly owing to surpluses accumulated during the first oil crisis. Public investment ensured a rosy growth rate suggesting that these countries would become true regional economic powers. Moreover, investment in civil infrastructure drastically improved living conditions, to the point, for instance, of transforming Libya and Iraq into countries of immigration.

Iraq: the oil rent and the Baath party (1968–1980)

The July 1968 revolution definitively secured control of the country for the Baath party. A Command Council was established and on 9 November 1969, this body became "the supreme decision-making body of the country... Saddam Hussein, deputy secretary-general of the Baath, was elected vice-president of the RCC (Revolutionary Command Council), making him second in command of the new regime" after President Ahmed Hassan Bakr.[25] While on the political scene a violent conflict had begun with Barzani's Kurdistan Democratic Party (KDP), on the economic level the Baath party set up a development programme that would deeply alter Iraq's social and economic structures. From 1968 until the war with Iran in 1980, Baath party action was organised in three stages:

[from] July 1968 until early 1970, its efforts focused mainly on forming a strong and disciplined mass party and installing its members in all the important posts of the state apparatus (...). In the second phase, from early 1970 to the end of 1973, the Baath applied itself simultaneously to resolving the oil question via nationalisation and undertaking agrarian reform

(…). The third phase, from 1974 to 1977, involved the liquidation of the military aspect of the Kurdish problem through an alliance with Iran, and an economic take-off.[26]

Nationalisation of the oil sector provided the regime with the means to finance these policies. Living conditions were improved to such an extent that "at the end of 1970s Iraq had become the largest property market in the entire Near and Middle Eastern region… The outlook for the future seemed bright and promises much. By and large the Iraqi population was optimistic".[27] Nationalisation of the oil sector helped the Iraqi regime to develop a huge petrochemical industry: the construction of two new pipelines, the port of Mina al-Bakr, the development of a national fleet of 18 tankers, the construction of new refineries, etc.[28]

From 1972, when Iraq took control of its oil resource, to 1980, revenue rose from $575 million to $26 billion. On the eve of the war with Iran, the Iraqi regime had $30 billion in reserves and a production capacity of 3.4 million barrels per day.[29] Iraqi crude oil, which was discovered very early on, has been a stake in the rivalry between great powers since the dismantling of the Ottoman Empire.[30] Law 80, passed on 11 October 1961, and the founding of INOC in 1964 were certainly early signs of Iraq's desire to take possession of its resources. But it was not until after 1972 that the Iraqi regime truly began to draw profits from its oil. The Baath party had made it a central element of its strategy, as demonstrated by its slogan: "Arab oil for the Arabs". Thus the Party stated, "it was the Socialist Baath Party which invented the slogan, 'Arab Oil to the Arabs', and the nationalization of 1 June 1972 was the first coup carried out by the Arab people on imperialism since the defeat of June 1967".[31] In January 1974, President Bakr declared during the 8th Baath Party Regional Conference: "the total liberation of Iraq's economy and resources from any foreign control has been and will remain at the base of our development strategy".[32]

The Baath party would henceforth employ this financial wealth to finance its "socialist" programme. Driven by a nationalist ideology and anti-imperialist sentiment, it used the oil windfall to bolster its social distribution policy. And in fact, during the 1970s, Baath socialism brought about a real improvement in living conditions. The number of doctors increased from 1 per every 3,320 inhabitants in the early 1970s to 1 per every 1,837 inhabitants at the start of the 1980s. Similarly, the number of hospitals doubled in the course of this same decade.[33] As a result, life expectancy rose from 49 years to 67. In the field of education, Baath policies experienced the same success as in health care: the number of elementary schools doubled in ten years from 5,617 to 11,280, while the number of secondary schools increased from 921 to 1,891. The number of girls in school went from 34 per cent in 1970 to 95 per cent in 1980.[34] The Baath party takeover in 1968 raised Iraq out of poverty: in 1969, per capita GDP was $225. It was the golden age of the Baath: at its height it appeared to be an honest and effective party. In truth, it managed to establish its authoritarianism effectively just by improving the population's living conditions. Its exclusive control over the state enabled it to limit "waste" of the oil rent, but the revenue became *de facto* "the exclusive province of Ba'th party members".[35]

Libya: Coup d'état and revolution (1969)

The 1969 coup d'état led to major changes in the hydrocarbon sector. Just before Muammar Qadhafi seized power, Libya was the world's fourth largest oil exporter and production was in the vicinity of Saudi Arabia's at 3.5 million barrels per day. With low extraction costs ($0.30 per barrel), Libya was an extremely attractive country. Law number 24 of 5 March 1970 replaced LIPETCO with the National Oil Corporation (NOC), an "independent body operating under the supervision and control of the Minister of Petroleum in order to achieve the development plan objectives in the oil sector".[36] Law number 69 of 4 July 1970 granted the NOC a monopoly on imports and exports. During the years 1972–73, the Libyan government nationalised the oil-gas sector and put an end to the hegemony of over forty-two foreign companies exploiting crude oil since it was discovered in 1959.[37] Revenues went from 663 million Libyan dinars (LD) in 1973 to 3,800 billion in 1979—that is, they multiplied sixfold in scarcely six years. But although in the mid-1970s Libya was "on the verge of occupying fourth place in world oil production", it "lacked any industrial base; such is the contradictory situation that plagues Libya today".[38] Most of Libya's

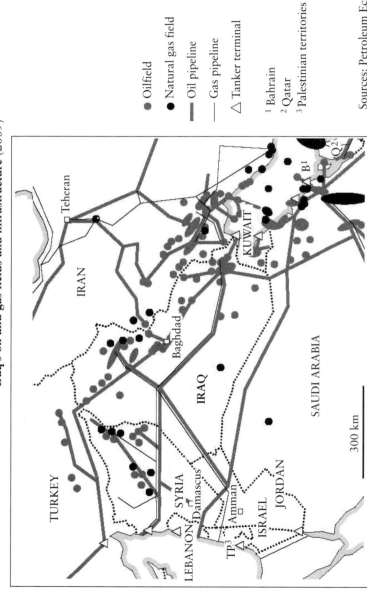

Iraq's oil and gas fields and infrastructure (2009)

- ● Oilfield
- ● Natural gas field
- ── Oil pipeline
- ── Gas pipeline
- △ Tanker terminal

[1] Bahrain
[2] Qatar
[3] Palestinian territories

Sources: Petroleum Economist, *World Enery Atlas 2009.*

Atelier de cartographie de Sciences Po, April 2010.

known oil reserves (79 billion barrels out of 113 billion of known reserves) were discovered between 1957 and 1967, under the Idris monarchy (1951–69). Five sectors were considered of key importance: the oil and petrochemical industry, agriculture and water, the iron and steel industry, infrastructure, education and health care.[39] Immediately after the 1969 revolution, Libya was a country with no industry, it had only one refinery and its agrifood sector was very limited. The 1972–75 Plan was the first three-year plan that emphasised the importance of industry. The Libyan authorities envisaged the development of heavy industry based on petroleum products. Two major developments illustrate this, the Ras Lanuf petrochemical complex (which refines 11 million of the 18 million tonnes of crude oil processed annually by Libya) and the Misrata steelworks. However, the industrial sector as a whole still only represented 10 per cent of GDP.

The new regime's legitimacy was basically reliant on the redistribution of wealth and hence the improvement of living conditions. Egalitarianism is only comprehensible if one recalls the situation of Libya under the Idris monarchy. During this period, the country was one of the most disadvantaged in the region: 94 per cent of its population was illiterate, it had no medical doctors and infant mortality reached 40 per cent. With an annual per capita income of $35 between 1951 and 1959, Libya was considered one of the world's poorest countries.[40] By bringing an end to the monarchy with a coup d'état and instituting a "distributive state",[41] Muammar Qadhafi stood as the people's benefactor. Nationalisation of oil and gas would provide a growing increase in revenue and ensure an improvement in living conditions for the Libyan people. The 1973–75 development plan, for instance, led to the construction of 115,552 housing units, twenty-one hospitals, thirty-nine dental clinics, sixty-one maternity wards, and 102 health centres.[42]

In 1973 the population of Libya was estimated at 2,052,372. In 1995, it had grown to 5.6 million, of which nearly one-third (1,719,692) was under the age of 15. The rejuvenation of the population was inherent in an annual population growth rate of 4.21 per cent, one of the highest in the Arab world. Combined with this population growth was rapid urbanisation:[43] the urban population represented 20 per cent of the total population in 1950, 26 per cent in 1960, 45 per cent in 1970, 62 per cent in 1980, 79 per cent in 1990 and 80 per cent in 1995.[44] The revolution sedentarised the Bedouin and revolutionary socialism gave them jobs in the public sector. 75 per cent of the active population is in fact employed by the state, which has become the sole potential employer for thousands of students: in 1951, Libya had only one university, in Benghazi, but by 1995 it had thirteen. Enrolment rose constantly to reach 269,302 students in 1999, compared with only 13,418 in 1975.[45] The oil rent thus also fostered the development of a system of patronage, obliging the population to negotiate with the revolutionary organisations for access to goods and services—which did not, for all that, reassure the regime as to the people's allegiance. In 1975, RCC members were already criticising the revolutionary fantasies of the regime. Hervé Bleuchot recalls that one RCC member, Omar Al-Mehishi, at the time already considered that "dissent has become widespread". In practice, he said, "the head of state can now only trust members of his tribe, and army officers have been replaced by people from Sirte".[46] Thus the Libyan anomaly that John Davis had pointed out—"The Revolutionary Command Council is not a family, and it does not claim ownership of the state"[47]—vanished with the Qadhafi clan's taking exclusive control of state property.[48]

Algeria: Socialism and industrialisation

The coup d'état of June 1965 brought an end to Ben Bella's presidency and placed power in the hands of Colonel Houari Boumediene, the real chief of the army. Like Libya and Iraq, Algeria immediately set up an ambitious development policy that set out to improve the living conditions of the people, whose numbers were put at 11,820,125 in 1966. For the new regime, the colonial legacy still weighed too heavily on Algerian society. The development policy thus seemed to be a healthy reaction aiming to foster the "passage from a capitalist society of exploitation based on selfish profit, domination of the wealthy and class struggle to a socialist type of society based on social justice, equal opportunity and respect for the general interest... and requires that structural transformations necessarily be allied with the transformation of behaviours and mentalities. This cultural revolution is a long-term battle".[49] Algerian socialism was careful to distinguish itself from the USSR version and above all to point out that it shared common values with Islam. For Houari Boumediene, "Socialism does not proceed from any materialist metaphysics and is not connected to any dogmatic conception that is foreign to our national genius. It is identified with the fulfilment of Islamic values".[50] This reminder did not prevent fundamentalists from accusing the regime of taking an atheist turn and moving far from true Islamic values.[51] But for the regime, socialism was "the only way to do away with unemployment, ignorance and social shortcomings. It is synonymous with justice and fairness and it is this message that the Prophet brought us; furthermore, our fight for liberation, which is a people's revolution, requires the application of socialism to eliminate poverty and social disparities".[52]

Fundamentalist criticisms actually carried little weight regarding the success of the Boumediene regime. The successful nationalisation of the hydrocarbon sector in 1970–71 endowed the regime with the financial means to ensure its development policy. Throughout the 1970s, growth rate hovered around 7 per cent and the gross rate of investment exceeded 35 per cent. GDP (in millions of current dinars) reached 80,573 DA in 1977, whereas it was only 13,130 DA in 1963.[53] This exceptional growth rate made Algeria look like a "Mediterranean dragon". Industrialisation and agrarian reform were the two pillars of Algeria's development strategy.

In the collective memory, this decade appears as a golden age, a period when Algeria promised to become a regional power guided by a strong and respected state and bolstered by a prosperous economy, which itself was drawn by the success of "industrialising industries". Under the influence of G. Destanne de Bernis, Algeria espoused the words: "Developing countries can only hope to catch up to countries that began their industrialisation over a century ago if they decide to plough ahead and focus immediately on the most modern production processes".[54] The complex and sophisticated strategy of "industrialising industries" aimed to create a dynamics of full economic integration (of metallurgy, mechanical and electrical industries) to establish industrial exchange. The aim was to have the Algerian economy produce its own industrial facilities to the greatest extent possible. This strategy was also based on the theory that "industry should not rely mainly on export, but should help to turn the Algerian economy inward". Algeria's ambition was to manage to build an industrial sector that could manufacture producer goods more than consumer goods.[55] The success of this model depended on the capacity for trickle-down of industry to agriculture, lasting coordination among government departments involved in implementing it and, especially, sustained financial investment. The construction of natural gas liquefaction complexes (Arzew, Skida), oil refineries (Alger, Arzew, Hassi Messaoud), a mercury plant (Bou Ismail), a hot rolling mill (Annaba) and fertiliser and plastic manufacturing units had to meet the goal of giving the petrochemical industry the most modern means of production. In short, the country indeed had to plough ahead. More than in Muammar Qadhafi's Libya or Saddam Hussein's Iraq, Boumediene's Algeria was a perfect illustration of oil nationalism and its faith in industrial development. In contrast to Algeria, in the 1960s South Korea's industrialisation strategy had given precedence to import substitution industries and relied on exports; heavy industry was developed later.[56] Algeria chose the opposite route of heavy industrialisation first without having had the time, owing to the drying up of investment after the collapse of oil prices in 1986, to develop substitution industries.

But even before the vulnerability of its industrial strategy was fully realised, the Boumediene regime already inspired ambivalent sentiments, a mix of fear and hope. Most justified the regime's authoritarianism because of its outstanding performance. Its use of the oil rent seemed fair because it was employed for substantial social and economic redistribution. Moreover, in addition to his aura of charismatic leader, Boumediene displayed an ethic of justice and a condemnation of corruption that sustained the perception of a state that, however authoritarian, was honest. The oil rent was presented as a just reward for the sacrifices the people had made to give birth to the Algerian nation. Consequently, it could only be used in the "general interest", and Boumediene issued a warning to those who did not see things that way: "As for those whose only aim is to make money, they should realise once and for all that they have no place in the government, the party or the army".[57] He reiterated this message on a number of occasions, as in 1976: "Those who have opted for wealth can step back and keep their distance from the Revolution". But was it politically astute to isolate those who were "interested in riches"? Was that not, on the contrary, the best way to encourage theft?

Boumediene's death hailed the end of a dream. Behind the strong state and promising economic outcomes of the exceptional decade were concealed the shortcomings of a young nation carried away by its enthusiasm. Boumediene had managed to inspire a vision of the future, to impose an obligation to succeed in order to move Algeria away from its colonial past. The FLN's anti-colonial discourse remained credible as long as it could put its revolutionary legitimacy into practice: seizure of unoccupied property, nationalisation of the oil sector, the agrarian revolution, the transition to socialism were all events that fuelled the revolutionary dream. But at the end of the 1970s, the vacuity of the FLN discourse became evident well beyond circles that criticised the revolutionary experience. Boumediene's departure revealed the failures, drawbacks and shortcomings of a development policy that Algeria could hardly afford to finance.[58]

The illusion of a hardworking Algeria came to an end. Unemployment remained massive owing to the yearly arrival of increasingly large numbers of people on the job market. The failure of the agrarian revolution found an outlet in mass emigration of peasants to the land of the former colonial power. Algerian society was sinking not into the tranquillity of a fair society but into the throes of bitterness and feelings of jealousy. This state, which according to the official rhetoric came into existence on the backs of the million and a half martyrs of the revolution, had become the instrument of wealth for a minority who had taken possession of the heritage of the war for independence and placed it in the hands of the "revolutionary family".[59] The artificial barrier constructed to protect the state from those who were "interested in money" would be broken down by the development of a state bureaucracy that instituted a system in which corruption spread to all echelons of the administration. Boumediene's dream thus turned into a nightmare during the "dark decade", as Chadli Bendjedid's opponents called his rule, followed by the bloody decade of civil war (1991–98). The oil rent had created a development process that suddenly ground to a halt. All that remained were the usurped "vacant property", diverted farmland (via the agrarian revolution), and pillaged public investments (in the context of industrialisation). The oil rent itself, the only source of available revenue, would also soon become the object of organised and structured plunder in the context of "state capitalism" and for the benefit of a "bourgeoisie that had invested the entire state apparatus".[60]

Financial abundance and "despotic potential"

Capture of the rent by nationalist revolutionary organisations brought an end to the race among major powers for access to oil reserves. Until then, two models were superimposed: an "imperial model" that had led the major powers into constant rivalry for the control of territories with abundant reserves, and a "semi-colonial" model in the wake of the Second World War, in which oil companies exploited the reserves of independent states with limited sovereignty.[61] Thus the monarchies in Iraq (1930–58) and in Libya (1951–69) benefited from royalties in exchange for foreign company control over exploitation of their reserves. In this context, the consumer states—the major powers—no longer took direct control of the reserves but acted through their oil companies. These had a grip on entire geographical areas within independent states, as in the case of the Anglo-Iranian Oil Company in the Middle East.[62] This semi-colonial regime considerably limited the development of a rent conducive to making the rulers of independent states autonomous. During the 1950s and 1960s, their dependence on foreign oil companies forced them constantly to negotiate to obtain a better distribution of earnings. But once the hydrocarbon sector was nationalised, it began to produce abundant financial resources. The fight among major powers for access to reserves turned into a struggle among national actors for the control, use and distribution of the rent. Exclusive control of it ended up being a guarantee for the continuity of the coalitions that ruled these regimes.

Starting in 1970, the oil rent was used to satisfy the utopias of the socialist regime in Algeria, the Baath regime in Iraq and the revolutionary regime in Libya. But the coalitions of alliances—"public

Oil and natural gas fields and infrastructure in Algeria and Libya (2009)

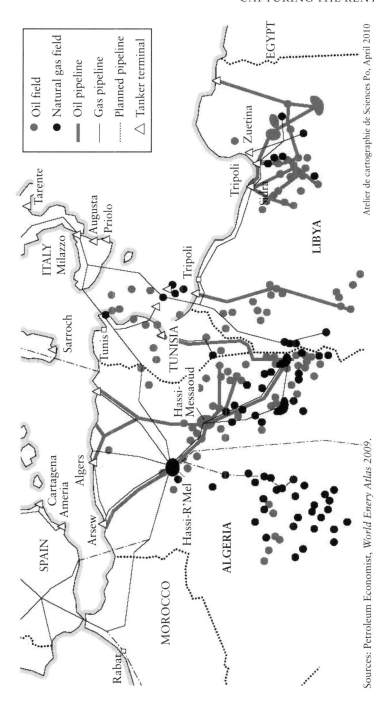

Sources: Petroleum Economist, *World Enery Atlas 2009*.

Atelier de cartographie de Sciences Po, April 2010

officials, military and security elites and their allies in the private sector"[63]—that ruled them gradually drove these regimes into bankruptcy and economic ruin. For their populations, faced with "devastation", the oil rent had become synonymous with a curse, given the extent to which it dehumanised those who had privileged access to it. In Algeria, there is a term, *hogra*, to describe this feeling of contempt in which the elites hold the "people". In Iraq, the Kurds in the north and the Shia in the south experienced the limits of distribution by the Baath regime as violence, which used "deportation as its supreme weapon".[64] In Libya after the overthrow of the monarchy, the region of Cyrenaica, cradle of the Sanusiyya, ended up deprived of any public investment, and its population of any hope of seeing its living conditions improved. In fact, financial abundance primarily enabled these regimes to develop their "despotic potential", the seeds of which were already contained in their revolutionary political organisations. As E. Kienle points out, "more recently the rising external resources of these states and thus their growing external dependence have further increased their degree of autonomy vis-à-vis their own societies resulting more and more in internal despotism".[65] Should it thus be concluded that the abundance of revenues resulting from the nationalisation of the hydrocarbon sector fostered the radicalisation of these regimes?

The answer is yes. Let us consider the "despotic potential" of the Baath party: it only fully blossomed after 1973, and it was hydrocarbon revenue that gave the party undivided domination over resources, thus making it slide into despotism. "As long as oil revenue remained fairly modest", Marion-Farouk Sluglett notes, "the despotic potential inherent in this type of state was not yet very manifest, but it became totally obvious, particularly after the 1973 price boom, that the oil rent played a decisive role in increasing both the economic and repressive power of the Iraqi state, and more particularly, the power of those who controlled this state".[66] With the bulk of resources in its hands, the party could destroy those who threatened it or those who entered into dispute with it and justify this brutality as a result of ideological purification. Financial abundance, which grew out of the first oil crisis, reduced to nought any possibility of seeing the Iraqi republic evolve toward a pluralist regime; the party had available all the means and resources it needed to eradicate its rivals, enemies or opponents.[67] In short, the oil rent is viewed by some as the direct cause of the Iraqi state's slide into violence: "In the 1940s and 50s, Iraq's oil resources were sufficient to allow expansion of the mechanisms of the state, modernisation of education and other services, and the gradual development of the country's infrastructure",[68] but after 1973, the Baath had 20 times more revenue (increased from $500 million in 1972 to $10 billion in 1977); this "enormous increase in power of the men in control of the state" reduced to nought the threat posed by protest movements and organisations.

In Libya, the violence of the revolutionary government manifested itself quite clearly after 1973. Four periods can roughly be identified in the construction of the instruments of power. The first period goes from the takeover of power in a coup d'état in 1969 to the Zuwara speech in 1973. In the course of these four years, the instruments of power rested on four main political structures: the Revolutionary Command Council, the government, the army and the Arab Socialist Union. Decisions were made in a collegial fashion among members of the RCC, presided over by Muammar Qadhafi. The constitutional proclamation of the Libyan Arab Republic on 11 December 1969 affirmed that the RCC was the highest authority of the Libyan Arab Republic. During this period, Libya undertook a series of administrative, political and economic reforms and drastically altered its diplomatic relations. The Zuwara speech[69] on 16 April 1973 ushered in the second period. Muammar Qadhafi announced the formation of popular committees and stated, "The Popular Revolution begins today". This initiative aroused a constantly growing resistance: in addition to criticism of Muammar Qadhafi's total control over the revolution, there was disparagement of regional policy failures, and concern about the risk of war with Egypt. In 1977, a third period began: the regime established revolutionary committees in charge of orienting and working to attain revolutionary goals. Hervé Bleuchot compares them to the "Red Guards" of the Chinese revolution. The regime thus had a new arbitrary power instrument and was prepared to use violence, thereby tightening its grip.[70] At the end of the 1970s, there was no longer any doubt that the popular revolution was in the clutches of an authoritarian regime and that all political, economic, military and diplomatic decisions totally escaped the political institutions representing the "people"; the government and the General People's Congress were in any event converted into bodies that represented first the RCC and second the "directives" of "the Guide" (qa'id). Now, as in Iraq, the revenues available to the Libyan revolution were also 20 times greater than at the time of the coup d'état of 1969; collegial decisions were thus no longer necessary. Furthermore, the regime had the means to kill "stray dogs", political opponents in exile who denounced the monopolising of national wealth by the revolutionaries.

In Algeria, the June 1965 coup brought Ben Bella's (1962–65) "third-worldist" experiment[71] to an end and, unlike in Iraq where Baath civilians controlled the military, it placed the military back at the centre of power: "Political power was now concentrated at the level of closed circles. Military security under Boumediene's direct authority was the decisive and determinant element of the new power".[72] Without truly achieving the effectiveness of the Baath in Iraq, Military Security was perceived as "a veritable parallel political system [...] that functioned in practical terms as an organisation supervising all areas of activity in the country".[73] The new regime that grew out of the coup d'état benefited from the increase in oil revenues which "doubled after 1965 and tripled up to 1971. Afterwards, revenues benefited from the leap in 1972–1973, which multiplied them by about seven".[74] However, unlike in Iraq and Libya, the profusion of revenues after 1973 did not accelerate a concentration of power. Oil revenues enabled the regime to strengthen the coalition that ruled Algeria (senior civil servants and army officials, state corporation heads, the walis): "the focus of its problem was to prevent any other stratum from setting itself up as the new dominant class". Armed with these revenues and revolutionary legitimacy, the regime could do without democratic institutions, "and this explains the lack of participation, of democracy, of a national assembly as well as the near ineffectiveness of mass organisations".[75] Thus financial abundance in fact enabled a balance to be maintained between "two bureaucracies (civilian and military) whose interests were complementary."[76] This type of political operation spared the Algeria revolution from sliding into an Iraqi-style dictatorship. The shaky balance between civilian and military bureaucracy in fact gave rise to a mafia-style phenomenon of "encystment",[77] in other words an organisation capable of securing transactions in a context marked by lack of legal protection and the arbitrariness of state-controlled power.[78]

Who controls the rent?

How is it possible to manage at once the revolution, the redistribution of wealth, political stability, the desire for enrichment, conflicts and rivalries, and clan struggles? The socialist and Baathist revolutions were soon confronted with regulating conflicts fuelled by the repercussions of the oil rent. As they lacked any political institutions that could secure negotiations among the various groups, paramilitary organisations quickly stepped in to oversee and act as regulators. Inside the Republics, various bodies would set the rules of the game through violence, define the legitimate actors and work towards political stability by intimidating and eliminating insubordinates. In short, these bodies put order in the revolution so as to be able to redistribute the revenue from the oil rent.

Financial abundance inherent in the capture of the rent literally transformed the landscapes of these countries. Geographers and city planners have highlighted the deep changes that have occurred: new towns, modern infrastructure and petrochemical complexes. Demographers and economists identified the "social revolutions" taking shape: urbanisation, increased internal migration, education on the rise and the emergence of a middle class. The oil rent had managed to provide for these "revolutions" by financing the many projects that were supposed to destroy the "remnants of archaic societies". Redefinition of the geographical and economic landscape was to be completed by a reconfiguration of behaviour, customs and mindsets. The aim was not to create a "new man" or to make a "great leap forward", but to modernise tradition, to make Islam and socialism, and nationalism and development, compatible. But what political frameworks could be used to implement such a programme? "Western-style democracy" was unacceptable to these three countries. The arguments used to reject it varied but all were based on the idea that it was not compatible with the revolution. In Libya, political parties were banned in the name of individual sovereignty: "representation is a fraud", stipulated the Green Book. In Algeria, Houari Boumediene compared party pluralism to "sects" and preferred to rely on FLN activists and cadres. In Iraq, Baath ideology viewed the party as a "guide for the people" during the socialist transition period. Between the people and the party, there should be "complete voluntary mutual responsiveness".[79] The party had secured a monopoly over people's representation as well as the exclusive control of the state. The people, who were immature, first had to learn the basic rules of democracy; they had to be educated before their emancipation could be envisaged. In Algeria, "socialist villages" were to embody the revolution under way in which people could learn "basic democracy". In Libya, it was to be expressed in the *Jamahiriyya* (State of the Masses), represented through local grassroots committees. "Committees everywhere", cried Muammar Qadhafi to explain the "Third Universal Theory". In the 1970s, participatory democracy theoretically stood out as the most appropriate method of governance to best express the ideals of socialist revolutions. In Iraq, it was the party, made up of 25,000 full members and 1.5 million activists,[80] which, again theoretically, was supposed to provide for the building of a "modern state" by destroying tribal affiliations and diminishing religious and ethnic barriers.

Theologians pointed out the incompatibility of these socialist revolutions with the values of Islam, maintaining that the leaders' progressivism was actually very remote from traditional Islam. Muammar Qadhafi, invoking his right to *ijtihad* in order to ban polygamy in July 1978, drew an angry response from the Libyan *ulama*: "Go back to the Qur'an", they said, "for in it we find passages and principles for a better organisation of society and especially for balanced relations between man and woman". By granting women the right to divorce if they found themselves sexually unfulfilled, revolutionary Libya made the cover of Western feminist magazines which viewed Muammar Qadhafi as the champion of women's liberation in the Islamic world. The attempt to dissociate Islam as an institution from the Qur'an as the revealed word was a revolutionary approach at the time, which was justified by the "authentic and fundamental" dimension of the revolution. But in Algeria, the socialist revolution's preoccupation was to fill "empty stomachs" and not to confront the revolution with a revolutionary interpretation of Islam. For Houari Boumediene, "people don't want to go to heaven with an empty stomach. People who are hungry don't need to listen to verses. I say that with all the consideration I have for the Qur'an that I learned at the age of ten. People who are hungry need bread, people who are ignorant need knowledge, people who are sick need hospitals".[81] The oil rent, therefore, was primarily supposed to provide bread, knowledge and hospitals; in other words it should enable people to reach paradise in better shape. In Iraq, the constitution of 1970 stipulated that the "natural resources and basic means of production are owned by the people". The oil rent should thus be used to meet basic needs. Agrarian reform, in fact confiscation of land, was also part of this quest for better redistribution under the party's exclusive control.[82]

These regimes thus gave the impression of having managed to lift their populations out of poverty, modernise Islam, and make the socialist revolution compatible with development. They seemed to be to the Arab world what Japan was to Asia, an avantgarde fostering the renaissance of a region—the Arab world—which had slid into decline after reaching its peak. These countries inspired a certain fascination, their "success" was touted by those who believed in their achievements. The image of Algeria, Iraq and Libya at the time was one of emerging countries confident in the future and in the men that led them. Geographers' maps, city planners' drawings, economic outcomes and statistical data were "proof" of the success of the Arab socialist revolutions. And yet, much of this success owed nothing to the "revolution" or to "socialism": it was mainly based on the oil rent, the engine of this dynamism, but also its greatest threat. During this entire period, the virtual dependence on this sole source of external revenue was not yet a point of discussion; the disciplined and efficient use of it aroused admiration. Although it would have been legitimate to question the criteria for choosing those who defined its use, the debate was not considered timely. Worse still, those who raised the question and wished to examine it were instantly cast off into the category of counter-revolutionaries.

In fact, behind the scenes, this success relied on stringent super-vision of society by paramilitary forces that were accepted only because they were so effective. Although the Baath party in Iraq reassured its supporters, its ability to control the political scene naturally made its adversaries and opponents anxious. The era of coups d'état was a thing of the past:[83] "The strength of the Baath lay not only in the capacity its leaders had affirmed for the past ten years, but also in the perfect organisation of overseeing its forces. Some of them are moreover kept within the People's Army, a veri-table militia, that was formed on 8 February 1970".[84] This system would demonstrate its destructive potential as well as the difficulty of uprooting it a few decades later. Complementarity between tribes, the party and the army ensured that the regime had the strong framework it needed to survive.[85] In Libya, the *Jamahiriyya* led to the formation of "committees everywhere", but it also organ-ised revolutionary committees in charge of overseeing the order of debates. Founded in 1977 by Major Abdel Salam Jalloud, the regime's second in command at the time, the revolutionary com-mittees, led by officials appointed directly by the Guide, literally formed a political police force in charge of reinforcing the Grass-roots People's Committees. Their mission was to eliminate oppo-nents, silence protesters and impose on the Grassroots People's Committees the political directives to follow.[86] In a rare moment of compassion, Muammar Qadhafi denounced their excesses: "They have deviated, harmed, tortured. The revolutionary does not prac-tice repression. On the contrary, I want to prove that the commit-tees are lovers of the masses".[87] In Algeria, a fearsome instrument was organised in Military Security: "its networks", wrote Mohamed Harbi, "have penetrated administrations, the FLN, the police, and chosen representatives at the municipal and regional level. The role of Military Security is preponderant in co-opting elites, organising congresses and public debates. Fear has become a factor in the exer-cise of power".[88] Military Security performed the function of regu-lating conflicts and rivalries, it distributed wealth and privileges to its allies, helped its former partners go into business and eliminated insubordinates. Like the Baath and the revolutionary committees, Military Security served as a violent secret organisation that aimed to establish political stability and secure transactions. Financial abundance had led to collective enrichment strategies in states lacking democratic institutions and therefore incapable of establishing formal rules of the game. Concentration of political and military power in small circles meant that wealth could be redistributed in a selective but controlled manner. In short, the Baath, the revolutionary committees and Military Security all fulfilled the functions usually attributed to mafias: making transactions secure in a market lacking any instruments of protection.

Was such control over their citizens a sign of the leaders' apprehension about the rapid transformations affecting their societies? Did the "Asian" growth rate (an average of 7 per cent from 1973 to 1985) make them fear the emergence of a "bourgeois counterrevolution" instigated by the middle class? Was such supervision not instead a display of strength to intimidate all those who might have the intention, or even the ambition, to challenge the exclusive control of the rent by these closed circles that had managed to take possession of it? As Marion Farouk-Sluglett reminds us with regard to Iraq, even if the rate of urbanisation rose from 35 per cent in 1947 to 65 per cent in 1977, "beneath this facade, patriarchal values as well as family, clan, and tribal ties continued to be reproduced under the dictatorial regime".[89] Were these revolutions political takeovers or "confiscations of independence", as Ferhat Abbas wrote about Boumediene's Algeria? Did these dictatorial regimes and these "totalitarian socialisms" demonstrate in a premonitory fashion that they could only lead to violence?[90] This historical period, an extremely important one in the formation of political systems, was characterised by the unexpected meeting between socialist revolutions, hoped for and borne by nationalist revolutionary elites, and the financial abundance inherent in the nationalisation of hydrocarbons and then the first oil crisis. It should be remembered that the price of a barrel of oil went up from $2 in the early 1960s to $40 at the end of the 1970s. This indicates just how much the organisation of a revolution was necessarily subject to very strong rivalries. Access to regulatory bodies (Military Security, revolutionary committees, the Baath party) was akin to a guarantee not only of protection but more especially of rapid enrichment. The countless economic projects, some more realistic than others, were in fact indirect operations for reinvesting revenue from the rent. Public investment was colossal in the 1970s, but there were no legitimate political institutions capable of exercising control over this expenditure, any more than there was a free press capable of giving an account of the arbitrages underlying the chosen projects. Was the revolution merely an alibi, an illusion, an arbitrary regime necessary to capture property and the oil rent? Although these questions are difficult to answer, by the end of the 1970s all illusions about these revolutions had vanished. The regimes had certainly set up mechanisms that ensured political stability and central regulatory bodies (the Baath party, revolutionary committees, Military Security). But they also oriented these revolutions toward unbridled authoritarianism, dictatorship, even tyranny. These central regulatory bodies held all the more sway since oil revenue rose continually, thus providing the means to finance a sophisticated and effective repressive apparatus that could prevent possible coups and crush potential adversaries. Of the three regimes, Iraq's became both the most sophisticated and the most violent: "The rulers turned the party itself into a true instrument of the state, tightly controlling the army and creating several competing security services equipped with the most modern means of surveillance and coercion. Anyone inside or outside of the party who disagreed with the ruling group formed around Bakr and Saddam Hussein was either ousted or eliminated".[91]

Conclusion

Does capture of the rent by revolutionary organisations and management of revolutions by security organisations explain the political blindness of these regimes at the end of the 1970s? The certainty that oil prices could only increase reinforced the grip security services had on the state, thereby depriving the state of the tools it needed to steer itself. Thus, although this period appeared as a golden age in the collective imagination, in retrospect it appears as a pivotal period in the political trajectory of these countries. It enabled the fusion of central regulatory bodies (Baath militias, revolutionary committees, Military Security) with the rentier economy. At the end of the 1970s, the state was the sole owner and agent of a large segment of goods and services. The agrarian revolution had expropriated landowners, urbanisation had turned farmland into real estate, the over-valuation of national currency and foreign exchange control encouraged currency speculation, trade regulations gave rise to a corporation of goods and produce importers: financial abundance had reduced to nought the original values of socialist revolutions. The hydrocarbon sector had become the sole source of external revenue which in turn irrigated the meanders of networks made up of clients and protégés that the central regulatory bodies strove to maintain by periodically flushing out anyone who could weaken the proper functioning of this mechanism. In the space of ten years, from 1970 to 1980, these regimes managed to make their populations forget the poverty and distress in which they lived before the time of financial abundance. Furthermore, the exponential increase in oil prices suggested that oil wealth was infinite. The effectiveness of central regulatory bodies fostered selective redistribution of wealth that introduced a period of enviable political stability. These achievements would not fail to blind the sycophants of these new economic, oil and military powers, who saw themselves managing to redefine a new world economic order and reorganise the landscape at the regional level to be more in line with their ambitions.

2

THE ILLUSORY POWER OF OIL

Assured of a bright future in the early 1970s, twenty years later Iraq was ruined and laid to waste, Algeria bankrupt and in the throes of civil war, and Libya under an embargo. Oil nationalism, under which an entire generation had grown up convinced that this gift of nature had endowed them with wealth and power, had driven these countries into an impasse. Invested with every virtue, oil was to be at once the weapon against underdevelopment, the key that would open the door to modernity, and the sinews of war against imperialism and Zionism. In short, for these countries it was the just reward bestowed upon all those whom contemporary history had mistreated and humiliated. But actually, capture of the rent in the 1970s would make them blind. The sudden influx of financial abundance in states with vulnerable political institutions had the effect of making their rulers totally unreceptive to the demands of their societies. The scale of the projects undertaken rested on the belief that oil wealth was unlimited and the rise in oil prices was exponential. This conviction nourished excessive economic projects and fuelled ambitions for regional economic and military supremacy. It also led to immoderate spending. Moreover, the sudden enrichment inherent in the nationalisation of the oil and gas sector made these countries' foreign policy more aggressive and relations between ruling authoritarian coalitions and society more violent than ever. In other words, oil wealth had created an "irrational and symbolic universe" that fostered "societal autism".[1]

This book posits that the oil rent responded to a yearning to dominate that formed under colonial occupation. The bitterness accumulated during that period produced a deep sentiment of vengeance against the former colonial powers. The new regimes, unable to rival the former rulers from a military and economic standpoint, vented their bitterness on their neighbours: Morocco for Algeria, Tunisia and Chad for Libya, Iran and Kuwait for Iraq. Symptomatically, these three countries had the same ambition of achieving military supremacy and economic domination over their region. This ambition was, however, doomed to fail as well: defeated by Saudi Arabia in their attempt to gain control of OPEC[2] (which, in conjunction with their economic decisions and extravagant spending, led them into a major financial crisis in the late 1980s) and powerless to crush their neighbours, these three regimes then turned all their ability and power against opponents within. Far from collapsing or agreeing to hand over power to the political party coalitions who laid claim to it, the authoritarian regimes resorted to brutality to remain in place, and used violence to rebuild the foundations on which to consolidate their power.

The trappings of power

The political choices of the 1970s oriented these countries' trajectory towards an illusion of power. The oil rent and subsequent financial abundance reinforced decisions previously taken by these non-democratic regimes; despite the flagrant evidence of failure in the late 1980s, the flow of money inhibited self-examination. Coercion and distribution had silenced the political scene, which bowed to revolutionary parties guided by "charismatic" leaders. As the national communities began to split, showing signs of its potential for violence, these regimes deployed their influence across the regional, even the international stage. The success of the 1970s had galvanised the leaders. Algeria, Iraq and Libya changed rapidly through urbanisation, literacy campaigns, and industrialisation. The colonial past seemed far away for these young states that had decided to overhaul the social and economic structures inherited from that period. The failure of land reform did not yet emerge as a major preoccupation. The population in these three countries had doubled, but the oil rent enabled them to afford massive imports of foodstuffs. Economic contradictions began to come to light, but the results achieved during the 1970s could only strengthen the factions among the governing bodies that considered that political voluntarism had lifted the countries out of "underdevelopment". Those who pointed out that these achievements were highly relative given the total dependence on hydrocarbons were countered by the sycophants of "Arab socialism" in fierce denial of reality. They argued, for instance, that the Iraqi health system was one of the best in the Middle East and that patients even came from abroad to receive care, that Tunisians migrated to Libya in search of work, that the Moroccans envied their Algerian neighbours, etc.

These economic results favoured a social compromise that contributed considerably to the regimes' stability. As Jean Leca points out, "The Algerian social compromise may be summed up as follows: oil revenues and access to foreign loans have permitted the generalisation of salaried employment, the creation of jobs without any corresponding extension of production..."[3] It was during this period, moreover, that the theoretical and political framework explaining and justifying the action and vision of the ruling coalitions was formulated: in the proceedings of the 8th Baath Party Congress in 1974, in the Algiers Charter of 1976,[4] or again in the Green Book of 1977.[5] For many observers, these documents were the explanatory matrix for the regimes, and an astute reading of them would reveal the various currents. However, the impression of unanimity within the regimes and the grip that the Baath Party, the FLN and the revolutionary committees had on the societies' instruments of expression made it difficult to perceive harbingers of their fragility, apart from notorious opponents in exile or in prison. The impression these countries conveyed was one of emerging powers. But in fact, control over their society's means of expression was only partial, owing both to the regimes' inability to satisfy their hegemonic ambitions and the cunning with which social actors circumvented and transformed apparatuses of control. That said, the oil rent had indeed provided financing for a system of allocation which, without being impermeable to the economic situation, had nevertheless enabled these regimes to ensure their legitimacy, thereby confirming the correlation between rentier state and political stability, at least until the late 1980s.[6] By ensuring the material wellbeing of its citizens without taxing them, the rentier state seemed vaccinated against all forms of protest. Theoretically, distribution of the rent was supposed to depoliticise transactions between the state and its citizens and thereby offer social peace in exchange for the lack of interference in political decisions. Following this line of reasoning, political change became scarcely imaginable. Yet, in the late 1980s, insurgencies came to destabilise these regimes and prompt a reinterpretation of the political effects of the oil rent. It is nevertheless important to remember that before experiencing domestic protest, these regimes had implemented an ambitious and costly regional policy that did not fail to arouse concern among their neighbours.

Surges in military spending

Carried away by the diplomatic success of the nationalisation of the oil-gas sector and the fallout from the first oil crisis, the Algerian, Iraqi, and Libyan regimes launched into ambitious foreign policies. The oil rent afforded extensive military spending and greater involvement in conflicts. The regimes justified this spending by referring to the state of war against the "Zionist enemy", even when the arsenals accumulated were rarely used against Israel. Military spending swelled constantly: in Libya, it represented 12 per cent of total public expenditure in 1970, 23 per cent in 1975 and 34 per cent in 1980; in Iraq, it was 41 per cent in 1970, dropping to 32 per cent in 1975 and doubling to 66 per cent in 1985, at the height of the war against Iran. In Algeria, it was 14 per cent in 1970, then 18 per cent in 1975 before falling to 6 per cent in 1981, only to pick up again and reach 37 per cent in 1992[7] at the start of the civil war. With the oil counter-crisis and the collapse of oil prices in 1985, this spending soon became unmanageable for governments and incomprehensible to populations with growing social demands.

The objectives of the massive investment in the defence sector varied depending on the country. Libya aspired to become the hub of revolutionaries the world over, which explains the disproportion between its military spending and its actual involvement in military action, a disproportion that could be explained by the distribution of weapons to international insurgent groups involved in the fight against imperialism, colonialism or "Zionism".[8] Revolutionary Libya was thus becoming a wholesale military barracks. Saddam Hussein's Iraq was striving to become a recognised regional power: "In brief, we want Iraq to play a leading role in the area especially in the Arab homeland. We want Iraq to play a leading role in the consolidation of anti-imperialist policies at the international level".[9] The quest for independence was an abiding feature of the regime. Iraq wanted to shake the role of mere customer of the armaments industry to take on the role of a weapons producer country on the model of emerging Latin American nations in the 1970s like Brazil and Argentina. Algeria's military spending, though much lower, was also substantial. Here regional preoccupations took precedence over Middle Eastern concerns: for the Algerian regime, it was essential to maintain military superiority over Morocco, which was gradually taking over the Western Sahara.[10]

This spending did not for all that transform these countries into military powers in the 1980s, any more than industrial investments allowed the take-off of a competitive industrial sector. In fact, the army in Algeria and in Libya fulfilled a domestic police role more than that of a force for expansion abroad. Only the Iraqi army, headed by Baath Party civilians, embarked on wars of invasion, in Iran and later in Kuwait.[11]

Libya: A wholesale barracks

Muammar Qadhafi's Libya illustrates the blindness that the oil rent can cause. It was considered one of the poorest countries in the world in the 1950s, but the Qadhafi regime—buoyed by its revolutionary ideology—led a population of five million inhabitants, moreover obliged to live in only 3 per cent of the territory, single-handedly to confront "the imperial power" (the United States), "the colonial powers" (France and the United Kingdom) and "the Zionist power" (Israel). For many observers, only Muammar Qadhafi's irrational behaviour could explain this bellicose attitude. But although Muammar Qadhafi's Libya was not as large and powerful as the USSR, in the 1970s it was nevertheless the world's fourth largest oil exporter. The regime thus had the means to match its ambitions and prove its credibility. The oil rent reinforced the illusion of power that had led the regime to project itself as an emerging regional power. Whereas most Libyan men and women would have been satisfied with a successful and socially bearable economic regime, Muammar Qadhafi decided to bring the population of the *Jamahiriyya* to the forefront of international concerns. Under the aegis of Muammar Qadhafi, Libya turned into a "terrorist state" warmly welcoming all the world's revolutionaries in the framework of its policy of supporting revolutionary organisations.

The construction of a terrorist infrastructure at first aimed to eliminate all internal and external enemies of the Libyan revolution. Libya's revolutionary policy in Africa openly targeted those African regimes that harboured Libyan opponents or established diplomatic relations with Israel.[12] Later, the revolutionary regime, galvanised by the rise in oil prices, embarked on a policy of supporting communist, separatist and fundamentalist revolutionary movements in Latin America (including Guatemala, El Salvador, Ecuador and Colombia) and in Asian countries such as Bangladesh and the Philippines. The revolutionary regime set up training camps and centres for instruction in the techniques of subversion and terrorism (these included the so-called April 7 camp and the Sidi Bilal, Bin Gashir and Ras al Hilal camps). Over thirty terrorist and revolutionary movements are thought to have gone through these camps between 1970 and 1993.[13] Finally, the regime's support for the Abu Nidal organisation, which had perpetrated the 27 December 1985 attacks on Rome and Vienna airports, was for the United States government the real argument for enacting a policy of economic and military sanctions against Libya. It is not easy to draw up a full roster of Libya's terrorist activities, but "more than thirty countries" are believed to have been affected by "Libya-sponsored attacks".[14] It was in this context that the notion of the "terrorist state" developed,[15] encompassing a whole range of threats identified by American national security policy

This policy took shape in the early 1980s[16] with the creation in 1982 of the Libyan anti-imperialism centre, known as Mathaba International, the real think-tank or backbone of terrorist policy. It prospected in areas of tension to detect emerging markets for international terrorism. Since the Middle East itself was the sphere of influence for such regional powers as Syria and Iran, little scope remained there for Libya. The revolutionary regime thus decided to invest in new markets in South-East Asia, such as the Philippines, in Latin America and in Africa. Libyan agents offered training in guerrilla and terrorist tactics to many new movements, but also provided support for more well-established organisations such as the IRA in Northern Ireland. The director of Mathaba International was Mussa Kussa, whose vast personal networks enabled him to form ties with a variety of international figures.[17]

The Libyan regime's ambitious terrorist policy was based on wide-ranging support for political and military organisations fighting imperialism, Zionism and neo-colonialism. In practical terms, this policy formed Libya as an enemy of the United States, Israel, the United Kingdom and France. Between 1978 and 1986, owing to the rise in the price of oil, the Libyan regime had considerable financial resources at its disposal. The cost of this ambitious terrorist policy is difficult to evaluate, but the amount spent on arms purchases during this period is estimated at about $12 billion.[18] This policy was only one of the facets, no doubt the most destructive, of a far broader ambition: Libya was seeking to acquire the accoutrements of a military power. Furthermore, the regime did not limit itself to creating a terrorist infrastructure, it also embarked on a weapons of mass destruction programme and imported conventional arms.

In the early 1790s, the Libyan regime sought to acquire atomic weapons from China. After being rebuffed by the Chinese, Libya turned to the black market[19] to set up a "basic research and development" facility for its nuclear reactor at Tajura. Starting in the 1980s, the development of chemical weapons got under way. Construction of the Rabta complex (known as Pharma 150), with the aid of private foreign companies,[20] and later Pharma 200, near the town of Sebha, enabled the regime to produce chemical agents. Under the embargo, the chemical weapons development programme continued with the construction of the Tarhuna complex, there too owing to private foreign investment. Already in the 1990s, a number of reports by American agencies detailed the various strategies used by the regime to put together the industrial infrastructure needed to produce chemical and biological weapons.[21]

In the field of conventional weapons, the regime imported military equipment in vast quantities that were disproportionate to the size of its security forces. In the early 1980s, the USSR and France were Libya's main suppliers of tanks and combat aircraft. In 1986 Libya possessed an impressive fleet of over 3,000 tanks and 500 fighters or fighter-bombers. Quantitatively, the country was emerging as a leading military power in the region, but in practice it was unable to use its military arsenal effectively. Libya did not have the necessary personnel and was obliged to bring in foreign technicians to maintain and even to use it. The Libyan regime's military shortcomings became clear in the war against Egypt in 1977, and with the American air raid of 1986 and the expansion of the Chad conflict in 1987. Paradoxically, the over-equipped Libyan army inspired Muammar Qadhafi's suspicion: "The regime fears and distrusts the military, and thus imposes conditions on it that limit its effectiveness".[22] Between 1992 and 2003, international sanctions further deteriorated the military arsenal purchased for a small fortune a decade earlier.

Iraq: "Champion of the Arabs"

Oil revenue enabled the Baathist regime to finance the implementation of an expansionist policy that called into question the configuration of the Iraqi state endorsed by the League of Nations in 1920. In short, even if the seeds of Iraqi expansionism were contained in the British building of the Iraqi state, capture of the rent in the 1970s was fertile to their development within the Baath Party.

After working for Arab recovery of control over oil—the Baath Party slogan was "Arab oil for the Arabs"—the Baath proclaimed itself champion of the Gulf Arabs against the Shah and later the Islamic Republic. At the same time, Baghdad was striving to become the "capital of the Steadfastness Front" against Israel, whose 4 September 1974 accord with Egypt was denounced as "a serious setback for the Arab cause". Between 1968 and 1989, Iraq spent $90 billion in arms purchases. As it was for Libya, the USSR was its principal supplier.[23] Unlike Saudi Arabia, which during the same period spent $62 billion, the Iraqi Baath had set up a military industry that was likely to make it autonomous in certain defence sectors. As Abdelkader Sid Ahmed pointed out in the 1980s, "There is a strong contrast between huge arms purchases and the lack of any Arab weapons industry".[24] The regime's aim was to apply the same methods to the defence industry as those that had worked for the oil industry. Thus, between 1972 and 1987, a team of "armourers" led by Kamal Hussein attempted to give Iraq the foundations of a defence industry. It was a policy that distinguished this authoritarian regime from the others in terms of performance: "military industrialization conveys the image of an industrial sector that recognizes competence and productivity".[25]

Between 1973 and 1983, total currency inflow was estimated at $47.5 billion. On the eve of the invasion of Iran in 1980, the Iraqi government had about $30 billion in available reserves. The nationalisation of the hydrocarbon sector and the first oil crisis had enabled Iraq to increase its annual oil revenue from $487 million in 1968 to $13 billion for the year 1979. The Baath had the financial means to back its power. "Baghdad could not have gone to war against Iran", writes J.F. Luizard, "if its oil resources had not provided the bases for its weapons capability".[26] The oil rent played a fundamental role in the projection of the Iraqi regime's power. The government unwisely believed that the constant rise in oil prices—to which it owed considerable economic achievements throughout the 1970s—could only continue during the following decade. The war against Iran was bolstered by the belief in a rapid, flash victory that would have provoked the collapse of the Islamic Republic. But the latter's survival scuttled Baath expectations and led the regime into an even less sustainable war economy,[27] after which the oil counter-crisis would sound the knell for Iraqi financial prosperity and plunge the country into debt. At the end of the conflict, Iraq found itself with a debt of $100 billion. Stable and prosperous before it entered into war, Iraq was ruined when the conflict ended.[28]

Although devastated by human losses and financially ruined, Iraq at the end of the conflict with Iran in 1988 had become a feared military power in the region. But paradoxically, its military potential rested on an economy in crisis, unable to absorb the tens of thousands of demobilised soldiers. The regime's vulnerability at home was to some extent protected by the regional dread that this

THE VIOLENCE OF PETRO-DOLLAR REGIMES

army aroused, with the experience of seven years of war and equipped, by the "West", with sophisticated weaponry. In fact, and thanks to the oil rent, Iraq was able to ensure a continual weapons supply. In contrast to the conflict between Ethiopia and Eritrea, for instance, the Iraq-Iran war had demonstrated the advantages of the oil rent in terms of getting the bank loans necessary for the purchase of arms. In 1990, the regime's domestic vulnerability was such that it provoked the invasion of Kuwait on the grounds that the emirate was working to undermine Iraq's oil power and thereby seeking its financial ruin. The annexation was presented as healthy for Iraq's economy: "Sa'dun Hammadi, the minister of economics, appeared on state television after the invasion of Kuwait to tell hungry Iraqis that the occupation of Kuwait would enable them to repay their colossal foreign debts in a mere two to four years".[29] Donning the appearance of the last true Arab nationalist, Saddam Hussein sought in vain to mobilise the "Arab masses" by presenting the absorption of Kuwait as the forerunner of the necessary merger of an Arab world in danger in the face of Israel and its allies. Blinded by the power of oil, he also claimed that international sanctions would not last because "we have 20 per cent of world reserves. Sanctions will be lifted not for the sake of our eyes, but for the sake of our oil".[30] And yet it was indeed the threat of the possible union of the world's second and third largest proven oil reserves at the time that prompted the "international community" to free Kuwait in 1991, plunging Iraq into the throes of a total embargo. With the oil rent, the Baath Party had managed to improve the population's living conditions, only to send it back, after the annexation of Kuwait, to the "Middle Ages".[31] After the financial windfall, the military experience acquired in the fight against Iran ended up being thrown away in the Kuwait venture. Unlike the Argentine and Brazilian military regimes in the 1970s, Iraq under Baath Party rule thus failed to curtail its ambitions, which led to the destruction of its power.

Algeria: Development first, then Morocco

Unlike Libya and Iraq, Algeria under Boumediene believed that its power could only be expressed in development at home.

Domestic concerns took precedence over projects abroad. Certainly, during the 1970s, Algeria had exploited the opportunities between the two blocs offered by the Non-Aligned Movement. At the United Nations General Assembly, for instance, it proposed a new model of economic relations between North and South, a scarcely revolutionary project if compared with neighbouring Libya's policies. As Houari Boumediene explained, "We could have employed subversion or even merely propaganda. We refrained from all that".[32] Algeria had faith in progress and development. Its definition of power was economic, but its domination was sometimes expressed with arrogance both at the regional and the continental level. The oil rent was supposed to enable it to catch up economically and become an engine for the Arab world and Africa. The Algerian elites were convinced of the excellence of their development model and never missed an opportunity to point out its superiority. Algeria's foreign policy had no revolutionary aims. The Algerian revolution[33] was not intended for export and the socialist model was willing to cohabit with very different regimes in the region, such as the Moroccan monarchy. The preoccupations of the first ten years lay more in regaining control of Algeria's underground wealth, and therefore facing an inevitable diplomatic confrontation with France.

Spain's cession of the Western Sahara to Morocco in 1976, however, altered the order of priorities on the regime's agenda. Between 1962 and 1972, Algeria did not have the financial means to devise a response to Morocco's territorial claims in Algeria's southwest. In 1963, "the sand war" demonstrated that Algeria's territorial outline, drawn up by France, was disputed by Morocco,[34] first by the Istiqlal party, which called for a return to Greater Morocco, then by the monarchy of Hassan II. The territorial dispute between Algeria and Morocco found its resolution in the Ifrane Treaty of 1969 by which the two countries pledged to respect the borders handed down from the colonial period. In actual fact, the clash between two newly independent states would feed distrust and bitterness. Thus when Morocco cleverly recovered the Western Sahara upon the withdrawal of Spanish troops, Algeria was faced with a dilemma: acknowledging a *fait accompli* or going to war. But unlike in 1963, in 1976 Algeria enjoyed an oil rent

51

which since the first oil crisis endowed the regime with substantial revenue.

Algeria's strategy towards Morocco would be similar to Pakistan's towards India in Kashmir: "an outsourced war"[35] in which the Polisario Front, at first backed by Libya, soon became a tool in the service of Algeria. Weapons spending would follow fluctuations in oil prices: between 1973 and 1977, it amounted to $710 million, a paltry sum compared with Libya and Iraq during the same period, but it increased noticeably between 1978 and 1982 to reach $3.2 billion, then stabilised between 1983 and 1987 at $2.5 billion, and then, from 1987 to 1991, at $2 billion. The USSR was Algeria's main supplier, with sales of about three-quarters of Algeria's military equipment.[36] Many observers expressed concern about this arms race in the region. But unlike the conflict between Pakistan and India, for instance, or that between Iraq and Iran, the Algeria-Morocco confrontation, through the intermediary of the Polisario Front, remained confined to desert guerrilla warfare, with little cost to public finances. In the face of Morocco's annexation of the Western Sahara, all Algeria could do was make this absorption "indigestible" or painful, and that is probably one of the main reasons for the conflict's longevity. With the wealth of its oil rent, Algeria could afford the luxury of providing for the Sahrawi population in makeshift camps and could criticise Morocco's indifference to the people's right to self-determination. From 1975 to 1991, from annexation to ceasefire, Algeria nevertheless obliged Morocco to budget for considerable military spending in relation to its GDP in order to maintain control over the Sahara. This war of attrition cost the monarchy about ten billion dollars, obliging it to maintain and deploy its army (130,000 to 160,000 troops) in the Sahara. In the words of Fouad Abdelmoumni: "the cost of this issue is quite simply Morocco's non-development".[37]

The Western Sahara conflict thus blocked economic development in the Maghreb region. But this loss penalised Morocco more than Algeria, which could count on its oil rent. Algeria's stance on the Western Sahara—that the Sahrawi people had the right to a referendum on self-determination—translated into a diplomatic impasse and thus military tension. In its economic rivalry with Morocco, Algeria, blinded by the illusions of the oil rent, considered that time was on its side. The abundance of hydrocarbon revenues enabled it to conduct an endless "privatised war" that, it thought, could not fail to ruin the Sherifian kingdom, to provoke internal revolt; in short to challenge the choice of annexation. But the oil counter-crisis of 1986, which translated into a collapse of oil prices, would demolish this strategy, reveal the spectre of financial bankruptcy and provoke riots in Algeria. Between 1991 and 1993, Algeria only spent $145 million on weapons purchases, and support for the Sahrawis fell by the wayside in the face of the threat that the Front Islamique du Salut (FIS) posed to the regime. The oil rent did not provide sufficient resources for Algeria to thwart Morocco's plan of annexing the Western Sahara. It is symbolic that in the late 1980s, the two countries were both in debt and both offered their populations a low standard of living.

The 1980s demonstrated the limits of oil wealth's ability to generate military power. The oil rent did not suffice to ensure their regional ambitions: despite its giant arsenal, Libya was defeated by the Habre regime in Chad, Algeria was unable to stop Morocco's gradual absorption of the Western Sahara, and Iraq's military power was crushed by the campaign to liberate Kuwait. On the other hand, it helped them to remain in power despite their military defeats, as can be seen in the case of Libya in 1987 and Iraq in 1991. Whereas the Argentine military regime collapsed after its defeat by Britain in the Falkland Islands,[38] the Libyan and Iraqi regimes overcame their defeats and showed a strong aptitude for survival. The oil rent gave them the opportunity to purchase the trappings of power, to provoke regional conflicts and lose them but to manage, *in fine*, to remain in power. During the 1980s, the Arab socialist oil republics discovered that oil was not the weapon of mass destruction that would upset the balance of power in the region. Quite the contrary, oil wealth proved to be short-lived when after 1986, the oil counter-crisis plunged these countries into an unexpected economic crisis.

The end of illusions: The oil counter-crisis

Until 1986, Algeria, Libya and Iraq were able to overcome the domestic and regional problems that confronted them: riots, separatist movements and regional conflicts were held in check. With an annual growth rate of 6 per cent between 1970 and 1985, Libya was able to forget its war against Egypt in 1977 and the setbacks to its Africa policy: Algeria quickly turned the page on the Berber riots in the spring of 1980, and Iraq managed to spectacularly rebuild the infrastructure destroyed during the war against Iran. Until the oil counter-crisis, these regimes gave an impression of stability and control over their destinies. But the drop in the price of a barrel of oil from $30 to less than $10 in the space of a few months provoked a sense of vulnerability among these regimes for the first time since 1973. They came to the cruel realisation that their stability relied primarily on the price of oil. Iraq, which began its war against Iran with $30 billion in reserves, was forced to accumulate a huge debt to sustain its war economy. Algeria refused to admit the failure of its economic model and had trouble acknowledging it was in crisis. The spectacular drop in oil prices put an end to the belief in "black gold" as an engine of development.

Stability in Algeria, Iraq and Libya rested on rentier economies, and calling into question the way they functioned could only provoke resistance among the authoritarian coalitions that had managed to benefit from them. In the face of drastic reductions in revenue, those in power found themselves obliged either to enact deep economic reforms or to maintain the system by incurring huge debt. The governments ended up using both levers. If there is one thing the 1986 oil counter-crisis confirmed, it is indeed the hypothesis that the oil boom of the 1970s undermined the leaders' forecasting abilities. The abundance of revenue destroyed any instrument for risk analysis among administrations and bodies in charge of evaluating economic policies. The belief in a constant and virtually irreversible rise in the price of oil made them lose sight of the precarious and fragile nature of these rentier economies.[39] With the same conviction and the same eagerness that had nourished the belief in an oil nationalism serving development, those in power now sought to impose sometimes radical economic reforms without measuring the social consequences of those reforms. Thus economic liberalisation would produce unemployment and inflation without improving economic performance. In the end, these reforms would engender a prosperous informal economy.

Improvised economic liberalisation

> As oil revenues declined in the 1980s, all oil exporters attempted to liberalize their economies by withdrawing subsidies, cutting state spending, and encouraging the private sector to assume a larger role in the industrial, trade and agricultural sectors... in the so-called "socialist" countries like Libya and Algeria, they were blocked through the concerted efforts of labour, ruling party cadre and bureaucrats. In contrast, Iraq emerged from its eight year war with Iran to implement the most wide-ranging privatization program in the developing world.[40]

The scope of reforms undertaken by the Iraqi regime caused economic chaos that was particularly worrying for the Baath Party given that in 1987, 96 per cent of the active population was employed by state companies. Thus the population found that unemployment plus inflation after eight years of war against Iran were particularly difficult to digest: "As the crisis deepened, the economic disaster became a political crisis".[41] In agriculture, the government implemented land tenure reform: 53 per cent of state-owned agricultural land was privatised, 46 per cent was leased by the state and only 1 per cent remained under its control.[42] Privatisation of public companies and agricultural land enabled the regime to rebuild a clientelistic base among the new elites: "Unlike the old commercial elite, the new private sector that emerged had strong political, financial and kinship ties with the regime".[43] The benefactor rentier state of the 1970s had ceased to function, as was illustrated by the abolition of taxes on the profits made by private companies, although they sustained the social security fund for workers; in 1989, all companies were exempted from taxes for ten years.

In Libya, the drop in oil prices starting in 1985 caused revenue to plummet: from $20 billion in 1981 to $5 billion in 1986. Whereas the country was engaged in a costly armament policy, this financial reversal considerably diminished *Jamahiriyya* finances. But the regime had managed to compensate for the loss of income principally through its petrodollar investments in international financial markets. In 1992, for instance, LAFICO managed a portfolio estimated at $8 billion. Though the Jamahiriyya contrived more or less to sustain its war effort in Chad, the Libyan people's standard of living continued to deteriorate, and restrictions on imports led to shortages, resulting in speculation in food. In consequence, the regime decided in 1988 to rescind the ban on private commerce to offset the inadequacy of the distribution system. From 1988, Qadhafi announced a number of reforms that had certain similarities to IMF recommendations: trade liberalisation, abolition of subsidies for certain commodities (wheat, tea, etc.), together with permission for agricultural producers to market their produce privately. In 1990, a second wave of measures was announced: closure of bankrupt state companies, reduction in the number of civil servants, laws facilitating foreign investment, and the public provision of loans for private businesses. In 1993, schemes to promote tourism were launched and the convertibility of the dinar authorised. This process of economic liberalisation came to a halt, however, when the United Nations Security Council decided to impose sanctions on Libya. The regime's priorities changed, with economic problems eclipsed by political and security issues.[44]

As for Algeria, its hydrocarbon revenues shrank by 50 per cent in 1986: from $10 billion in 1985, they dropped to a little more than $5 billion. As in Iraq and Libya, the government therefore sought to reduce state spending. Publicly refusing to have recourse to the IMF, it implemented a liberalisation policy aiming to give state companies greater independence, encourage foreign direct investment (FDI), overhaul the management and property rights of agricultural enterprises and change the law on currency and credit.[45] Two schools argued over the reform: some maintained that the crisis was due to the economic climate, that the economy had to adapt while waiting for oil prices to go up again; others believed that the crisis was structural, revealing the failure of economic policies, and that the remedy was a complete overhaul of the rentier economy. But the hydrocarbon sector seemed untouchable, so great was the fascination it continued to hold: it was responsible for the growth in external revenue from $0.2 billion in 1970 to $12.5 billion in 1980. Yet, with annual receipts maintained at around $5 billion between 1986 and 1990, the state could no longer meet current expenditure without going heavily into debt. Between 1985 and 1988, the total volume of debt doubled to reach $26 billion. Repaying it would bring Algeria to the brink of bankruptcy in the early 1990s, the service of the debt absorbing most of its oil and gas revenue. "The golden age" was over for most and the failure of the

Algerian development model became an illustration of the resource curse. In 1989, a reform-minded government finally set itself the task of "making irreversible institutional and economic changes"[46] with the IMF's discreet support. Resistance to such a plan was widespread, among both those who had benefited from the state's largesse and those who had profited from it and were now, in the context of the crisis, accused of corruption and embezzlement.[47] Eager as they were to carry out economic and political reforms at once, the reformers ended up losing control of the transition with the overwhelming and unexpected victory of the FIS in the municipal and legislative elections of 1990 and 1991. The Islamist threat hanging over the regime relegated reform to oblivion.

The oil counter-crisis thus destabilised these states' distribution mechanisms. Confronted with social demands and protest movements, the Algerian, Libyan and Iraqi regimes were subjected to serious challenges to their legitimacy. The drop in revenues and rise in social demands inherent in the tripling of their populations and the resultant transformation of the demographic spread obliged the rulers of these countries to redefine their economic policies. Even if the economic crisis did not bring the authoritarian regimes down, it did usher in a new period of instability[48] that would lead to internal conflicts. In fact, short of funds but with a massive stock of weapons, the regimes used violence, sometimes in the framework of a civil war, to reassert their authority. For the people, the benefactor state turned into a "barbarian", tyrannical" or "dictatorial" state, depending on the case. In fact, the regimes were able to demonstrate that despite their economic and military incompetence, they were far more robust and imaginative than their opponents believed when it came to repression. For these regimes fighting for their very survival, exiting authoritarianism was certainly not a priority on their political agenda.

Is the oil rent conducive to crushing revolts?

In the early 1990s the military oil regimes, made vulnerable by the perverse effects of implementing economic liberalisation policies, weakened by their military defeats, challenged by Islamist and separatist movements, ended up turning against "their society". Ensnared in international sanctions and criticism, Iraq, Libya and Algeria were subject to embargos, a total one for Saddam Hussein's regime, partial for Muammar Qadhafi of the *Jamahiriyya*, and moral for the Algerian generals. These countries, considered as models of development in the 1970s, had become "pariah states"[49] that the international community found distasteful to associate with, at least in public. Under the embargos, humiliated on the regional front and strongly disputed from within, these regimes would brutally repress opponents and protesters behind closed doors. By a terrible reversal of history, these regimes, which had grown out of coups d'état and were inspired by egalitarian ideology, turned into infernal machines that aroused fear or revolt in most of their citizens. These Arab socialist republics were challenged by opponents harbouring plans for an Islamic state. If oil wealth had blinded the regimes and led them to financial ruin, it had also destroyed their ability to perceive and anticipate transformations in their society.

The brutality of these regimes towards their opponents illustrates the ideology of combat that inspired the ruling elites. Convinced it was the only legitimate guardian of the state, the Baath Party in Iraq demanded Sunni Arab solidarity when it crushed the Shia revolt of March 1991. The brutality of the repression matched the scale of the regime's worries; it had been defeated in its confrontation with the Coalition forces, and perceived the insurgency as a challenge to the legitimacy of the state founded in 1920 on a Sunni Arab base.[50] In Algeria, the defeat of the FLN in the 1991 legislative elections and the likely establishment of an Islamic state frightened the army, which not only saw the electoral process escape its control but moreover foresaw in the Islamist discourse the prospect that the "generals" would become the expiatory victims of the new Islamic state.[51] For the army, the self-proclaimed last rampart of the state, the Islamists would bring about a revolution that would sweep away the post-colonial Arab socialist republic. The systematic destruction of Algerian Islamists is reminiscent of the slaughter of Indonesian Communists in 1965:[52] it aimed to "purify" a social and political body perceived as marred by the blemishes of history and culture.[53] In Libya, the crushing of the Islamist guerrilla had similar motivations: for Muammar Qadhafi, the Islamists were society's political "AIDS", that absolutely had to be destroyed in order for the regime to survive. Libyan Islamists, for the first time since the 1969 coup, brought violence against the regime inside the country. Until then, opposition movements had been cast out of the territory (into Egypt and Chad) and were the result of a political complex of regional alliances. Libyan Islamists considered that they had to cleanse Libya of the *Jamahiriyya*. For them, "the just society" Muammar Qadhafi had planned had sunk into corruption and debauchery. It was time to "purify" Libya of the "sickness" personified by Muammar Qadhafi.[54]

The brutality of the repression was to be efficacious thanks to profits generated by the oil rent. It had encouraged rapid urbanisation and the construction of modern infrastructure (highways, airports, etc.), which largely facilitated the task of the repressive forces. Urban density, for instance, enabled Republican Guard helicopters in Iraq to carry out a slaughter among the population and install terror very quickly. Likewise, the Algerian and Libyan maquis scrub offered little chance of surviving aerial bombardment. In contrast, for decades the Sudanese regime had been experiencing huge difficulties in silencing its opponents; but when the pipeline to the Red Sea was brought into service in 1998, the regime's external revenue increased, enabling it to finance militias, thus improving its ability to retaliate against the "rebels" and giving it bargaining power.[55] Improvements in infrastructure during the 1970s turned out to offer an effective instrument in the repression of the early 1980s: the territory had become useful, the cities accessible and easily controlled by regimes that had developed an effective repressive apparatus. On the other hand, the regime had to ensure that the insurgents would be incapable of sabotaging the hydrocarbon industry, especially the network of oil and gas pipelines that connected the oil fields to export terminals. In short, the spectre of acts of sabotage and kidnapping so common in Nigeria,[56] or attacks on oil company facilities such as Chevron in Sudan, had to be averted.[57]

Can the oil rent thus be said to facilitate the crushing of insurgencies? In fact, the 1990s confirmed the hypothesis that authoritarian oil regimes had a decisive advantage in their confrontation with rebels. Hydrocarbons, unlike diamonds or gold, guaranteed regimes that exploited this sector a monopoly on production and sales. Certainly, guerrilla organisations can always divert barrels of oil here and there, as they do in Nigeria and Iraq, but over time they cannot benefit from the revenues of this sector as it requires an industry capable of producing.[58] Moreover, although Islamist rebels may sometimes enjoy popular support, it will never translate into recognition from the international community, owing to the fears aroused in the world energy market by the spectre of their seizing control of oil resources. For such technical and political reasons, regimes have the necessary conditions to achieve victory over rebels in the more or less long term, depending on the level of brutality they are prepared to use. The crushing of insurgencies in Iraq, Algeria and Libya bears out this hypothesis.

Doomed insurrections

In March 1991, a violent uprising broke out in Iraq that for two weeks posed a threat to the regime. From south to north, populations driven by feelings of anger and a sense of injustice in the face of the dramatic defeat inflicted on the Iraqi army directed their rancour at the symbols of the Baath Party and its regime. The dream of widespread insurrection, nourished for so long by both Kurdish and Islamist opposition movements, became a reality, even if its spontaneity totally escaped these movements' control. Thus, owing to its "total lack of preparation", the uprising was doomed to fail and was inevitably destroyed. Indeed, Saddam Hussein's regime, unlike its opponents, was well prepared: "...by 1991, Saddam Hussein arranged his forces to face a three-edged threat, from the north, from the south and from inside the capital, presuming that at least one would arise in militating insurrection".[59] By the end of March, the Republican Guard had crushed the insurrection and massacred the rebels from north to south, leaving the uprising no time to organise or bring together all those within the army or in the ranks of the opposition who shared the conviction that the regime should not survive the new assault it had just made on the Iraqi people.

The founding moment of the revolt was the regime's "abandonment" of the army following the military campaign to liberate

Kuwait. The massacre of soldiers on the "highway of death" (Al Mutla) by Coalition air forces blew a wind of revolt, even among the army ranks. The army in southern Iraq, which was over 80 per cent Shia Muslim (although only 20 per cent of the officers were Shia), was the hardest hit by Coalition air attacks. It was behind an uprising that aimed to bring about regime change. But the fear of seeing the insurrection lead to the establishment of an Islamic state united those who believed keeping Saddam Hussein in power was a lesser evil than an Islamic republic. They were few in number but worried enough to remain united in the destruction of their enemies. Thus the regime's weakness in the face of the external enemies that had just chased it out of Kuwait, was offset by an incredible ferocity and brutality against its own people.

With a lesser degree of violence, the Algerian regime displayed a comparable attitude. Unable to stop Morocco's annexation of the Western Sahara, stricken by the failure of its economic model and shouted down by rioters who never missed an opportunity to denounce the monopolising of the oil rent by a minority, President Chadli Bendjedid offered to put an end to the FLN-state in hopes of allaying these sources of bitterness. In contrast to Iraq, Algeria did not go to war against Morocco. It opted instead for a democratic transition, which, however, would lead to civil war. The Algerian revolution had produced an FLN-state whose "sons" fought against "Islamic socialism" and dreamed of instituting a genuine Islamic state.[60] Having won two elections that it had not demanded, the FIS realised the power of its party and by the same token the vulnerability of the regime. The FLN's electoral defeat implied unconditional surrender. The fear of becoming the expiatory victims of an Islamic state founded on virtue led army leaders to confront "the ungrateful people" with a selective memory.

Unlike the Republican Guard in Iraq, the Algerian army, with its 160,000 troops, was not prepared for an armed rebellion. An army anti-terrorist squad of 80,000 men was formed in record time to lead the fight, in addition to volunteers prepared to form militias. But once the Islamist party was disbanded and its activists put in jail, the army still had to face a guerrilla resistance of about 30,000 combatants. In 1994, now better reorganised, the army launched its "total war" against the armed groups and managed to eradicate them. The Islamist guerrillas, divided into several tendencies, at first enjoyed considerable popular support, suggesting that they might be able to overturn the regime. In 1994, the possibility of the Algerian regime's collapse worried chanceries in neighbouring countries. The guerrilla "emirs" were convinced that time was on their side and that the regime would fall sooner or later under the *jihad's* battering. After the nationalist fight against colonial rule, the Islamists claimed to be fighting to establish an Islamic state. But in 1998, the guerrillas were defeated; the war had left 150,000 civilians dead and displaced over a million and a half. As in Iraq, the military rulers remained united in adversity and managed to convince sceptics that an Islamist state was more dangerous than keeping the old regime. The victorious army did not fail to repeat that one of its missions was to save Algeria from the many plots threatening it. As one general claimed,

> There is no denying that the Algerian army, in its unity and cohesion, enjoyed the trust of the national forces, that this army was truly a rampart that prevented the FIS as well as the opposition associated with it from succeeding. I don't know which groups and parties were linked with the FIS. But we can imagine. They are not solely Algerian. It is not political doubletalk to say these groups and parties are also foreign.[61]

Morocco, without being explicitly named, was considered an objective ally of the Islamists. Defeated at the polls in 1990 and 1991, the regime took its military revenge between 1993 and 1998, putting down a guerrilla campaign with strong popular support. Like the Iraqi regime, in adversity the Algerian regime had displayed an extraordinary aptitude for combat, particularly against its "lost children", which is how the regime viewed the Islamists.

In Libya, the armed rebellion against the regime was not blessed with a context as favourable as in Iraq after the military defeat in Kuwait, or in Algeria after the electoral process was brought to a halt in January 1992. The political conditions for a successful insurgency did not exist. Only international sanctions could suggest that the *Jamahiriyya* had been weakened by international isolation. When in 1995 Islamic insurgents launched a revolt against the regime, they believed that international sanctions would deeply and durably weaken it. The Islamist opponents, like those in Baathist Iraq and socialist Algeria, accused revolutionary Libya of being apostate. The Libyan Islamic Fighting Group (Al Islamiyya al Muqatila bi Libya, LIFG) first came on the scene in 1995. It called for a *jihad* against the Qadhafi regime to put an end to the plight of "Libyan Muslims": "There is no doubt that the tragic situation which is hurting Libyan society is not hidden from any person with even the least concern for the situation of the Muslim. So the absence of the Islamic regime—which is a guarantor for the achievement of salvation and peace in this world and the next—is what brought us to this situation".[62] Between 1995 and 1998, the LIFG conducted guerrilla operations against security forces in the Benghazi region, prompting a strong response from the regime in the form of bombing raids on the mountainous region of Jebel al-Akhdar where the Islamist militants had their hideouts. The regime associated them with the imperialist threat: "Our revolution", Qadhafi proclaimed in 1993, "is a fundamental revolution, a revolution of authenticity. We are the leaders of an authentic and fundamental revolution; only the revolution and pan-Arabism can combat imperialism and its local allies that are the Islamists".

Although the regime had been taken by surprise, it reacted swiftly. The geographical hardship confronting the guerrillas (their only place of refuge was the mountainous area of Jebel al-Akhdar), combined with limited inhabitable land (3 per cent of the country), enabled Libyan security forces to bring the counterinsurgency operations to a successful conclusion. Moreover, the building of modern infrastructure facilitated troop transport and the alternate use of air and ground forces to put down the rebels. To combat the Islamists, as in Iraq, the regime mobilised the Revolutionary Guard, seconded by foreign mercenaries, rather than the army. To their great astonishment, the insurgents discovered the reaction capacity of a regime it believed to be running out of steam:

> The regime is passing through a phase of unprecedented hysteria and is massing all its military and security might in attempt to annihilate the LIFG. The Libyans have not bombed their own country since the Italian occupation. But we are witnessing today the Libyan air force bombing the Mujahideen positions in the Jebel al-Akhdar, the heart of the anti-Italian resistance. This area is today one of the many strong points of the LIFG. Meanwhile, Qaddafi is attempting to conceal from public opinion the real nature of these clashes by

disguising this military offensives as raids on drug traffickers and the like. At the present moment, he has 10,000 troops in the region, including Serbian forces brought in from the former Yugoslavia.[63]

Between 1995 and 1998, a major security operation was carried out in the Jebel al-Akhdar region. Roadblocks were set up every 10 kilometres for security forces to check the identity of all passengers. The brutality of the repression clearly indicated the ambition to destroy the protest by all possible means. For example, the use of heavy weapons to put down the Abu Salim prison mutiny in Tripoli[64] left a lasting impression in people's minds.

Between 1995 and 1998, the LIFG failed to escalate its violent uprising into a full-blown insurrection. It did not succeed in generating a legitimate protest movement transcending tribal and regional affiliations. Although its violent actions were mainly confined to Cyrenaica, the LIFG did not manage to create the narrative necessary to discredit the regime: to gain acceptance for the idea that the government's repressive policy was a continuation of the Italian colonial regime. Furthermore, the LIFG had underestimated the regime's capacity to react and defend itself. Like the armed Islamist movements in Algeria, the LIFG had mistaken vulnerability for weakness. The Qadhafi regime was vulnerable under the embargo, but this did not mean it was unable to strike back. The LIFG did not have the opportunity to crystallise resentment against the regime by politically exploiting a specific injustice (such as the cancellation of the electoral process in Algeria) or even a feeling of humiliation (like the feeling aroused by the defeat of the Iraqi army). The declaration of the *jihad* in 1995 failed to arouse any widespread protest. The regime's reaction finally proved fatal to the Islamists' armed revolt. The LIFG, like other Islamist guerrilla movements, discovered at its own expense the survival tactics of a vulnerable regime.

Recourse to paramilitary organisations

The armies in these countries, pampered in terms of military equipment during the period of financial abundance, were neglected by the governing coalitions after the oil counter-crisis in favour of paramilitary organisations, which were better suited to counterinsurgency. After being praised to the skies for their role as a "rampart"—against the advance of the desert in Algeria (the army being employed in reafforestation) or against the Iranian revolution in Iraq or against imperialism and colonialism in Libya—armies became the symbol of regime failure. Yet they had absorbed a considerable share of the revenue during the oil boom (1973–85): $102 billion in Iraq, $35 billion in Libya and $20 billion in Algeria. Inspired by the Soviet model, these armies were formatted for a fairly static system of defence. Most of the troops were conscripts, and the national army was presented as a symbol of the nation.[65] The consequences of these political decisions would be felt during the 1990s. International sanctions imposed on the regimes in fact led to deterioration of their military equipment due to the ban on weapons purchases. From a political standpoint, they witnessed the emergence of paramilitary organisations that threatened their position in the regimes' security apparatus, which in Iraq and Libya were likely to sideline the army. Given the need to combat enemies from within, the capabilities amassed for external conflicts lost all value. Symbolically, during the 1990s, the ruling coalitions seemed to find paramilitary forces more powerful and more reliable. Like the economy, the security apparatuses were undergoing profound changes tending towards more flexible structures because they were based on ties of clan, tribal or regional allegiance. The national army seemed to have vanished, put under embargo like the state. Although national defence remained a concern at the regional level, regime security seemed better ensured under the watchful eye of paramilitary organisations.

In response to Iraq's invasion of Kuwait, the Iraqi army was destroyed by Coalition troops and its strategic ambitions reduced to naught: "The regime's choices were strictly circumscribed by the aim of achieving military parity with Israel and strategic superiority over Iran. This was not, in itself, evidence of expansionist ambitions; rather, Iraq sought to become strong enough militarily to forestall aggression from any regional power".[66] The world's fourth largest army vanished, leaving the regime only with the Republican Guard, which became the true pillar of the regime under embargo. Made up of members selected from the clans most loyal to Saddam Hussein, it ensured the regime's defence by destroying the enemies within and dissuading those who felt nostalgic for the army from trying to overthrow the regime. The objective of supplanting Egypt as the regional Arab power would crumble after the strategic error of invading Kuwait.[67] The Iraqi army, which the Baath Party in the war against Iran had raised to the rank of symbol of the Arab nation, would come out of it seriously crippled. This army was primarily Sunni; its violent actions against Shia Arab tribes, the Assyrians, the Kurds and then the Communists fitted into a context of developing an Arab nationalist sentiment. The state's Sunni Arab ethnic orientation then became apparent, even if it was not legalised by any constitution.[68] The nation-state was based on Arabism, as during the British mandate Sunni Arab elites became dominant in place of the Persian elites of the Ottoman era. The Baath Party takeover of power in 1968 considerably accelerated this process. Unlike previous repressions, the one in March 1991 demonstrated the regime's terrifying brutality, spawned by the power bestowed by the oil rent.

In Libya, international sanctions caused the army to collapse, as it found itself deprived of the means to maintain its military equipment.[69] Under the embargo, its 45,000 troops gradually lost the importance they had had in the 1970s and the early 1980s. In 1991, the Defence Ministry was abolished. The army had not been mobilised to combat armed Islamist dissidence. Attempted military coups between 1993 and 1995 placed the army in disgrace in favour of the Revolutionary Guard and paramilitary structures to defend the regime. The Revolutionary Guard was in charge of regime defence, the Republican Guard had the mission of protecting Qadhafi and his family, and security squads were to control the main cities. The repressive function of this security apparatus was patent. The development of a feeling of vulnerability under the sanctions had caused the *Jamahiriyya* to retreat toward its instruments of repression. Threats hanging over the regime had caused it to contract around figures that Muammar Qadhafi considered trustworthy. More than competence, absolute allegiance was sought, a far better guarantee of the regime's security.[70] As Mansour O. El-Kikhia writes, "there are a large number of Qathafa junior officers headed by a core of colonels who are individually and jointly responsible for the preservation of the regime."[71] Such tribalisation of power fostered consolidation of the regime in a context of great vulnerability.

In Algeria, a new army corps of 15,000 men was created in 1993, made up of units from the army, the gendarmerie and the police. Its numbers very quickly reached 80,000. But despite its effectiveness, this army corps was incapable of defeating the guerrillas. The army thus took the risk of calling on militias to back its war effort. The military institution feared that the militias would turn into independent forces that would refuse to comply with army strategy. In 1994, militias incorporated in the fight against the guerrillas were also organised. Three types of them appeared: first, self-defence groups, literally armed wings of political parties and regional associations; secondly, resistance or patriotic forces incorporated into gendarmerie units (equipped by the government, and auxiliaries of the Interior Ministry); lastly, private militias serving local notables. Actually, the civil war went in hand with a militarisation of society that soon became cause for concern. For the Algerian army, democratisation was as negative a choice as the decision by Saddam Hussein's regime to invade Kuwait, plunging the Iraqi army into disarray. The Algerian generals feared that the electoral process had provoked chaos: "Algerian society must make some serious choices about the direction its future is to take… The country is faced with reckonings that are a fundamental stage in the consolidation of Algeria's destiny as a modern nation".[72] The Islamist insurgency was careful to distinguish between the army and the regime. It even offered the army a way out by making a deal with it: "the army must understand that its future—that is to say its status as a modern powerful army that respects the Constitution and is respected by the people… more than ever [lies in regaining] control of itself and halting this bogus electoral process that is currently plunging the country into chaos".[73]

For the army, the civil war was the worst of ordeals. Not only did it threaten the institution owing to the number of conscripts in its ranks (80,000 out of 160,000), it also risked estranging the "people" or turning them against it, whereas they were a component of its legitimacy. Lastly, in the fight against the Islamists, the success of the militias was a double-edged sword, for although it ensured security throughout the land, it also strengthened their control on the ground. It was thus essential to prevent the civil war from taking root. The army was aware that the longer the conflict lasted, the more its ability to compel the militias to obey it was likely to be curtailed. The army could not be sidelined as it was in Iraq and Libya (it was a basic component of the regime) and it could not mobilise tribal organisations in order to function and survive. For the Algerian regime, the solution involved rebuilding the militias and recomposing the "revolutionary family". This family acted as a "tribe" and its members shared the immense privilege of having paid with their blood to make Algeria free and independent. The revolutionary family was a social organisation with complex and deep ramifications spread throughout the country. This social organisation, which formed one body with the state and considered itself an integral part of the regime, remained convinced that "it is Algeria"—and that the country's riches belonged to it. Oil is its blood as well as its reward. Starting in 1998, once assured that the Islamist guerrilla had been defeated, the army set about demobilising the militias.

The Algerian, Iraqi and Libyan regimes all demonstrated that in a vulnerable situation, recourse to mass repression was a political instrument of survival. Freed from any moral or diplomatic constraints, resorting to brutality was all the easier since control of the oil rent had enabled them to finance the cost of using violence. These examples confirm studies that underscore how difficult it is to topple regimes that have a monopoly over control of the rent. Indeed, in such a context, rebel movements seem doomed to fail because the abundance of revenue enables regimes to carry out a costly but effective counterinsurgency policy, even in times of financial and economic crisis. The only way to establish a relatively equal balance of forces would have been for the insurgents to destroy oil production facilities in order to reduce the regimes' income. But implementing such a strategy requires technical means that the insurgents did not have. Furthermore, investments by the regimes in security protection of oil production sites made any attempt to destroy or sabotage them vain. Thus, having been the symbol of development and the pride of the nationalists, oil wealth turned into fuel for authoritarian coalitions living on borrowed time.

Conclusion

The oil rent did not produce the desired metamorphosis. The nationalists in the Baath Party, the FLN and the *Jamahiriyya* believed that capture of the rent would give them power, impose their economic supremacy and assert their military hegemony. In fact, the oil rent blinded them, made them careless and arrogant. Seeking to acquire the outward signs of wealth, they eliminated all those who condemned such usurpation. Despite military defeats and political crises, the generation of oil nationalism of the 1970s did not want to admit defeat. While the USSR and the Eastern Bloc countries were collapsing and Latin America was gradually ridding itself of its military regimes, this generation continued to believe that it embodied the people. Yet many changes had occurred in the course of twenty years and investments made in the 1970s were beginning to bear fruit: record literacy rates were achieved, rising from 34 per cent in 1960 to 60 per cent in 1990 in Iraq, from 46 per cent to 79 per cent in Algeria; life expectancy at birth in Libya went from 46 years in 1960 to 61 in 1990, from 48 to 65 in Iraq, from 47 to 65 in Algeria; the mortality rate per 1,000 births within the first five years was declining everywhere, falling from 269 to 112 in Libya, from 222 to 86 in Iraq and from 270 to 98 in Algeria. All the human development indicators showed a constant improvement in the population's standard of living. Certainly, economic growth had been lower than population growth during that period, and so unemployment remained on a large scale, particularly for young people under the age of thirty who made up most of the population. Following the oil counter-crisis, the drop in revenue forced the rulers to institute liberalisation policies aiming to reduce state spending and reform an unproductive and costly agricultural sector while food needs were constantly rising. From a sociological standpoint, the generation born after oil and gas industries were nationalised was entering its twenties and aspired to change. Islamism was the dominant ideological offer; the Islamic state was the new political utopia rallying the people. In this context the Iraqi republic, the FLN-state and the Jamahariyya stood as obstacles. Incapable of negotiating a happy and peaceful outcome, the regimes would destroy those who threatened them and plunge those who challenged them into the inferno of international sanctions for Iraq, the purgatory of partial sanctions for Libya and the vain hope of the end of the FLN-state in Algeria. The 1990s therefore began with the conviction that oil was a curse, it was that "excrement of the devil" denounced by the founding father of OPEC, Juan Pablo Pérez Alfonso.[74] If oil was a godsend, it was for another reason: it provided for the fusion of the rentier economy and authoritarian coalitions and thus gave rise to resilient mafia-type regimes.

3

OIL RENT AND MAFIA REGIMES

A favourable context for regime transformation

The revolutionary period gave the security services an opportunity to play a strategic role in regulating the oil "market" and protecting transactions during the period of financial abundance (1971–85). The sudden collapse in oil prices in 1986 derailed the economic and foreign policies previously pursued by the Algerian, Iraqi and Libyan governments. It plunged these countries into deep political crisis. Destabilised by the scale of social and political protest, the central security agencies no longer managed to permeate the heterogeneous coalitions that ruled these authoritarian regimes at the time. In short, the mechanisms developed to ensure exclusive control over the oil rent became jammed, thereby undermining the complex political frameworks that had ensured a certain degree of stability. 1986 thus ushered in a period of instability, which resulted from the violent means used to reconstruct and create new mechanisms of regulation and consolidation. Confronted with the sudden scarcity of resources and the threat of falling from power, the authoritarian coalitions broke apart to recombine as groups whose loyalty was no longer based on belief in the revolution (socialist or pan-Arabist) but on ties of clan and tribal allegiance. The basic motivations of these regimes were laid bare, revealing the vacuity of revolutionary political organisations, even for the central security agencies. The nationalist and socialist revolutions have had their day and no longer offer an adequate political framework.

In the late 1980s, in an international and national context threatening to these regimes, there began a process of reconstructing new coalitions, based no longer on managing and distributing the rent, but on the transfer of ownership of state goods and services to the open market. The auctioning off of the state's property bought new protagonists on the scene and, by the fact of this new competitive context, a surge of violence. Indeed, the need to guarantee the security of property transactions made in the context of liberalisation and privatisation policies brought about the emergence of "mafias".[1] These criminal organisations fulfil regulatory functions, to some extent supplanting the role played by central security agencies throughout the 1970s. They foster the organisation of new coalitions that no longer aim to capture the oil rent but to take control of land, real estate, and industrial and commercial property that the new economic situation now offered. This situation plunged the people into even greater instability and poverty. State property, valued by the rentier economy, became a fundamental stake in the battle to reform the authoritarian coalitions. An economy of plunder thus took hold in a context marked not only by political violence but also by international sanctions.

In the face of this test, the heterogeneous coalitions formed during the period of financial abundance shrank, eclipsed at first by the most loyal social groups. Financially independent, vaccinated against diplomatic and clan retaliation from the political and ethnic standpoint, oil regimes now used violence to build new authoritarian coalitions bearing resemblance to criminal or mafia organisations that must be underscored. Nationalist and progressive rhetoric lost even more credibility owing to the criminal practices of leaders in both security and administrative organisations. Like criminal organisations, these regimes flourish with the expansion of poverty: the scarcity of resources thus fostered the development of "sultanistic" behaviour among the ruling elites.[2] And yet, the latter had partly built their legitimacy on recovering the nation's resources, which had been unfairly exploited by the former colonial powers or through their oil companies. The new context, characterised by international sanctions and a major crisis among rentier economies, caused a deep transformation in the authoritarian regimes of the three countries: under embargo, stripped of their ideology, they turned into mafia regimes adapted to their new environment. They began to function as criminal enterprises "able to gain a foothold in a territory, amass huge economic resources, control large segments of the local society and dominate it using a military apparatus".[3]

There is much to learn from an analysis of the embargo periods in seeking to understand the type of transformation that affected the regimes of rentier states. International sanctions encouraged them to use guile and cruelty to survive. In a context of increasingly scarce resources, they ended up seizing what remained and destroying even more brutally those who disputed their rule. Made vulnerable by the regime of sanctions but threatened by the same challenges, they managed to stick together. This is why, and against all expectation, the Algerian, Libyan and Iraqi regimes managed to endure the oil counter-crisis, maintain a certain degree of cohesion within their repressive apparatuses and finally emerge victorious from the confrontation with their Islamist opponents. These regimes thus demonstrated their remarkable aptitude to adapt to an environment as uncertain and dangerous as ever. At the end of this period, only the Iraqi regime disappeared, but it was not its inability to destroy all those that threatened it from within that led to its downfall; it was an unforeseeable event, the September 11, 2001 attacks, that would provoke in American foreign policy a blend of fury, thirst for revenge, utopia and a "grand strategy".[4]

The economic reforms enacted in the mid-1980s modified property rights of agricultural land and public companies, import licences and access to foreign currency. Until the oil counter-crisis, the state held a monopoly over access to its resources. "Coalitions [seeking] to exploit sources of revenues"[5] ensured the regimes' stability, which thus rested primarily on their ability to portion out the allocation of revenue. But after 1985–86, modification of property rights led to the appearance of new actors that aimed to gain access to the resources thus "freed", while the state lost a share of its monopoly because of sanctions.[6] Selling off public property was therefore simply a means of redistributing investments made using the oil rent over the course of two decades. The aim was indeed to sell or distribute goods and services financed during the period of abundance. Such transactions, protected by criminal groups, took place in a totally opaque manner. The phenomenon was facilitated partly by the fact that the population was so terrorised by the violence of the Islamist insurgents—who were trying to overthrow the authoritarian coalitions, that seizing control of public property was far from being a priority concern but also by the absence of an independent judiciary. It was in this unprecedented context that the new mafia regimes of the 1990s came about.

In the early 1990s, Iraq, Libya and Algeria were punished by the international community. There was a total embargo against Saddam Hussein's regime for having invaded Kuwait, and sanctions also against Muammar Qadhafi's regime, accused of supporting terrorism. As for the regime of the Algerian generals, though no official sanctions were levied, it was isolated diplomatically owing to the vast human rights violations perpetrated during the war against the Islamists. This decade put an end to any illusions engendered by oil nationalism. During this period, traditional "Khaldunian and Mameluk"[7] modes of domination re-emerged, precisely those that the political voluntarism of the progressive elites criticised in the wake of the socialist revolutions. In the 1970s, the myth of "strong states" that would modernise and transform "archaic" societies was replaced in the early 1990s by the perception of "weak" or "bankrupt" states. Once feared for their politics of power, Iraq, Libya and to a lesser extent Algeria made their neighbours and their own populations afraid of their potential collapse. In fact, under the threat of a dual constraint—external in terms of sanctions and internal with the emergence of violent movements led by Islamist dissidents—the people were mainly afraid that their country would take a road similar to Afghanistan.[8] Thus, if the 1980s underscored the limits and aberrations of an oil-based politics of power, the 1990s began with a deep sense of disenchantment and powerlessness.

The battering of violence and the regime of international sanctions erased the progress made over the course of the previous twenty years. The mirage of the "strong state" that had grown out of the marriage between a rentier economy and an authoritarian regime vanished as it revealed its extreme vulnerability. From a political standpoint, the ideology that had legitimated it waned in the face of the dramatic cost its hegemony forced society to bear. Economically speaking, the state, which claimed exclusive ownership of resources, proved incapable of making them fructify and distributing them equitably. Bankrupt, it abandoned social programmes and allowed the majority of its people to slide into instability and poverty. On the international scene, these states were filed under the category of "rogue and terrorist states" to be contained. Placed under embargo, "the strong state" would shrink to nothing, making way for regimes whose survival capacity would nevertheless turn out to be surprising. In fact, the regimes would demonstrate an unexpected ability to adapt in extremely adverse conditions, thereby bearing out the findings of research on the resilience of authoritarian oil regimes. Even if international sanctions reduced these regimes' access to resources and thereby weakened their nuisance potential on the international scene, they actually reinforced the regimes' grip on their populations.

Iraq: total embargo and the end of the "robust state"

Iraq, whose potential was so often lauded in the 1970s as a symbol of the rebirth of Arab power,[9] provides a dramatic illustration of the illusions of the "strong state". Until 1990, "the economy, education, and the health care system showed results that were envied by neighbouring countries. The army, which absorbed a considerable share of the state budget, formed the country's principal institutional framework… While not democratic, Saddam Hussein's Iraq was a strong state".[10] The strength of the Iraqi state was to vanish, however. Between 1991 and 1996, Iraq was subject to a virtually total embargo under the terms of United Nations resolution 687 (3 April 1991). The decision resembled collective punishment more than economic sanctions properly speaking. Iraq was subject to the harshest embargo of the century. Not even the Treaty of Versailles went as far. Certainly, the victors of World War I amputated German territory, forced the vanquished to pay reparations, bridled its military power, but nothing prevented Germany from re-establishing normal trade relations and rebuilding its infrastructure. The Security Council banned imports of material needed to get Iraq's water treatment and electric plants going again on the pretence that it might have a "dual", civil and military, use. Certainly, Iraq was allowed to export a small quantity of crude oil at a price set by the UN, but the attitude of the United States made it virtually impossible to supply food for the country. Basic medication and food were blocked on the pretence that they could be used to manufacture chemical weapons. Owing to a lack of aerosols, asthma became a deadly illness. An estimated 500,000 children below the age of five paid for the rigour of this embargo with their lives. In 1996, when interviewed on the American television programme *60 Minutes* about the human cost of sanctions, Madeleine Albright, caught off guard, declared, "We think it's worth it". In 1995, the FAO and UNICEF announced that four million Iraqis lived in a state of "pre-famine" and that the lives of a million of them, particularly children, were threatened.[11]

The regime nevertheless managed to circumvent these sanctions, thereby disproving the hypothesis that sanctions weaken such a regime.[12] F. Rigaud describes the three phases of economic improvement that the regime enjoyed.[13] 1995–96 was a period of inflation: the government's distribution method was printing money, which provoked the collapse of the Iraqi dinar ($1 came to be exchanged for 1,500 dinars). Secondly, the government used the strategic stocks it accumulated during the war against Iran and goods it lifted from Kuwait when it invaded the country. In short, the regime lived on its reserves. It was during this same period that the government encouraged smuggling and deregulated foreign trade. The second phase, 1997–98, was characterised by a foreign trade boom reflected in mass imports of consumer goods and commodities. The market improved and the shortage of goods and commodities in the years 1993–95 gradually receded. The third period began in 1998 and was characterised by the state's disengagement: privatisation of the socialist sector, business self-financing, financial self-sufficiency, remuneration of civil servants on the basis of their productivity, etc. The regime was able once again to meet a portion of the population's needs.

After some years sanctions were eased: in 1996, the Iraqi government was allowed to sell $2 billion of crude oil every six months and in 1998, the authorised amount was raised to $5 billion; in 1999, the ceiling was removed entirely, the harm having already been done. In order to supervise the "Oil-for-Food" (OFF) resolution and control the conditions under which the resolution was applied, a host of inspectors was mobilised. 25 per cent of the revenue went to Kuwait to pay war damages. Crude oil dealers handled most of the sales of Iraqi oil (83 per cent), their largest customer being the American market (60 per cent of UN-controlled exports). But far from improving governance, the system gave rise to a huge swindle: "Under OFF Iraq sold $64.2 billion worth of crude oil. It also generated $1.5 billion in kickbacks on humanitarian goods contracts and $229 million in illicit payments on the oil contracts through manipulating OFF. It also cultivated an international network of patronage by awarding oil allocations to individuals and groups with payoffs of $130 million to those individuals and groups".[14] As for the regime, it managed to wrest $ 2.5 billion per year in revenue from UN control, mainly by developing contraband with the neighbouring countries. Thus an estimated 110,000 barrels per day (bpd) were exported to Jordan, using over 2,000 trucks, and 80,000 bpd to Turkey and 40,000 bpd to the Arabian peninsula, mainly to Dubai. It was Syria that benefited most from this contraband, receiving about 250,000 bpd of crude. Syria, an enemy neighbour and oil producer, could thus export its production and meet domestic demand with the influx of Iraqi oil. In a context of extreme resource scarcity, the regime proved able to extract the annual revenue it needed to survive whereas the embargo, far from weakening it, enabled it to tighten its grip on a society that was all the weaker as it was ravaged, without hope and "left to its own devices".[15]

Libya: Partial embargo and derailment of the revolution

Subjected to a partial embargo because of its policy of supporting terrorism, the Libyan regime, like Iraq's, placarded all the big cities in the country with the slogan, "We shall overcome the sanctions". And in fact, it managed to do that, just like Iraq did. In the 1990s, the embargo was at the root of considerable hardships and especially a deterioration in the standard of living of the Libyan population which, with a minimum wage of 250 dinars,[16] could no longer provide for its basic needs. The central distributive function, the basis for the government's legitimacy, was no longer fulfilled. The Libyan distributive state, whose *leitmotif* was founded on the principle "partners, not employees", and which promised social and economic egalitarianism that was to ensure political equilibrium, found itself with one of its pillars destroyed. In September 1996, the Libyan authorities submitted a report to United Nations Secretary-General Boutros Boutros-Ghali outlining the economic, social and health consequences of the sanctions against Libya: "All infrastructure development programmes and plans have been adversely affected, thereby dashing the hopes and aspirations of the Libyan Arab people".[17] The Libyan authorities explained that regarding health care, over 15,750 people required specific medical treatment and the sanctions prevented more than 8,500 foreign doctors from coming to Libya. The case of children infected by the AIDS virus would serve to illustrate the ill-effects of the embargo on the population. From an economic standpoint, the report emphasised the damage done to transport and communications. The government estimated the overall cost of the sanctions at $24 billion in 1998.[18] The impoverishment of Libya under the embargo is undeniable: in 1991 GDP was $32 billion; it dropped to $21 billion in 1999. This was reflected in a collapse of Libyan purchasing power, as annual per capita GDP dropped from $7,500 in 1991 to $4,000 in 1999. Between 1992 and 1999 the Libyan population had to face a host of new problems: the ban on international air travel generated feelings of isolation and marginalisation; the deterioration in living standards led to anti-government protest; the collapse of the Libyan currency and the emergence of an informal currency market produced inequalities that a society fed on egalitarianism had trouble accepting.

But at the same time, the collapse of the dinar brought large profits to some. Resale of state-subsidised commodities on the private market at uncontrolled prices was a source of great profit, to the dismay of Libyans who found the stalls of the public markets empty.[19] Businessmen sought to sell subsidised commodities to foreign merchants who paid in hard currency or in dinars obtained on the black market. The practice of illicitly re-exporting Libyan goods and commodities was akin to an economy of plunder that some leaders profited from: "Libya", writes Emmanuel Grégoire, is flooding West Africa with cheap (because subsidised) foodstuffs including Asian rice, noodles, wheat flour, couscous, soy oil, milk powder, tomato concentrate, biscuits etc. as well as manufactured goods (fabric, spare auto parts, household appliances, light construction materials, mattresses, rugs, wool blankets, etc.). A few all-terrain vehicles and trucks are also being resold in Black Africa. A stolen state car market has in fact developed, with Arab and Toubou middlemen selling them in Niger, Mali, Chad and Mauritania... A large American cigarette market is also operating from Benin and Niger into Libya.[20]

Because of the embargo and the illegal re-exporting of Libyan commodities, a lucrative cross-border black market sprang up that transformed Libya into a "warehouse state" and Tunisia into a strategic crossing point. Between 1988 and 1997, 18.8 million people crossed the Ras Jdir border post on Libya's Tunisian frontier.[21] The Libyans in fact now travelled to other destinations from Tunisia's Djerba airport. The Tunisia-Libya border became a conduit for smuggled goods handled by the Touazine tribe in Tunisia and the Nouayel in Libya, as Hassan Boubakri's research shows.[22] The ensuing local prosperity sparked envy and fury among the Libyan population, which saw subsidised imports sold at higher prices in Tunisia. Nor was smuggling confined to Tunisia and Egypt. Libya, as well as Algeria, was involved in cross-border smuggling reaching down into sub-Saharan Africa.

The decline of living standards under the embargo, as well as the extent of Islamist protest, obliged the regime to devise a more effective policy of social control. The creation of Popular and Social Commands (*al-Qiyadat al-Sha'biyya wa al-Ijtima'iyya*) in 1998,[23] made up of tribal chieftains, notables and senior-ranking military officers, was part of this process. The aim of these new political structures was to diminish the authority of the Revolutionary Committees, now viewed by the public as predators. At the same time, the regime thus introduced new intermediary bodies able to strengthen its authority over those tribes critical of the direction the *Jamahiri-yya* was taking. For instance, in Misrata, Derna and Benghazi, "tribal associations" were set up whose role was to reorganise and institutionalise tribal affiliations. The Popular and Social Commands' brief was to revitalise local political life, which had up to that time been entirely controlled by the Revolutionary Committees, to the detriment of the Grassroots People's Committees, which theoretically represented the people. The desire to reassert control at the local level represented a response to the gradual erosion of the mechanisms of control exercised by the "people" of the *Jamahiriyya*.

The official handover of local power to the "tribes" to some extent indicates the failure of the *Jamahiriyya* as Muammar Qadhafi had conceived it. Whereas he aimed to create a political authority whose bases rested on the "people", it was finally local notables and chieftains who were authorised to govern the towns. This method certainly offers a degree of effective political control and, as Lisa Anderson had demonstrated, is in line with the Ottoman "tradition" that was revived during the Italian colonial period.[24] The invention of tribal chiefs during these periods lent the current political structures new local power intermediaries with a considerably broadened purview. Moreover, from 1998, a real "cultural revolution" in public morals took place. Drinking establishments cropped up in the major cities and a steady flow of prostitutes ended up in bars and hotels. The rigidity that had characterised social relations since proclamation of the *Jamahiriyya* seemed to crumble. Whereas in Iraq under the embargo prostitutes were reported to be "decapitated", in Libya they managed to work their way in, proof of the social changes underway. The ban on liquor consumption and prostitution had initially been a reaction to the supposed debauchery rampant under the Idris monarchy. The colonel's takeover had also been presented as progress with respect to what the Muslim Brotherhood perceived as a social deviation detrimental to Islam and to Libyan dignity. The social rigidity promoted by Muammar Qadhafi was thus connected with a desire to purge the social body from the "vices accumulated under the monarchy". The effects of this policy were soon palpable among Libyan society which, under the yoke of revolutionary fervour, had lapsed into impenetrable boredom. Feelings of frustration were accompanied by a powerful outburst of xenophobia towards African immigrants as well as by jealousy of Tunisia's economic success, and bitterness over the perception of the *Jamahiriyya*'s relative failure. The Libyan Revolution lost some of its arrogance under the effect of the embargo. The Libyan population feared that the regime would adapt to these sanctions which in the end did little to penalise it.

Algeria: The moral condemnation of the generals' regime

During the 1990s, the generals' regime had a bad press. Unlike Iraq and Libya, the regime did not face sanctions ordered by the Security Council. Even if European leaders and Western diplomats avoided being seen in the company of the Algerian generals, Algeria remained open to international trade. In fact, the regime was a victim not of a UN Security Council resolution, but of moral condemnation as a result of its strategy for eradicating the Islamist guerrilla resistance. Thus, in the space of scarcely ten years, in the 1990s, all of the capital of sympathy accumulated during the war of independence (1954–62) was dilapidated. Repression against the Islamists and massacres of civilians caused unease among all those who out of affinity had refrained from criticising the FLN-state too openly. But between 1993 and 1998, the Algerian authorities became people not to be associated with, and few political leaders dared be seen with those responsible for halting the January 1992 electoral process. This ostracising suited the Algerian regime, as it could more easily implement its survival strategy behind closed doors.

Three challenges threatened the regime. First of all, the emergence of an Islamist insurrection, with a following estimated at 30,000 in 1994. Divided into a number of tendencies, it enjoyed considerable popular support in the beginning and was deemed capable of overthrowing the regime in 1994. The emirs of the guerrilla movement were convinced that time was on their side and that the regime would eventually collapse under the battering of the *"jihad"*. Secondly, in 1995 the regime was threatened by the establishment of a political opposition that coalesced in talks held under the aegis of the Sant'Egidio Catholic community in Rome. The Front des Forces Socialistes (FFS), the Front de Libération Nationale (FLN), the Front Islamique du Salut (FIS) and the workers' party formed a political platform to find "a peaceful outcome to the political crisis". These parties had represented 80 per cent of the voters in the December 1991 elections; their votes mattered. They especially represented a rejection of the army's appeal for "civil society support" for halting the electoral process. The military officials were demanding that civil society—represented by trade union officials, political party officials of the Rassemblement pour la Culture et la Démocratie (RCD) or the Communist party (Ittihad)—exert "pressure" to prevent the establishment of a "theocratic state". Whereas the pacifist coalition advocated a peaceful way out of the crisis, the military establishment's answer was the policy of eradicating the Islamists.

The third threat to the regime was the risk of financial bankruptcy following the collapse of crude oil prices. The "war economy" advocated by Belaïd Abdessalem prevented the government from meeting its debt repayments. Not only was there a risk of defaulting on payments, but civil servants were likely to demobilise because of fears that their wages would go unpaid. In addition, the establishment of a strategy came at a financial cost that the government seemed unable to afford.

To vanquish the Islamist guerrilla resistance, the regime waged total war, which was immediately decried by human rights organisations. In 1997–98, violence reached its height with massacres in the villages of Beni Messous and Bentalha: claimed by Islamist groups, these massacres were nevertheless ascribed to the army which once again found itself in the dock.[25] The president of the Algerian League of Human Rights accused it of "abandoning populations in danger". For the first time, the Algerian tragedy came out in the open. It became a concern for the European Union, which sent out a fact-finding mission on the situation in Algeria. The United Nations Human Rights Commission also requested a debate on the Algerian conflict and did not hesitate to accuse the regime of practicing "state terrorism". The potential for internationalisation of the Algerian tragedy came to haunt the army, which saw it as a plot hatched by "Algeria's enemies".[26] But, as in Iraq and Libya, the regime held fast. Its civil administrations continued to function as best they could and the security apparatuses maintained the necessary cohesion for a counterinsurgency.

On the other hand, the Algerian population, like the Iraqi and Libyan populations, was hard hit by the political and moral boycott inflicted on the country, adding to the effects of conflict. Amid widespread indifference, about 1.5 million Algerians fled their villages between 1993 and 1997.[27] Over 100,000 persons sought shelter on the outskirts of towns such as Djelfa, Medea and Chlef. This exodus, linked to the security situation, was moreover part of an overall context of pauperisation. In a report entitled "The Effects of the Structural Adjustment Programme on Vulnerable Populations",[28] CENEAP (the Centre National d'Etudes et d'Analyses pour la Population et le Développement) showed that pauperisation affected 35 per cent of the Algerian population at that time. Out of 31 million Algerians, 12 million lived on less than 18,000 DA per year, or 50 DA per day. Economic reforms and the retreat of the state allowed poverty to develop. With the collapse of purchasing power caused by devaluations of the dinar, 70 per cent of household spending was now devoted to food. The employment rate exceeded 30 per cent and illiteracy affected 32 per cent of the total population (including 40 per cent of the women). The effects on public health were immediate, with the return of diseases such as typhoid, tuberculosis and scabies.

The tragedy of the civil war (150,000 casualties) naturally traumatised the post-independence generation. The end of the FLN-state monopoly on what defined the Algerian national community first prompted reflection on Algeria's history and identity. Through violence, Algerian society rediscovered not only its political pluralism but also its fragility. The psychoanalyst Nourredine Toualbi pointed out in 2000 that in Algeria:

> the young generations are in a crisis of meaning. Their life trajectory is thwarted by the weight of countless existential impoverishments (social, affective, and sexual poverty). Destructive anguish can be feared as a backlash. These youths sometimes represent a danger for others as well—and perhaps they are dangerous especially for themselves, struggling with serious disenchantment in a supposedly egalitarian society that has not kept its promises.[29]

The 1990s deeply upset the balance that the state had previously maintained with society. In Iraq, in Libya and in Algeria this decade destroyed the image of the benefactor state. During the 1990s, the deep changes that could be noted generally did not fail to cause concern, and the dramatic deterioration of living conditions raised questions about the capacity of regimes to redesign projects for society that drew people's support. The dominant impression during this period is one of a breach between the coalitions in power and society. These states seemed to be on the road to ruin. Their trajectories offered comparisons that were unthinkable twenty years earlier: Algeria was no longer compared with Mexico but with Nigeria; Libya with Sudan and not an emirate in the Mediterranean; and as for Iraq, its trajectory was closer to Azerbaijan's than Japan's. For many observers, these countries threw away twenty years of effort, so much so that their populations came to believe that living conditions had been less harsh under the colonial regime. Oil wealth no longer held any illusions; oil seemed more like a curse. From the population's viewpoint, it was the most destitute who bore the brunt of the sanctions. They found themselves literally cast into poverty and instability because of an economic and financial crisis inherent in the oil counter-crisis of 1986.

Bankrupt economies

Thus, thirty years after the nationalisation of the hydrocarbon sector, oil wealth seemed to have gone up in smoke, leaving only the ashes of economies in a shambles. This financial collapse was triggered by the sudden fall in crude oil prices after 1986 (from $30 to $10 per barrel). Although states maintained the illusion of wealth for a while by going into debt, service of the debt soon led Algeria and Iraq down the road to bankruptcy. At a point when the population had tripled in 20 years, the regimes had neither the financial means nor a diversified economy to meet the basic needs demanded by the generation born during the period of financial abundance. In Algeria, the share of oil and natural gas earnings in export receipts went up from 93 per cent in 1975 to 95 per cent in 1999. The share of taxation on oil in budget receipts rose from 58 to 60 per cent during the same period.[30] In Libya, 99 per cent of export earnings came from hydrocarbons, which produced 80 per cent of budget receipts. The oil sector represented 74 per cent of GDP.

The inability to reform these rentier economies led their rulers to depend solely on revenue from this sector. When it was healthy, as was the case between 1971 and 1985, hydrocarbon export earnings enabled them to finance expenditures. But with the oil counter-crisis, the oil fields ended up serving as security to obtain bank loans. In fact, even when bankrupt, countries with large oil and natural gas reserves remained creditworthy. In Algeria between 1985 and 1988, the total debt thus doubled to reach $26 billion. On the verge of bankruptcy, the authorities negotiated short-term loans forcing the governments to devote most of their revenues to debt servicing. Thus, the ratio of debt service to export earnings went from 66.4 per cent in 1990 to 82.2 per cent in 1993. Forecasts for 1994 showed a rate of 93.5 per cent, making default inevitable.[31] In 1994, before the Paris Club and the London Club, Algeria was forced to reschedule $15 billion falling due between 1994 and 1997.[32] To crown the humiliation, in 1994, it had to agree to a structural adjustment plan (SAP), thus joining Tunisia and Morocco. Throughout the 1990s, Algeria lived with a growth rate of 1.3 per cent, lower than its population growth rate (2.2 per cent), making it impossible for millions of young people to join the workforce.

The collapse of oil prices in 1985 placed Iraq, at war with Iran and in a more critical situation than Algeria, in disastrous financial straits. Whereas the cost of the war continually rose, oil export earnings declined from $26 billion in 1980 to $12.5 billion in 1985, then to $8 billion in 1986. Weapons expenditure alone reached the astronomical sum of $90 billion. Iraq was unable to finance the war economy by increasing oil production during this period, owing to low oil prices. But, like Algeria, Iraq was granted bank loans that would generate "an odious debt"[33] contracted by the dictatorship.[34] Overburdened with debt, Iraq invaded Kuwait, provoking the second Gulf War. Whereas the regime had pulled off the feat of rebuilding 88 per cent of its infrastructure destroyed during its war with Iran, the military campaign to free Kuwait (110,000 air attacks and 90,000 tonnes of bombs) plunged the Iraqis into poverty with an inflation rate of 1,500 per cent in 1991.

By comparison, the Libyan situation could seem enviable. The drop in annual oil earnings ($22.5 billion in 1985 but $9 billion beginning in 1991) triggered a financial and economic crisis but not bankruptcy. It was less fluctuating oil prices than the UN Security Council that troubled the regime. In 1992, the Libyan regime was expecting the Security Council to levy international sanctions as severe as those inflicted on Iraq—that is, a total oil embargo which in all likelihood would have returned the country to a famine economy similar to the one that prevailed in the 1940s-50s, before the start of oil exploitation. Oil revenue represented the lion's share of current receipts and enabled the government to finance needs in terms of food (of which 80 per cent is imported). Unlike the case of Iraq, agriculture would not have enabled Libya to meet its needs under a total embargo: only 2 per cent of the land is arable. Libya was spared not by the Security Council's humanitarian concerns, but by the active support of Germany and Italy, its two main customers for crude oil. A sudden halt in Libyan deliveries would have caused a serious energy crisis in these two countries.[35] Libya had prepared for this eventuality though; the regime had transferred a few billion dollars into banks in the Middle East and spread some of its bank holdings over about a hundred offshore accounts.

The partial embargo (oil sales were allowed) did not produce a humanitarian crisis as it did in Iraq, but it reduced Libyan purchasing power: accumulated rises in consumer prices amounted to 200 per cent between 1992 and 1997.[36] With inflation at 30 per cent per year between 1995 and 1998, the loss of purchasing power for Libya's 700,000 state employees (out of an active population of 900,000), whose income had been blocked since 1979 at around 250 dinars per month, was hard felt. The emergence of a black market, which until then had represented up to 20 per cent of currency transactions at a rate ten times higher than the official rate, fed a prosperous informal economy. The government estimated the unemployment rate at 11 per cent of the active population, but it was actually 30 per cent. Owing to the threat of international sanctions the Libyan regime, unlike Algeria, was unable to secure short-term loans to finance this adjustment. As the country was not creditworthy, Libya's foreign debt ($4.5 billion in 1991–92) did not bring the regime to the IMF's doorstep, thus sparing it an excessive burden of debt. Servicing of the debt represented only 3 per cent of oil revenue in 1994, compared with 90 per cent for Algeria that same year. This is why in 1996 the regime could allow military expenditure to continue to absorb 33 per cent of oil revenue.

Charity and allegiance

From Syria to Tunisia to Morocco, many wondered how neighbours as rich as Iraq, Algeria and Libya had managed to sink into such a state of violence and poverty. In fact, unlike authoritarian regimes that do not have oil (whether revolutionary or not), authoritarian oil (and revolutionary) regimes are obliged to practice charity to justify their legitimacy. Having risen to power on the back of a revolution buoyed by oil nationalism, these regimes distributed goods and services to which the people were entitled and sought to restore the nation's dignity that had been trampled upon by colonial history.[37] But in exchange they demanded absolute obedience and allegiance, thereby defining the framework of revolutionary legitimacy. Without institutions able to exercise oversight in this transaction between the "people" and the "rulers" (independent judiciary, political parties, freedom of the press, etc.), exchanges and negotiations are arbitrary and opaque. In the framework of political regimes devoid of institutions that can manage state charity, expectations generated by oil wealth can only produce an economy of waste. This explains the paradox of regimes that are undeniably successful politically—if longevity is a measure of success—but whose economic failure is just as flagrant if gauged by the state in which their population lives.

The concentration of powers, and thus the lack of control over the rent, explain the development of corruption, which functions as a safety valve. Present at all echelons of society and in all professional activities, corrupt practices offer a means of satisfying needs that vary depending on the protagonists. The non-governmental organisation Transparency International ranks Algeria, Iraq and Libya as highly corrupt. Out of 145 states, Algeria is 97th, Iraq 129th and Libya 108th. The NGO does not hesitate to point out that Libya and Iraq "have reached an alarming level" of corruption.[38] Yet the legal mechanisms are not lacking, as the example of Libya illustrates. On 10 October 1999, at a conference in Durban on anti-corruption measures, Abdurrahman Musa al-Abbar, the Secretary-General of the Popular Committee at the Council for Popular Control, gave an account of the measures Libya had taken against corruption. According to the Libyan official these included "Law number 2 of 1979, concerning economic crimes, which is related to fighting all aspects of economic corruption in the state. Law number 6 of 1985 regarding prohibition of favouritism; and law number 3 of 1986 required the disclosure of the origin of assets, in a measure relating to the prohibition of improper gains. Law number 10 of year 1994 regarding purification".[39] But in the 1990s, these mechanisms could have no impact on deeply anchored, functional and efficient corruption practices that had taken root in the clientelistic system during the period of abundance, and which then became necessary, even vital in the time of sanctions.[40]

The massive influx of oil revenues in state without democratic institutions destroyed any chance of economic reform, even when such measures were essential to sustainable development. Thus, the difference in trajectory between Norway, also an oil state, and Libya can be explained by the democratic oversight exercised on uses of the rent in Oslo, whereas in Tripoli, arbitrary and opaque decision-making practices weakened economic performance. From a political standpoint, economic performance has never been the Libyan regime's primary concern; as with the FLN-state and the Baath party, oil revenue served first of all to consolidate the regimes. From that perspective, "waste" and "corruption", far from being problematic, provided a means of sustaining a system of patronage which, during the period of abundance, ensured the peaceful functioning of the political scene. But under the embargos and with the emergence of political violence, this system lost ground, "criminal enterprises" gradually taking its place. They were better adapted to an environment characterised by violence, poverty and especially transfer of ownership. The flexibility of mafia regimes would also help to rebuild social bases on different foundations to those of the 1970s. For leaders henceforth devoid of ideology, the "people" and its official representatives were no longer needed as incantatory figures. On the other hand, recourse to family, tribal and regional affiliations turned out to be decisive for these regimes' survival, as therein they found the cohesion and trust required for the proper functioning of their criminal enterprises. The 1990s is an illustration of the changing practices within the ruling coalitions: a shift from corruption to predation.

Regime consolidation mafia-style

Between 1986 and 2003 (the beginning of the third oil crisis), the authoritarian coalitions developed economies of plunder. The weakness of political institutions, the lack of control over the rent and the destruction of civil societies by embargos fostered the emergence of these mafia regimes. In the eyes of militants of the revolutionary cause, the national and socialist revolutions had been victims of the oil wealth, which had engendered a parasite contaminating the social and political body, not unlike narco-states. But in contrast to the drug economy, exploitation of hydrocarbons is not conducive to the development of a rapidly lucrative mafia-like economy. The hydrocarbon sector demands huge investments, first of all, and secondly, exports require a market in which the actors are obliged to show a certain degree of transparency. On the other hand, the use of export earnings is similar to the distribution methods used by certain criminal organisations such as the Colombian cartels in the 1980s. Cartel leaders distributed some of the gains from the drug economy in order to consolidate their criminal enterprises.[41] In an economic and social context similarly characterised by poverty and instability, drugs and oil have spawned narco-states in one instance and "oil mafias" in the other.[42] Revenues from drugs, like those from oil, have seeped into a web of liaisons and relations, leading to a confusion between regime and state, the latter no longer being an independent actor able to influence other social actors, but a powerful modern tool in the service of organised and armed minority groups. Moreover, thanks to oil, the emergence of these mafias benefited from a ready political framework in which the distinction between public and private space is weak.

The contrast between the image of integrity and the effectiveness of these regimes in the 1970s, and the corruption and predatory behaviour of the 1990s is striking. How can this discrepancy between perception and practices be explained? The political construction of the "developmentalist" narrative upheld by oil nationalism was deceptive: in the 1970s the regimes already practiced predation but it was concealed by or submerged in the abundance of resources produced by the nationalisation of hydrocarbons and by the sympathy some observers had for these young states. The regimes did not change, sanctions simply revealed practices that in the meantime, in a context of increased resource scarcity and national disenchantment, had become unacceptable and intolerable. In Iraq, Saddam Hussein had set up mechanisms for appropriating revenue from the rent that escaped all control:

In the late 1980s, he held absolute control over the state. The party machinery and the security services were in the hands of some of his own relatives. Laws took the form of decrees bearing his signature. Moreover, he now had the Oil Ministry as well as Industry and Military Industrialisation Ministry entirely under his thumb. Both enjoyed "autonomous" status: their receipts and expenditures were held secret and they reported only to the President.[43]

In Algeria, the mechanisms of appropriation were more diffuse. Thus neither President Boumediene (1965–78) nor his clan managed to take absolute control. As Ahmed Dahmani points out, after the coup d'état of 1965, "the system of corruption became more discreet [...]. Domestic and foreign trade was organised around concentrated centres of policy-making that obeyed unwritten rules and socio-political criteria: influence in the political-military apparatus, nepotism, regional clientelism". In this system, one actor stands out: "the military clique". "Army officers and security services officials are those who handle the most lucrative deals, usually through a front man".[44] This system would make Algeria a textbook case "to analyse the curse of wealth and the symptoms of a rentier economy: monopolisation of the rent by a class of state racketeers who use the control of power as a means of personal enrichment and systematic corruption".[45] In Libya, an opaque system embodied the "real" government in the eyes of Libyans: the Qadhafi family and its clans.[46]

Modification of ownership in the framework of privatisation was officially part of the liberalisation policy that aimed to reduce state expenditure and manage resources more efficiently. In reality, this policy put to a severe test the "coalitions" that shared the sources of revenue. As long as the state had a monopoly over the revenue by controlling the rent, the primary aim was to obtain the necessary resources to enter the networks that managed this windfall.[47] After the oil boom and the destruction of the non-hydrocarbon economy, the game boiled down mostly to managing imports, the volume of which depended on the country: from $10 billion annually to over $30 billion between 1970 and 2000. Dealers specialising in imports redistributed goods and merchandise, they irrigated a whole economy with "bazaars" and "warehouses". The national oil companies (Sonatrach, NOC, INOC) were usually protected from any form of political interference. In short, the oil industry, the sole source of external revenue, was sheltered and its staff pampered. Oil production was vital to these regimes' stability, even their survival. The mere idea of opening this sector to foreign investment provoked a wave of panic and uncertainty. In fact, the total lack of transparency regarding transactions fuelled wild speculation. The end of the monopoly caused fear that the rules of the game, which until then had provided for an equitable allocation of revenue among partners in the regimes, now favoured some actors to the detriment of others. In a period of great instability and vulnerability—due to embargos and Islamist violence—control of these transactions was likely to bring new coalitions to power. It was feared that the risk of seeing the coalitions split at the top over the question of privatising the petroleum sector would bring an end to the regimes' internal cohesion. And yet, the investments required to increase production made opening the sector inevitable, as only foreign companies could make these, because of the financial straits the governments found themselves in.

In Libya, in 1996, the Energy Minister Abdullah Al-Badri announced that Law No. 25 of 1955 on oil exploitation required amendment in order to bring the Libyan market in line with the needs of the international oil industry. In 1998, a preparatory committee chaired by Muhammad al-Kaylani, adviser to the Energy ministry, drafted a new oil bill.[48] Just two weeks after the embargo was suspended in April 1999, Abdullah al-Badri also confirmed that Libya had made a commitment to open up its energy sector to as many international companies as possible, in all transparency, noting that 96 blocks of territory would be put up for auction.[49] In Algeria, the "Ghozali law" was passed in 1991. It confirmed the need to open up the hydrocarbon sector, its author saying, "from the moment we are obliged to borrow money to meet our expenses, it would be better to sell off part of our property; it's our money and at least we don't pay interest on it".[50] As of 1995, Algeria became an attractive market. In early 2000, Sonatrach had signed over 50 "upstream partnership" agreements with foreign companies. Abdelaziz Bouteflika's election to the presidency accelerated this move with the drafting of preliminary legislation on hydrocarbons, which its critics saw as foreshadowing privatisation of the sector.[51] In Iraq, the regime remained bound by international sanctions to act only within the framework of the so-called Oil-for-Food resolution. Eight Production Sharing Agreements were signed with foreign companies in anticipation of the end of UN sanctions, but the Coalition Provisional Authority (CPA) that replaced the Saddam Hussein regime in 2003 would end up "cancelling all the energy contracts negotiated under Saddam Hussein".[52]

Modification of ownership rights was in fact to favour the transfer of public property to all those who were well integrated in the state networks of the rentier economy. The Baath Party, the revolutionary family and the Revolutionary Committees used their access to resources to personal ends. As Kanan Makiya points out, "Once the Baathist elite began to shed ideology, Iraqi officials began to use the powers of the state for personal benefit through criminal activities of one kind or another. State institutions became riddled with corruption".[53] The highest party organ, the Revolutionary Council, took 5 per cent of oil revenue and "according to Muhammad Zini, a former consultant at the Oil Ministry, this fund grew to $17.4 billion by 1990".[54] The selling off of public property predictably led to the establishment of a predatory system: "As privileged beneficiaries of privatisations and the new import-export supply chains, the Baath party cadres gradually set up a system of predation on the country's resources".[55] This system did not hesitate either to exploit the United Nations "Oil-for-Food" programme that was supposed to alleviate the population's suffering. Between 1997 and 2003, the regime is believed to have embezzled $8 billion.[56]

A predatory economy took firm hold in Libya, as in Iraq. To ease the burden of sanctions and because the regime could afford it, cash gifts were distributed to families in distress. In 1996, Muammar Qadhafi personally gave 300,000 families $5,000 each to cope with the difficulties due to the embargo. He took this money from the Oil Fund Reserve, a financial organ over which no control is exercised, which in 2002 amounted to $8.8 billion.[57] All Libyan opposition parties have condemned the regime's predatory practices. The largest of these, the National Front for the Salvation of Libya, says control over state finances has become urgent.[58] Dissipation of Libya's oil resources is a criticism often voiced. Muammar Qadhafi's "generosity" towards various African heads of state is legendary. For instance, the leaders of South Africa and Ghana were each presented with a Mercedes S500 at a cost of $100,000 apiece, while Kumba Yala, former President of Guinea Bissau, allegedly received cash payments of $1.35 million delivered in a suitcase. The Libyan Arab African Investment Co. (LAAICO) invested $4 billion in Africa, with more than 130 projects brought to fruition, and owns outright a number of industrial enterprises in Ghana, Gabon, Liberia, Zambia and Congo Brazzaville.[59] The head of the Council for Foreign Investments was none other than Mohamed Elhuweij, Muammar Qadhafi's banker and former Finance Minister. In the context of the prevailing economic crisis, the Libyan people were surprised by the extent of Libya's investment in Africa, while Libya itself remained in dire need. Many saw these investments as a means of reinvesting petro-dollars in safer destinations than before, in response to the sanctions.

Under the embargo, the revolutionary regime's instruments of power weakened. The highest political authority, the General People's Congress, applied Muammar Qadhafi's directives, while the Revolutionary Committees turned into criminal enterprises that plundered the state's resources. Before the sanctions, the signs of such deviations were obvious; under the embargo they became flagrant. The Revolutionary Committees involved themselves in financial speculation, illegal importation of luxury cars and the establishment of offshore companies. Even their appearance took on the style of "gangsters": leather jackets, automatic pistols, BMW cars. The regime seemed to be running out of steam, stripped of its revolutionary rhetoric, deprived of popular support, governed by ministers without portfolios or prerogatives, humiliated by an embargo that isolated it, and accused of international terrorism. The regime held on during the embargo only thanks to the tribal solidarity that was a feature of the government. Between 1970 and 2000, the regime received $350 billion from hydrocarbon sales alone. But there was no administrative or political structure to supervise the use of this financial windfall, as it was under the exclusive control of Muammar Qadhafi and his close associates.

The oil rent in Libya remains family and tribal property. Complex informal organisations sprang up to handle the process of

distributing, investing and spending this "bonanza". The maintenance of the Qadhafi family and tribal relations relies on their ability to restrict direct access to this strategic resource. Nationalisation
of hydrocarbons in the 1970s and later the controlled opening up
of the sector has given them complete control over energy
resources and a substantial increase in their income. Unilateral
control of the oil rent was a political imperative for the continuation of the regime. The opening up to foreign investors was accompanied by discussion about privatisation of state enterprises and
incentives to start private companies.[60] This is why liberalisation of
the oil sector after the sanctions were lifted did not lead to any sort
of *perestroika*—after the fashion of Algerian liberalisation at the end
of the 1980s, which ended up destabilising the FLN-state[61]—which
would have inevitably called into question the methods of domination used by the tribal coalitions in power.

President Boudiaf of Algeria, who had called this predatory system a "political-financial mafia", was assassinated on 29 June 1992.
What was he denouncing? Engrained practices of capturing the
rent in the context of the policy of importing pharmaceutical products and weapons, skimming profits from oil contracts and money
transfers to accounts abroad. Economic liberalisation and privatisation programmes only amplified this trend.[62] Ownership transactions were handled in a totally opaque way. Journalists avoided
"talking about anything that resembled embezzlement of public
funds or corrupt practices".[63] And in fact they had already paid a
high price, with over 60 journalists murdered between 1993 and
1997. Opacity was all the thicker since there was great confusion
between Islamist groups and the government. As one Algerian
lawyer, Abderrahmane Boutamine, pointed out, in "a fairly pecu-
liar situation, certain corrupt milieus and their mafia-like practices
have in recent years meshed with the schemes of legal fundamentalist organisations, even those that were secret at first. Today, terrorism and even Islamist subversion cover and protect the development of corruption and contraband."[64] The economist Fatiha
Talahite indicates that between 1986 and 1988, over $9.7 billion
"was allegedly transferred out of Algeria illegally". This amount is
believed to have reached $16.3 billion in late 1990, or nearly 55 per
cent of the foreign debt ($30 billion in 1990).[65] At the end of the civil

war in 1999, the assets of Algerian billionaires held abroad were estimated at $40 billion.[66]

Conclusion

The mechanisms of clientelistic redistribution that had ensured the stability of authoritarian regimes underwent transformations under the embargos. The authoritarian coalitions that up to that point had benefited from state revenue to establish their legitimacy no longer had the means enabling them to "paralyse the exercise of popular sovereignty in a lasting fashion".[67] Confronted with insurrections and international sanctions, the coalitions, instead of negotiating an "exit from authoritarianism" or imploding, severed the ideological and political ties that connected them with the "people", leaving their citizens to their own devices. For these coalitions, the issue was no longer to sustain the illusions of "Arab socialism" but to survive in an environment that made them vulnerable. The failure of rentier economies, in a context of war and violence, obliged them to institute reforms which, in haste and opacity, altered ownership of the rent by placing a segment of the "national property" on the "market". Without legitimate political institutions to guarantee these transactions, mafias emerged and ensured security for the new rules of the game. They replaced and fulfilled the function that security services had during the period of abundance.

Modification of property rights was reflected in political terms by a change in the coalitions' practices, which went from corruption to predation. In the 1970s and 1980s, corrupt practices were regularly criticised, and the petroleum sector offered many opportunities for corruption.[68] However, the shift from corruption to predation was only possible because of the vulnerability of the actors who controlled ownership transactions. The external constraints imposed by sanctions (freezing of assets and investments, travel bans) and the internal threats represented by the Islamist guerrillas menaced the regimes' very survival. They reacted swiftly and imaginatively, turning from popular socialist republics into mafia regimes, demonstrating exceptional flexibility and prowess. Whereas their states were financially bankrupt, they managed to get billions of dollars in capital out of the country. This feat relied on the assurance that the security apparatuses would remain loyal in those uncertain times. The passage from an authoritarian regime to an openly mafia regime required the destruction of the power of the conventional army, a legacy from the 1970s when the regimes had regional ambitions. For the military, the collapse of the state during the 1990s was synonymous with strategic vulnerability. How could a policy of regional power be sustained in such a ravaged political, social and economic environment? Huge investments in weapons were pointless if the armies had to move in a ruined economic environment and among an angry and bitter population. What perspectives did these armies have? One possible outcome seems to be the return of a providential figure who could restore the "order and grandeur of the past", after the fashion of Vladimir Putin in Russia or, more humbly, Abdelaziz Bouteflika in Algeria.

Consolidation of the mafia regimes during the 1990s fostered the development of an economy of plunder based on exploitation of resource scarcity. Under the embargos, political conflicts provoked deep disenchantment among the people deserted by those who had the resources to survive elsewhere. For those who remained, a sense of fatality and renunciation dominated. The 1990s destroyed all possible ways out: it seemed impossible to get rid of the regimes, be they authoritarian or mafia-like. At the end of the 1990s, the Algerian generals sought a way out of the impasse in which the victory stained with human rights violations had placed them. Muammar Qadhafi's regime negotiated the conditions for a suspension of the embargo so as not to become a Mediterranean Cuba. Saddam Hussein's Iraq was on life support with the "Oil-for-Food" resolution that left no political or diplomatic alternative other than a humanitarian approach. The issue for Algeria came with the rise of Abdelaziz Bouteflika, a former Foreign Minister under Boumediene, to the presidency. His reconciliation policy met with approval both in Algeria and among the international community. In Libya, Muammar Qadhafi resigned himself to handing over the two men accused of the Lockerbie bombing, which led to a suspension of sanctions until they were finally lifted. In Iraq, Saddam Hussein's son Uday was preparing to succeed his father. But the September 11, 2001 attacks were to alter the trajectory of these regimes. Algeria seized the opportunity to change the image of its war against the Islamists from an endless violation of human rights to an "avant-garde" resistance against Al-Qaeda. Muammar Qadhafi's regime demonstrated the full range of its flexibility by switching to the "good side", that of the United States at war against Al-Qaeda. Only Saddam Hussein's regime, incapable of escaping the propaganda that associated it with Al-Qaeda, would be overthrown in the name of democracy.[69] The third oil crisis of 2003 would have the ring of rejuvenation for these three regimes, recalling the potential and the assets boasted during the 1970s. In an international context marked by the fear of international terrorism and energy concerns, these regimes would paradoxically offer assurances of their ability to take part in the fight against terrorism and guarantees regarding the satisfaction of energy needs.

4

THE UNFORESEEN RETURN
OF FINANCIAL ABUNDANCE

Thirty years after the nationalisation of the hydrocarbon sector, the oil wealth accumulated seemed to have vanished, inasmuch as it was totally absent from indicators measuring well-being. In Iraq, it was dilapidated by the regime's bellicose folly; in Algeria, it brought contentment to a minority and destitution to the majority; in Libya, it was lost on the government's colossal projects and off-shore accounts opened by the ruling coalitions. Lack of control over the oil rent resulted in its dissipation. The inability to control oil revenue gave the impression of "a wheel spinning in the void", as Qadhafi claimed in a fit of feigned anger: "Thirty years ago", he shouted, "we decided to devote 30 per cent of the oil revenue to the operating budget, hoping that each year this percentage would decrease to 10 per cent or 15 per cent, to eventually reach 0 per cent... What happened? We have in fact reached the point where 100 per cent of our oil revenues have been entirely devoted to the budget. I must intervene today to halt this wheel that is spinning in the void and burning oil".[1] On the eve of the third oil crisis, the failure was plain to see. In an investigative report, *Jeune Afrique* magazine calculated that between 1973 and 2002, $360 billion had gone through the hands of the Libyan regime.[2] The journalist won-dered what it had all been used for and what remained of it. Unlike Qatar[3] and Malaysia,[4] the regime had wasted its revenue on sense-less projects that did more to damage the people's wellbeing than helped to improve it.

In 2002, Libya's GDP was estimated at $19.1 billion, whereas Tunisia's was $21 billion.[5] It was not until 2004 that Libya's GDP ($29.1 billion) exceeded Tunisia's ($28.2 billion).[6] As for Algeria, even if in 2002 its GDP was higher than Morocco's, it ranked 100th out of 162 and Morocco ranked 112th in the *Human Development Report* for that same year. The effects of Algeria's oil wealth were not palpable. But if Algeria is compared to Indonesia, another major crude oil producer, Algeria's failure is patent. Indonesia has not only managed to diversify its economy but has also "begun to exit" authoritarianism:[7] its GDP in 2002 ($172.9 billion) was three times higher than Algeria's.[8] Whereas between 1975 and 2000 the annual GDP per capita growth rate was negative in Algeria (-0.3 per cent), it was positive in Indonesia (4.4 per cent). Lastly, Iraq illustrates the dramatic regression of a wealthy country: in the late 1990s, it was one of the poorest countries in the world with an annual per capita GDP of $705, a level comparable to Rwanda, whereas in 1989 it had been $3,500. Over 81 per cent of the population lived on less than $15 per month.[9] Of all the authoritarian oil countries, Iraq is the one that experienced the deepest and most dramatic ordeal of devastation, displaying the regime's destructive potential to perfection. In 2003, just before the regime change, the annual per capita GDP was $449,[10] one of the lowest in the world.

The heritage from the period of financial abundance (1973–85) seems very meagre indeed. To console themselves, the leaders could certainly point out that other rentier states, such as the Islamic Republic of Iran[11] and Venezuela,[12] had to deal with similar ills. However, even taking this into account, unlike the three countries under study Iran, owing to its political system, maintained a degree of social and national cohesion that enabled it to dispense with internal violence, at least until the disputed re-election of President Ahmadinejad in June 2009. Similarly, even if financial abundance weakened Venezuela's democratic institutions and did little to reduce poverty, Hugo Chavez's policies did not lead his country into a regional war,[13] despite the many disagreements with Colombia. In short, although the oil rent did not enrich Iran and Venezuela, it did not totally blind their regimes, because of the existence of more or less democratic political institutions that forced them to have a semblance of political clear-sightedness.

What, then, are the effects of the political transformations at work (installation of a new regime in Iraq; restoration of a "strong" presidential regime in Algeria; challenges to the revolutionary regime in Libya) regarding the use of revenues from the third oil crisis? After 2002, Algeria, Libya and Iraq recovered their oil wealth. Skyrocketing oil prices, leaping from $30 to $147 per barrel between 2002 and 2008, have endowed these three countries with unhoped-for external revenues that have enabled them to accumulate reserves estimated in 2008 at $140 billion for Algeria, $100 billion for Libya and $50 billion for Iraq. But since the wounds of the 1990s were not yet healed and the illusions of oil wealth had evaporated in the meanders of poverty, this unforeseen return of financial abundance nevertheless aroused concern. What would the windfall be used for? Who would control it? Would it once again provoke or sustain violence and conflict?

A salutary third oil crisis: rebuilding the state and nation

At the start of the 2000s, the new authoritarian coalitions that had formed during the embargos sought to institute a market economy despite the unsuccessful attempts of the 1990s. In view of the devastation of their economies during this period, the relaunch of economic liberalisation appears to be an attempt to reintegrate the criminal enterprises that flourished under the embargos. Furthermore, with the rebirth of the oil-gas sector, the governing coalitions, under the influence of "energy specialists", were pro-Western elites who took as a model the rentier economies in the Gulf. Owing to the third oil crisis, they managed to marginalise the "Arab socialists" who represented the military-industrial complex influenced by the USSR model and were backed by the military. For the "energy specialists", oil nationalism had had its day and no one any longer dared believe that petroleum was the weapon that would vanquish "imperialism, neocolonialism, and even Zionism", as the Iraqi Baathists claimed. For these new elites,[14] the convergence of interests (the energy market) and concerns (the fight against terrorism) between the former OPEC hardliners and the United States after 11 September 2001 was a historic opportunity to be seized. Freed from anti-Western rhetoric—which Al-Qaeda had taken up as its own—

the liberal coalitions felt they were in a position to convert their countries to a market economy in order to join, belatedly, the category of emerging countries that Morocco, Tunisia, Egypt and especially the rich Gulf monarchies had entered.[15]

Nationalisation of the hydrocarbon sector, the nationalists' proudest achievement in the 1970s, no longer seemed to the post-embargo coalitions to be the answer to development. Thus, President Abdelaziz Bouteflika declared before the James Baker Foundation: "We have resolutely opted to end monopolies and establish a regulatory framework that guarantees fairness and transparency for all national and foreign operations".[16] When the Khelil bill on the "privatisation" of Sonatrach was debated, it aroused emotional protest from the old guard: "Hydrocarbons are the lifeblood of the economy"; "privatisation of the hydrocarbon sector would be tantamount to entrusting the circulation of one's own blood through the heart to another".[17] The national oil companies (Sonatrach, NOC and INOC), as symbols of oil nationalism at the heart of major conflicts of interests, escaped the logic of privatisation. Even if state companies were closed to the entry of foreign capital, the energy sector opened up to direct foreign investment. This opening increased the geopolitical importance of countries like Algeria and Libya in Europe's energy supply system, Europe being eager to diversify its sources to counter the monopolistic strategy of Gazprom.[18] Similarly, their new purchasing power lent credibility to their plans to modernise the decrepit civilian infrastructure after a decade of violence and sanctions. These countries thus became attractive once again for foreign investment, recalling the agitation that surrounded them in the 1970s when they were perceived as Mediterranean Dragons (Algeria, Libya) or emerging powers in the Middle East (Iraq). Yet democracy was still absent from Algeria and Libya; in Iraq, the installation of democracy remains fragile, and the question of controlling and distributing the oil rent is an explosive one, as is the issue of exploitation of the Kirkuk oil fields.[19] That said, even if the third oil crisis did not restore Iraq's "order and grandeur of the past", it got a state moving again that had disappeared in the clutches of mafia-style coalitions.

Evolution of crude oil exports in Algeria, Iraq and Libya (2004-2008)

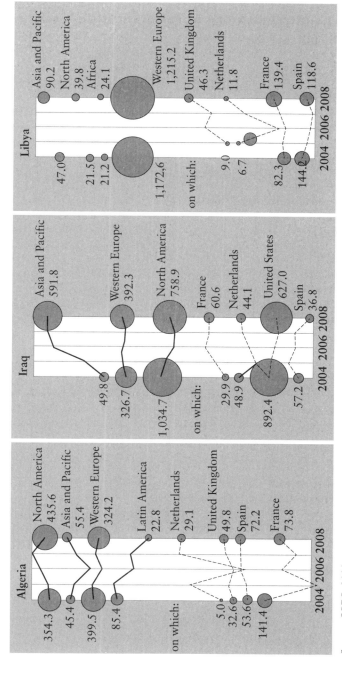

Source: OPEC, 2008.
Atelier de cartographie de Sciences Po, April 2010.

ALGERIA'S SPECTACULAR GROWTH
(sources: IMF, World Bank, UN Comtrade Data Base)

GDP (in billion US$)
2002: 55.9
2010: 162.7

Annual per capita GDP (in US$)
2002: 1,785
2010: 4,593

Average GDP growth rate
1975–2005: 0.1%
2005–2010: 5%

Total population (in millions)
1960: 11
1988: 24
2005: 32.9
2015: 38.1

Urban population (as % of total)
1960: 30
1988: 44
2005: 63.3
2015: 69.3

Life expectancy:
1960: 47
1990: 65.1
2005: 71.1

Fertility rate (number of births per woman)
1975: 7.4
2005: 2.5

Child mortality rate (for 1,000 births)
1970: 143
2005: 34

Total military expenditure in % of GDP
1962: 2%
1986: 1.9%
2000: 3.5%
2008: 3%

Rate of electrification in 2009: 98%

HDI ranking in 2009: 104

Algeria: National reconciliation and return of the state

In Algeria, the third oil crisis made it possible to restore a state that, according to Abdelaziz Bouteflika, had disappeared between 1994 and 1998. When he rose to the presidency in 1999, the state coffers were empty and power was dispersed between the "generals", who had won the civil war, and criminal enterprises, as discussed in the preceding chapter. Brought back to restore the civil peace in a devastated Algeria,[20] Abdelaziz Bouteflika benefited from the unforeseen and unhoped-for rise in oil prices. He was therefore able to offer Algeria not only national reconciliation, but a new economic takeoff.

The spectacular increase in oil prices between 2002 and 2008 left the government with $140 billion in reserves in 2008. In 2007, export receipts reached $56 billion and, in 2008, a record $81 billion. Never since the beginning of its short history had the state had such abundant financial resources. The third oil crisis meant it could repay the debt quickly,[21] undertake major civil infrastructure projects once again and especially rebuild a semblance of national cohesion damaged by years of civil war. In a context of economic growth and renewed financial abundance (annual per capita GDP went from $1,600 in 1999 to $3,400 in 2008, not to mention a huge drop in unemployment, from 30 per cent to 13 per cent),[22] Abdelaziz Bouteflika's presidency has become synonymous with prosperity and renewed confidence owing to the revival of state charity. Whereas during the 1990s the Algerians were violently at odds over the identity of the state and its evolution, today, in the framework of the national reconciliation policy, they are invited to return to the path of civil concord and put the "tragedy" behind them:

> You know, I don't expect congratulations for performing a miracle. I am trying to act with a modicum of good sense to get to the bottom of a tragedy which will soon have lasted for eight years. My personal feeling is that it is time for all this to stop. Life is not going to improve if we have 200,000 or 300,000 dead and three million victims of terrorism. So at some point things have to stop before they get worse. I'm trying to steer a narrow and tricky course through all the obstacles.[23]

Using "good sense", the president's office organised a national reconciliation programme that was based not on concern to obtain

105

justice for the victims or to uncover the truth, but on a desire to turn the page and forget the tragedy.

The national reconciliation policy focused on reintegrating thousands of combatants from the Islamist insurgency, disarming the militias, compensating the victims' families and granting amnesty to defenders of the state.[24] The Law on Civil Concord paved the way for a return to civilian life for the 6,000 Islamist insurgents who agreed to lay down arms in return for amnesty. This amnesty policy enabled the regime to dispense with a long drawn out truth and justice commission in favour of a short-term approach, that aimed to reduce the intensity of violence. At the same time, the big challenge to the regime was to integrate 500,000 people who had been armed members of self-defence groups and communal defence brigades.[25] The increase in oil revenue was a real boon for the regime, as in a context of massive unemployment, the economic and social integration of ex-combatants could have caused serious instability. The return of economic growth fostered job creation, particularly in the security sector with the surge in private surveillance and protection companies, thereby facilitating the retraining of these combatants. Some of these militias, which had powerful networks, sought to maximise their gains in the post-civil war period. Thus the "patriots" in the eastern part of the country, about 17,000 combatants strong, launched the initiative to hold a "patriots conference" to discuss "the patent failure of the Civil Concord".[26] After ten years of the militarisation of society, the question arose as to the government's ability to control and regulate the influence of these militias; the oil revenue helped to satisfy some of their demands. The regime still had to compensate the families of victims and the disappeared. The problem of the disappeared[27] illustrated the difficulty of implementing the national reconciliation policy, as it mainly addressed the problems of the survivors (Islamist combatants, defenders of the state accused of violating human rights). The disappeared were not taken into account by this policy; moreover, the issue reminded people of the expeditious methods used by the regime, that violated human rights. Although the government tried to demonstrate that the army and security services conducted "a clean war", the question of the disappeared raised and maintained the debate on the methods as well as the political and human cost of the victory over the FIS and armed groups. Thus, to put an end to this problem, Farouk Ksentini, President of the National Human Rights Commission of Algeria (CNCPPDH), indicated in an interview that he recommended and felt it was sufficient to compensate the families of the disappeared with "100 million centimes, plus a death certificate, to close the matter of the disappeared".[28]

The success of this national reconciliation policy rested on the launch of an ambitious programme to lift Algeria out of its economic slump. Added to the challenges of reintegrating Islamist and anti-Islamist combatants was the social and economic integration of a segment of the active population, because out of the 8.7 million people comprising it, 2.5 million were unemployed in 2000 (27 per cent). Pessimistic IMF forecasts readily predicted an unemployment rate of 37 per cent by 2010 if the growth rate excepting oil and gas remained lower than 7 per cent. The revenues of the third oil crisis were used both to finance the return of civil peace and to purchase social peace. The three year economic stimulation plan (2001–2004) sought to stimulate investment of $7 billion, after a decade of capital flight. "We never said", Prime Minister Ali Benflis claimed, "that this programme would make Algeria prosperous overnight. It is business that creates wealth. It must not be forgotten that this plan comes after ten years of terrorism and destruction. Whatever you do, it will always seem insufficient with respect to the ocean of demands to be met".[29]

A flourishing informal economy had in fact taken over to meet these needs since the state's disengagement. In 2005, this unobserved economy accounted for 16 to 17 per cent of the GDP and employed 50 per cent of the active population. Already in existence during the colonial era, it began to grow in the 1970 owing to the rigidity of the economy, particularly on the supply side. Controlled-price goods, for instance, were resold on the parallel market. Similarly, the monopoly on foreign trade increased opportunities to circumvent it. The Algerian authorities gave priority to the industrial sector, which represented the public sector. The private sector was abandoned to informal trade; but 70 per cent of the added value excepting oil and gas is produced by the private sector. The informal sector primarily developed in terms of distribution: goods imported by some 45,000 import/export companies redistribute their merchandise to private local tradesmen who resell it through informal networks. Other sectors are deeply affected by informal trade: agriculture, construction and public works, property and real estate.[30] Informal employment was estimated at 25 per cent of total employment excepting agriculture in 1985. It rose to 29 per cent in 1982, then to 33 per cent in 1997 and over 40 per cent in 2001. In Algeria, an ILO report indicates:

> Informal activities that have in particular invested the service craft industry and distribution are bound to remain in the future as long as economic liberalisation reforms are not totally completed, the declared private sector has not achieved a level of investment enabling it to provide strong and lasting stimulation for the job market and the unemployment rate has not come down to an acceptable level.[31]

Whereas in 2008 Sonatrach became the largest and most lucrative oil company on the African continent, reaping $81 billion, after $57 billion in 2007,[32] the rentier economy benefited only "600,000 to 800,000" persons.[33] In May 2008, the Energy Minister Chakib Khalil announced that Sonatrach would invest $45 billion in the coming years to reach a production level of 2 million bpd and 85 million m^3 of natural gas. Sonatrach is once again the engine of an economy that is struggling to diversify: 98 per cent of external revenue comes from the hydrocarbon sector, on which Algeria has never been more dependent. The housing crisis is not as critical as in the past and there is obvious improvement in road infrastructure. The UAE company Emaar Properties will invest $30 billion over twelve years in "health care cities" and tourist infrastructure: the government expected to attain 1.2 million foreign visitors in 2010, whereas Morocco is striving for 10 million. As in the 1970s, Algeria is a huge construction site. But unlike the past, it is Chinese companies and Chinese workers who deliver the commissioned goods in record time. This is because Algeria de-industrialised in the meantime, and no longer has enough qualified engineers and skilled workers. The bygone oil rent destroyed the human capital through a "brain drain".

Renewed oil wealth has enabled Abdelaziz Bouteflika's Algeria to make itself heard once again on the regional and international scene and reappear as an attractive emerging market for investors. For Algerians, Abdelaziz Bouteflika's presidency primarily means a semblance of state re-engagement after mafia rule. The Khalifa scandal illustrated the audacity of those who openly laundered the capital they accumulated during the decade of violence.[34] The anti-corruption campaigns following in the wake of this scandal helped show that the state was back. Between 1999 and 2009, Abdelaziz Bouteflika, aided by the price of oil, managed to restore, if not the legitimacy of institutions, at least order in business. However, his determination to pursue in 2009 the "task" begun in 1999 has raised doubts and concerns. His crushing victory in the May 2009 presidential election with 90 per cent of the vote was predictable, as the incumbent President's rivals did not have the state machinery or the logistics of a major popular political party to back them. Abdelaziz Bouteflika was bound to be elected by an overwhelming majority. The President wanted to recreate the illusion of a popular presidency on the model of Houari Boumediene (1965–1978). The main question in the election was therefore the rate of voter turn-out. The official turnout figure, 74.11 per cent, raised questions as to its reliability. In 1999, the "Bouteflika vote" indicated a desire to turn the page on years of violence and forget the tragedy of the civil war. In 2009, the presidential landslide suggested that there was no political void, that the nation had a chief of state who enjoyed the strong backing of the people: with the return of financial abundance Abdelaziz Bouteflika brought back "Boumedienism".

And yet, as some observers point out, if the per-barrel price is less than $70 beyond 2011, "the Algerian economy will be confronted with a serious upheaval leading to massive layoffs".[35] Since 1999, except for repayment of the debt, Abdelaziz Bouteflika's Algeria has not been able to shake its oil dependence. Rightly concerned by national reconciliation after the civil war, the President implemented an amnesty policy that functioned: the tragedy of the civil war was buried in the collective memory and there is a tacit agreement not to bring it up again. The fear of mutual responsibility has paralysed the former protagonists. It is a wound that has closed without being disinfected. The President's eagerness to go down in history as Algeria's "saviour" masks his inability to build legitimate political institutions. The renewal of patronage may function temporarily thanks to oil revenue. But the problems remain: dependence on oil, weak institutions, unemployment, corruption, etc., all ingredients that undermine the bases of future stability. Algeria is not Tunisia, and the state does not have the means to restrain the population or the ability to offer it a better standard of living. Without democratic institutions or legitimate opposition, the illusion of overwhelming support for the president will only delay Algeria's confrontation with the challenges it must face.

Restoration of "past grandeur" under Abdelaziz Bouteflika's presidency is only a partial answer to Algeria's problems. Even if this policy has led to improved security, it has not convinced the citizens during the meetings between the people and its representatives when elections are held. The extremely high abstention rate at the polls shows that Algerian voters do not believe political parties are capable of representing society; they view them as instruments in the service of a system that grants them a very slim margin for manoeuvre. Thus, more than the third oil crisis, it is the lack of democratic institutions that is a source of worry because, as the sociologist Zoubir Arous points out, there is considerable risk: "there are no organised forces capable of carrying out peaceful change. The path is therefore open to change through chaos".[36] In the May 2007 legislative elections, editorialists underscored the urgency of restoring the link between voters and political leaders. Yet the voter turnout was 35.51 per cent, one of the lowest on record since independence in 1962. Worse still, the "real" turnout was allegedly less than 20 per cent, according to the first secretary of the Front des Forces Socialistes (FFS), Karim Tabou, who had called for a boycott of the elections. In fact, in a column aptly entitled "Vote for Whom, and Why?" an Algerian editorialist pointed out that voters "penalised the political void and the transformation of parties into mere instruments and cogs in the machine of the system... That implies doing away with a façade of reasonableness to move towards real and effective democratisation".[37] The high abstention rate pointed up the inability of political parties to mobilise the electorate, as political parties seem to be an instrument in the service of a system of patronage that no longer meets people's expectations.

The lack of interest surprised the government all the more since its economic achievements exceeded even the most optimistic forecasts. With an economic stimulation plan of $140 billion in five years (2004–09), an average growth rate of 4.9 per cent, a 92 per cent increase in GDP and a rise of 29 per cent in per capita income, and an 11 per cent drop in unemployment, the governing parties should have inspired a wave of enthusiasm. Yet the opposite occurred and the FLN, for instance, lost seats. That indicates that the voters do not perceive the recent performance of the Algerian economy as a guarantee of lasting development but instead as the effect of the rise in oil prices. Algeria became richer, but its leaders did not manage to convince the citizens that they were the first to benefit. Paternalistic distribution of the oil rent is no longer popular, but it can nevertheless continue to nourish a small circle of voters in the framework of a clientelistic system.[38]

Libya: What to do with the revolution?

Having overcome the three challenges threatening it (armed Islamist dissidence, international sanctions and attempted coups), the Libyan regime managed to survive and seized the twin opportunities presented by the 11 September 2001 attacks and the invasion of Iraq in March 2003. A clever tactician, Muammar Qadhafi signed Libya up to the "Global War on Terror" and created an image of his country as a Mediterranean Eldorado. This conversion was accompanied by new rhetoric tailored to international community standards, peppered with terms such as transparency, the fight against corruption, and democracy. This transformation was the product of the new "national economic strategy" designed by Michael Porter, a Harvard professor. In the preface to a 200-page report drafted in conjunction with the Libyan Planning Council, he portrayed Libya as having such huge potential that it will have great influence in the future. According to Saif al Islam Qadhafi, "Libya will be a modern country with modern infrastructure and a high GDP. Its citizens will enjoy the best standard of living in the region. Libya will have closer relations with the rest of the world and with Africa, as well as a partnership with the EU. It will join the WTO. Libya will be the bridge between Europe and Africa".[39] But would Libya be democratic? The question did not come up at any point during the interview.

To accomplish its destiny, the regime first had to rejoin the international community by getting the sanctions lifted. To do so, it

LIBYA: A NEW EMIRATE
(sources: IMF, World Bank, UN Comtrade Data Base)

GDP (in billions of US$)
2002: 19.1
2010: 50.0

Annual per capita GDP (in US$)
2002: 3,512
2010: 8,300

Average GDP growth rate
1975–2005: 1%
2005–2010: 5%

Total population (in millions)
1960: 1.3
1988: 4.2
2005: 5.9
2015: 6.9

Urban population (in % of total)
1960: 23%
1988: 68%
2005: 87.9%
2015: 90.3%

Life expectancy:
1960: 47
1990: 61
2005: 72.7

Fertility rate (number of births per woman)
1975: 7.6
2005: 3

Child mortality rate (per 1,000 births)
1970: 105
2005: 18

Total military expenditure as % of GDP
1962: 1.2%
1986: 12.0%
2000: 3%
2008: 1%

Rate of electrification in 2009: 97%
HDI ranking in 2009: 55

agreed to pay compensation to the aircraft sabotage victims' families, but did so without ever acknowledging responsibility for the incidents. A Foundation was created to pay compensation to associations defending the families: $2.7 billion to the families of victims of the Lockerbie bombing and $270 million to the families of the victims of the bombed UTA flight. This foundation also set out to "humanise" the regime by altering its image in the international press. As in Algeria, a liberal coalition represented by Saif al Islam undertook efforts to bring Libya over to the "good side", that is, the United States and its allies. For the reformers who comprised this coalition, Libya, rather than repeating the errors of the past, should exploit its comparative advantages in the post-11 September 2001 context, and offer its new allies the energy supplies they require, as well as cooperating on security.

Libya's conversion was swift and affected all areas. It emphasised the convergence of its interests with those of the United States and Europe. It terminated its WMD programme and encouraged other countries to do the same. It liberalised its petroleum sector and offered Europe guarantees for its energy supply. The new elites that emerged in the fields of oil and security, trained in the United States, gradually sidelined the "revolutionaries" trained in Eastern Europe. These new elites believed that Libya must firmly attach itself to the West. The question was, how to dismantle the revolutionary regime without causing a stir? The old regime still had its "guard dogs" who were resistant to change. In short, what was to be done with the revolution? How could the *Jamahiriyya* be made effective? The reformers saw communist China as a model: combine the legacy of the revolution and the Green Book with a market economy. On 21 August 2007, Saif al Islam called for the end of the revolutionary era and the conversion of the Revolution into a constitutional state. In 2008, he called on reputed professors to take part in drafting a Constitution for Libya, paving the way for a succession to Muammar Qadhafi without actually altering the non-democratic nature of the regime.[40]

In 2007, the government authorised the creation of private media, although most of them belonged to the Ghad Foundation, which was headed by Saif al-Islam himself. In April 2008, this Qadhafi scion explained that Libyan society should have "several media that denounce corruption, fraud and violations of the law. These companies should be independent and not answer to the Ministry of Information, the Parliament, the government or even Seif el-Islam" (*Magharebia*, 3 June 2009). This media liberalisation gave the impression that Libya was leaning towards reforms that would open up the political system. But in May 2009 came the crackdown: a government decree nationalised the private media (the al-Libi satellite channel, Eman Al Libye radio, the *Quryna* and *Oea* newspapers), ending the experiment with free expression in the media. In consequence in December 2010 Saif al Islam announced his withdrawal from political activity, thereby ceasing to promote political reform in Libya. However, on 10 December 2010, his Ghad Foundation published a report on human rights in Libya, underscoring "a dangerous regression" in the situation of civil society organisations.

As soon as the sanctions were lifted, the regime began to shed its revolutionary heritage. For instance, in January 2005, Muammar Qadhafi issued a directive to the General People's Congress requesting the abolition of the People's Court, which conducted secret political trials. The Libyan League for Human Rights remarked:

> The abolition of the "People's Court" and the exceptional laws is undoubtedly a commendable step in the right direction but should be followed by other measures if the purpose of their abolition is to remedy the deplorable human rights situation in Libya. In fact, respect for human rights has been obstructed not only by the "People's Court" but, more particularly, by the total lack of an equitable and independent judiciary.[41]

The abolition of these revolutionary courts was a response to campaigns led by human rights activists, but for the people, the main problem resided in the regime's political organisation. Although in 2000 Muammar Qadhafi decided, in a moment of anger, to "abolish everything", the problems nevertheless remained:

> You (members of the General People's Congress) want to stick to your old ways to justify the waste of oil... The present system shall be no more. Once the Basic People's Congresses have been held and the General People's Congress has met, what is known as the General People's Committee shall be no more. Hereafter, there is no "government"... The entire system is abolished! Henceforth, we shall work with the communes and the *Sha'abiyat*. You shall no longer be answer-

able to any higher authority in Tripoli, Kufra or Sirte for anything you do within the *Sha'abiyat*: planning, budgeting and finance. Power will henceforth belong to the people, the communes and the *Sha'abiyat*.[42]

A dismayed Muammar Qadhafi decreed mandatory decentralisation:

> At the *Sha'abiyat* level, you have everything you need and secretaries for every sector: health, education, agriculture and industry. Therefore there is no need to refer upwards to anyone with higher authority. Now you alone must shoulder your responsibilities. This system will endure for fifty or a hundred years, until you have grasped it. Only then can we return to the system of the General People's Committee (the government).

In the process, 31 *Sha'abiyat* were established, whose powers theoretically embraced the management of local resources, including budgeting and other matters. The Basic People's Committees were distributed among the 31 *Sha'abiyat* to guarantee, once again in theory, representation of the people. Each *Sha'abiyat* had its people's committee, its executive authority, together with secretariats for education, health, etc.[43] The decentralisation policy, however, raised the problem of resource allocation to the Libyan people: since the towns did not levy taxes, they remained dependent on the transfer of revenue from the capital. Thus, the regime merely exposed local officials to the people's ire. The period of sanctions left scars that all could remember, such as the fights that would break out around state-subsidised bakeries. To make the *Jamahiriyya* effective, the reformers believed that a shift to a market economy was subordinate to institutionalising the Revolution: guarantees must first be enshrined in the future constitution to reassure the "revolutionaries" before building a more open economic framework. In that regard, the liberalisation of the Libyan economy was closer to the Chinese "communist capitalism" than to the Soviet *perestroika*.

These transformations aroused concerns among the "revolutionaries" who were afraid of opening a Pandora's box.[44] The *Jamahiriyya* was a powerful instrument of personal enrichment for those who served it, and it operated with the utmost opacity. Any questions raised about such an economic system would cause unease that Muammar Qadhafi would need to address. On the 37th anniversary of the Revolution, Muammar Qadhafi gave a speech that

115

reflected a fear of uncertainty, its aim being to reassure the pillars of the regime, the Revolutionary Committees: "Be prepared at any moment to crush enemies within who might attempt to hinder the people's progress ... When we led the revolution, we did not want power for ourselves, we assumed it for the people, and we will allow no one to rob the people of it".[45] The fear of seeing the reformers' plan for a revolutionary capitalist Libya derailed, opening a window of opportunity for opponents to the regime, was patent. The Revolutionary Committees still had in mind the petition signed by 108 members shortly before William Burns visited Tripoli in March 2004, calling for radical change:

> The creation of constitutional rule chosen by the people their own free will, and the dissolution of all legislation, structures and organizations that deviate from or contradict this constitutional legal framework; the establishment of democratic principles, the rule of law and the independence of the judiciary; the guaranteeing of political participation in the decision-making process, the democratic selection of leaders, and the implementation and respect of the principle that governments change; the release of all political prisoners of conscience, and the shedding of light on the fate all citizens who have been kidnapped or have disappeared; the abrogation of all laws that were established to cause oppression and curb freedoms, etc.[46]

Events in Benghazi provide a good indication of their concern. On 17 February 2006, in front of the Italian consulate, demonstrators led by the Revolutionary Committees began chanting anti-Italian slogans in protest against the provocation of an Italian minister who had worn a T-shirt reproducing one of the notorious Danish anti-Islamic cartoons. But soon anti-Qadhafi slogans were also heard and the overwhelmed police force fired on the crowd, leaving eleven dead and over sixty wounded. Following this incident, the regimes' dignitaries all went to Benghazi to calm the situation. The Minister of the Interior was dismissed for "excessive use of force" and a number of Muslim Brothers from the Benghazi region, imprisoned since 1998, were freed. In March 2007, Muammar Qadhafi delivered one of his revolutionary addresses intended to reassure the revolutionaries that no political reform was in the offing and that democracy and political parties were deviations to be condemned. Finally, he launched into a diatribe against the Italian colonial period (1911–43) and demanded financial compensation for its consequences. It must be surmised that his voice was heard, for on 30 August 2008, the Berlusconi administration offered an apology together with $5 billion in compensation in the form of investments over a twenty-five year period.

The tension surrounding political transformations had little effect on the economic opening up of the Libyan market. Once sanctions were lifted, Libya was the focus of attention for international oil companies, which view the country as one of the last Mediterranean Eldorados.[47] Already in September 1999, the Finance and Planning Minister, Abdel Hafiz Al Zalaytani, had said that between 2001 and 2005 the government would invest $35 billion (60 per cent from the state, 40 per cent from FDI) in the oil and electricity industries. He said that over the coming twenty years, the country would need approximately $150 billion in investments, of which 60 per cent would be provided by the state. Libya's projects were certainly vast, but not out of proportion to its financial capacities. For the authorities, these were undeniable assets that should be exploited since Libya had moved over to the "good" side. As in Algeria, the hydrocarbon sector attracted most of the investments in Libya. In September 2006, the government issued its third international invitation to tender: twelve offshore permits and twenty-nine onshore permits were put up for auction in the oil-rich Sirte and Ghadames basins as well as in the exploration basins of Murzuk, Kufra and Cyrenaica. This third invitation was in line with the policy of opening up the hydrocarbon sector initiated by Shukri Ghanem. In September 2004, in an unusual move, Shukri Ghanem's government put the exploration rights of fifteen offshore and onshore areas up for auction. This procedure was intended to be the most transparent method for selecting foreign partners. Shukri Ghanem's cabinet moreover announced that the process would be a departure from the opaque and arbitrary procedures that had characterised decision-making in Libya. This new way of proceeding was supposed to demonstrate the new authority acquired by the Shukri Ghanem government over the complex decision-making process. The Prime Minister had succeeded in convincing Muammar Qadhafi's unofficial immediate circles that Libya had to change its methods if it hoped to persuade foreign investors to return. The new government wanted to demonstrate that the modernisation of Libya's economy and infrastructure necessarily had to go hand in hand with changes in commercial practices. But the concessions granted in the framework of EPSA IV (the Exploration and Production Sharing Agreement) demonstrated that Libya continued to use the oil sector as a diplomatic weapon. United States companies were granted nine of the fifteen blocks put up for auction. The political and diplomatic aim was achieved. In May 2006, the United States and Libya re-established diplomatic ties. The US-Libya Business Association led by David Goldwyn had met its objective: Libya was once again open for business with Amerada Hess, Chevron, Conoco Philips, Occidental and Marathon.

Although the oil sector was the government's priority, it did not neglect civil infrastructure, which fell into disrepair under the embargo. A meeting under the auspices of Phoenicia Group Libya LLc was held in late September 2007 in Geneva, bringing together government officials and investors. At stake was an ambitious infrastructure development plan to build airports, highways, schools, hospitals and a 4,800 km regional (trans-Africa) railway network linking Tunisia and Egypt as well as the cities of Sebha and Sirte, and extending to Chad and Mali. Revenue from the oil rent has enabled Libya to pursue a sustained investment policy. The air transport industry took advantage of it to renew its fleet: it purchased twelve Airbuses (eight with an option) for Afriqiyah Airways and two business jets sold by Bombardier Inc. More important still were the agreements signed between EADS and the Libya Africa Portfolio for Investment led by Beshir Saleh to build a training and maintenance centre, an Air Academy and a meteorological centre. The idea was to make Libya a regional hub for Africa and the Middle East. The government aimed to create a trading area from Zuwarah to Bukamash. The project, called The Road to the Future and backed by Saadi al Qadhafi, was introduced in September 2007. He claimed during a press conference that it should make the Libyan coast an area comparable to "New York, Monte Carlo and Hong Kong". It included a whole series of projects: the Socialist Port Authority, which manages seven commercial ports, planned to enlarge the Port of Misrata to reach a capacity of 6 million tonnes of merchandise per year. The Railway Executive Board planned a railway construction programme for lines from Sirte to Benghazi (600km) and Benghazi to Tobruk (470km), and an underground railway in Tripoli.

The third oil crisis restored Libya's attractiveness. The regime, which celebrated its fortieth anniversary in September 2009, recovered an aura that it had believed lost for ever, thanks to its dollar reserves ($100 billion in 2008). After Berlusconi tendered apologies for Italy, the President of the Swiss Federal Council apologised for the treatment of Muammar Qadhafi's youngest son, Hannibal, by the police in a palace in Geneva.[48] In September 2009, the Scottish courts released Ali Basset al-Meghari, even though he had been found guilty of the Lockerbie bombing, on "humanitarian" grounds. Lastly, Libya occupied the presidency of the United Nations Security Council for one year. In 2009, the Libyan regime rediscovered all the charms and advantages of oil wealth.

Against all expectations, in February 2011 the Libyan population began demonstrating to demand Muammar Qadhafi's departure. Inspired by the success of movements in Tunisia and Egypt, the demonstrators took the risk of defying the regime. Predictably, government forces did not hesitate to retaliate with violence, which caused the protest movement to turn into an insurgency. Taken by surprise, the regime seemed on the verge of collapse before regaining control of the situation and retaking the "liberated" cities that had fallen into the hands of the insurgents. In the space of a few weeks, Libya slid into violence and the Qadhafi regime again became a pariah for the international community. In March 2011, the UN Security Council, on the basis of resolutions 1970 and 1973, imposed sanctions against the regime and authorized measures to protect civilians. Then, in October 2011, after a seven-month NATO intervention, the regime was overthrown and Muammar Qadhafi was lynched by rebels after his capture.

Iraq: The violence of state and national reconstruction

In May 2003, President George W. Bush announced that the war in Iraq was over and that a new era had dawned for the Iraqis. Freedom, democracy and development were the expected outcomes of liberation. In the post-trauma context, the Bush administration

119

accused the regime of Saddam Hussein of acting in complicity with the Al-Qaeda network[49] and producing weapons of mass destruction likely to be used by terrorists.[50] The Iraqi experience has since become the symbol of a new policy to impose democracy by force with a view to "liberating" Arab Muslim societies subjected to dictatorships.[51]

In fact, the Bush administration's post-war plan ran up against serious obstacles: lack of enough troops to make Iraq safe, increasing rejection of the occupation forces by the Iraqi population, development of torture, etc.[52] Symbolically, on 30 June 2004, Iraq recovered its sovereignty and the US administrator Paul Bremer left Baghdad. Legislative elections were held in January 2005. Approximately 14 million voters were called to the polls to elect the 275 members of the Provisional National Assembly, the members of the Baghdad City Council and seventeen regional councils and the 111 members of the autonomous Kurdistan Parliament. More than 120 political parties were registered to participate and 7,000 candidates were signed up on 109 lists to vie for election in a totally proportional system. The list sponsored by Ali Sistani, the Unified Iraqi Alliance, won 48.1 per cent of the votes and 140 seats; the Kurdistan Alliance 25 per cent and 75 seats, Prime Minister Ayad Allawi's list 13.8 per cent and 40 seats, while the list of President Ghazi al Yawer only obtained 1.7 per cent and five seats. On 15 October 2005, a referendum on the Constitution laid the foundations for a new Iraq.[53] This "transition" terminated with new legislative elections on 15 December 2005, confirming first and second place for the political forces of the Unified Iraqi Alliance and the Democratic Patriotic Alliance of Kurdistan. Sunni Arabs, after boycotting the first legislative elections on 30 January, took part in those held on 15 December 2005 under the banner of the Iraqi Concord Front.[54] Having enjoyed complete control under Saddam Hussein, the Sunnis became a minority in the Assembly and marginal in the oil-rich regions where the Kurds dominated in the North and the Shia in the South. They lost both power and petroleum. Saddam Hussein was executed in December 2006 and Iraq slid into a period of violence that claimed over 80,000 lives between 2004 and 2008, intensifying the suffering of a society that had been ravaged by over a decade of sanctions (1991–2003) followed by a war of liberation.

Amid violence, the governing coalition fashioned a new political system in order to replace the makeshift post-Saddam Hussein political arrangement, which suffered from a legitimacy deficit. On 30 January 2005 the foundations were laid for a democratic authority as, for the first time since the end of the old regime, the Iraqis were called out to vote and choose their government. The refusal of the Sunni leaders to participate underscored the long path that remained ahead to achieve a true representation of all the components of Iraqi society. The government rejected calls made by political figures and parties to postpone elections owing to the lack of security, because of the power vacuum this would inevitably create. The transition period coincided with a crystallisation of ethnic and religious identities. Three political constructions gradually emerged and took on identitarian features that threatened Iraq with implosion. Among the eighteen provinces, three major regions took shape: Kurdistan in the North, the Shia area in the South and the Sunni provinces in the soft belly of the Centre. Clearly, the Kurds, who for years had managed their autonomy within Iraq,[55] were envied by the Shia whose passive resistance to the US occupation was a strategy not unlike that of the Kurds. The plan to create a region that would group together the provinces of the Middle Euphrates was explicitly outlined in the unified conference on the Provinces of the Middle Euphrates in Najaf. The perspective of a federal style of government for Iraq would trigger a process of regrouping Shia provinces on the Kurdish model. Only the Sunni provinces remained on the sidelines of this evolution. Engaged in a strategy of armed resistance, the Sunnis rejected a political evolution that marginalised them. Not only relegated to a minority in a federal space, they would also have been deprived of oil resources, which are located in the area of Kirkuk and Basra.[56] Moreover, the Sunnis perceived the building of a new Iraqi security structure by coalition forces as discriminatory. The redeployment of Kurdish *pershmerga* and certain Shia militias in the Iraqi security forces made them fear that specific ethnic and religious groups would be operating under the cover of the national armed forces. This Sunni fear of seeing the budding state apparatus fall to the service of those formerly excluded was to nourish pre-emptive violence. Initially, the violence was perpetrated by offshoots of the Saddam

Hussein regime (Saddam's Fedayeen, etc.) and Islamist groups affiliated with Al-Qaeda (Ansar el-Islam). During the year 2003, a local armed resistance developed that took the Sunni Arab cities near Baghdad (Ramadi, Fallujah etc.) as its stronghold.[57] Added to that was the Shia resistance from the start of the insurgency in March 2004, led by the followers of Imam Moktada Sadr.[58]

The official end of the war came with the emergence and development of a guerrilla resistance that the US troops were unable to "destroy" and that undermined the plans for rebuilding Iraq.[59] And in fact, out of the $18 billion in aid for the reconstruction of Iraq, only 2 per cent was used in 2004. The political and security conditions prevented the Iraqi economy from getting started again. Insecurity and unemployment rose to become the symbols of the post-Saddam Hussein era. Regime change came along with economic reform and a radical modification of ownership rights[60] that favoured the "plunder of national resources to the benefit of a new ruling elite".[61] The murder of judges in charge of investigating corruption and criminality—over fifteen were killed in 2006—by criminal organisations anxious to protect the new owners became systematic, as had happened in Algeria in the 1990s. As Bilal A. Wahab points out: "The security vacuum following Iraqi liberation further bolstered opportunities not only for the existing mafia but also for new criminal gangs".[62] Like the rebel groups in the Niger Delta, the Iraqi guerrilla resistance was not to be outdone. Between 2003 and 2006, 40–50 per cent of its income came from smuggling oil. The end of Saddam Hussein's regime and the inability of the American authorities to establish political order brought to light the desire of Iraqi political actors to control their main resource: oil. From Kurdistan to Basra, from the guerrillas to the government, the control of oil trade became a vital issue. *The Peninsula* reported, "The Fadhila Party controls the governor's office as well as the oil industry in Basra. When the new Prime Minister Nuri al-Maliki decided not to give the oil ministry to the Fadhila party on announcing his new cabinet in May 2006, the party threatened to stop oil exports".[63] The end of Baath party control over the oil fields resulted in fierce and violent competition among the new political actors: "A Shia political source told a reporter, 'He who owns Basra owns the oil reserves... It has a strategic position so why would anyone give it up'".[64]

Control over oil resources thus became one of the new government's priorities, its revenue between 2003 and 2005 having reached over \$33 billion owing to the rise in oil prices. This increase, caused by the third oil crisis, was extremely useful for projects that would help it to consolidate its power. The format initially planned for Iraqi troops called for approximately 226,700 men distributed as follows: "71,000 police; 40,000 Iraqi Civil Defence Corps; 40,000 army personnel; 25,700 border patrol personnel; 50,000 facilities protection". In January 2004, total numbers came to 206,600,[65] but in January 2009, this figure increased to 600,000 men, which did not fail to raise a number of problems. Priority given to security has been to the detriment of reconstruction. Except for the security and energy sectors, other economic activities are losing ground. For the majority of the people, the public health situation remains a concern and the social situation is appalling, with an unemployment rate that varies between 25 and 50 per cent of the active population.[66]

Between 2005 and 2009, the regime enjoyed the success of the counterinsurgency strategy conducted by American troops. In November 2008, the parliament's ratification of the agreement to maintain US troops in Iraq until 2010–11[67] made it possible to strengthen security cooperation between the United States and Iraqi forces.[68] Thus the Iraqi regime will theoretically be able to deploy its armed forces as US troops pull out. The risk of collapse now past, it must face terrorist violence, as Algeria did in the 1990s.[69] Since Sunni Arab tribes have turned against Al-Qaeda, exasperated by the organisation's "hegemonic" ambitions,[70] its ability to do harm has been undermined, and the regime has been obliged to integrate a portion of the allied Arab tribes into its security apparatus. Prime Minister Nuri al-Maliki said that 20 per cent of the 53,000 "Sons of Iraq", the Sunni Arab tribal organisation that fought against Al-Qaeda, would join the armed forces, and the others would be paid "until a job is found for them".[71] With 600,000 men and \$80 billion in oil export earnings in 2008, the regime could begin to meet part of the "ocean of needs" of its population.

Iraq has recovered the affluence it enjoyed in the 1970s. The external "odious debt", which represented nearly 500 per cent of GDP in 2004, was brought down to 60 per cent of GDP in 2008 following

IRAQ: BASIC NEEDS TO BE MET
(sources: IMF, World Bank, UN Comtrade Data Base)

GDP (in billions of US$)
2002: 20.3
2010: 83.8

Annual per capita GDP (in US$)
2002: 449
2010: 4,005

Average GDP growth rate
1975–2005: –
2005–2010: 5%

Total population (in millions)
1960: 6.8
1988: 18.8
2005: 28.0
2015: 35.9

Urban population (in % of total)
1960: 43%
1988: 73%
2005: 66.6%
2015: –

Life expectancy:
1960: 48
1990: 59
2005: 57.7

Fertility rate (number of births per woman)
1975: 7
2005: 4.9

Child mortality rate (for 1,000 births)
1970: 88
2005: 125

Total military expenditure in % of GDP
1962: 8.7%
1986: 32%
2000: –
2007: 2.5%

Rate of electrification in 2009: –
HDI ranking in 2009: –

negotiations with the Paris and London Clubs, and repayments are now only 8 per cent of external revenue. The government is now in a position to meet the most immediate needs of the population. Imports rose from $20 billion in 2004 to $37 billion in 2008. The arrival of food and other products from Syria and Turkey on the Iraqi market has considerably enhanced food security. In 2005, according to the UN World Food Programme, 47 per cent of the population was affected by "food insecurity"; in 2008, this percentage had dropped to 3.1 per cent.[72] The benefits of abundance are perceptible in the Iraqis' basic needs. But it will take "hundreds of billions of dollars"[73] before it recovers the civil infrastructure it boasted in the 1980s. Continuing violence may remain a handicap for investment, and corruption is a serious hindrance to reconstruction. Moreover, the oil bonanza whetted appetites within the Iraqi government, which presents a serious challenge to the coalition in power, especially as it appears to lack the means to regulate its main source of external revenue. The main challenge facing the new Iraqi government will be to establish political institutions with sufficient legitimacy to impose fair distribution of oil revenue between the oil-rich regions and the political parties by the force of law.[74]

A fragile rebirth

Out of steam in the third oil crisis, the regimes finally made it brilliantly through the decade. In 2009, Muammar Qadhafi celebrated the fortieth anniversary of the Revolution and savoured his diplomatic successes. Furious at the arrest of his son Hannibal in Geneva, he accused Switzerland of being a "world mafia" at the G8 summit in Aquila, Italy in July 2009. The third oil crisis restored the power of the word to the Libyan regime after years of silence under the embargo. In the April 2009 presidential election in Algeria, Abdelaziz Bouteflika was elected to a third term by a landslide. With civil peace restored, Algeria recovered an economic growth rate on a par with the 1970s and a confidence that seemed to have previously vanished. Following the example of Libyan demands regarding the Italian colonial record, Abdelaziz Bouteflika's Algeria expects official apologies from France before it will consider a treaty of friendship between the two countries.[75] In Iraq, in February 2009, the list sponsored by the Prime Minister Nuri al-Maliki, "Coalition for the Rule of Law", came out in the lead in the provincial elections. For the first time, political organisations representing the Sunni Arabs agreed to take part in the elections, thereby acknowledging the government's authority.[76] Boosted by the oil rent, the new regime has managed to reduce poverty, but without achieving civil peace. Vulnerable and fragile, its fate most likely rests on its ability to redistribute the income from its immense oil reserves in order to offer a devastated population better living conditions. However, to do so, the government must solve the issue of how to distribute oil field property rights among the various regions and make its offer when auctioning the blocks attractive enough to convince international oil companies to invest in exploration and production.[77]

With their wealth regained, these three countries have become vast construction sites. As in the 1970s, roads, highways, ports, airports, underground rail networks, hospitals, universities, factories, housing and other buildings are under construction, giving the landscape a considerably different aspect from that of the 1990s. Luckily for their citizens, the third oil crisis occurred in a context of ideological void. Unlike the 1970s, the regimes no longer have the bellicose ideological energy that led them to dissipate most of the petroleum windfall in military undertakings. Moreover, having learned from the bitter experience of oil price fluctuations, they have given up on colossal projects, seeking instead to meet the most immediate needs of their populations (housing, water, electricity, transport). Lastly, and unlike in the 1970s, room for criticism of the way the oil rent is used has developed in the media, in public opinion and among the elites. This rebirth is fragile, though, and the hydrocarbon sector, once again a strategic resource, is at the centre of development policies. The dynamism of the oil sector has stimulated economic growth: in Libya, between 2003 and 2008, the average rate was 8 per cent, in Algeria 7 per cent and in Iraq 5 per cent. However, as in the 1970s, this economic growth is entirely dependent on the hydrocarbon sector: over 98 per cent of revenues in these three countries come from natural gas and oil exports. So when oil prices collapsed in 2009, fear of the effects of a new counter-crisis resurfaced.

Dependence on hydrocarbons is compounded by political violence. From the riots in Kabylia in 2001 to the Mozabite revolt in 2009, Algerian society is regularly rocked by social and ethnic violence, driving home the vulnerability of its cohesion. Moreover, and like Iraq, although the civil war has faded into the past, its derivatives continue to prosper. The installation of the Consultative Council of Al-Qaeda in the Islamic Maghreb (AQIM) has had deadly consequences. For the first time in Algeria, the technique of suicide bombing was made part of a struggle against the regime.[78] On Thursday, 6 September 2007, a suicide attack targeted the presidential cortège in the city of Batna, killing twenty-two and wounding over a hundred. On Saturday, 8 September, another suicide bombing was perpetrated against the coast guard barracks in Dellys by a fifteen year old boy; the toll was twenty-eight dead. On 11 April, a triple attack killed thirty and wounded over two hundred in Algiers. After the bloody 11 April 2007 attack, an AQIM communiqué declared:

> We tell the apostates and their Crusader masters: We bring you tidings of the arrival of Islamic youth who love death and martyrdom the way you love your life of debauchery and delinquency; by Allah, we will not lay down our swords or savour life until we have liberated every inch of Islamic land from the Crusader, apostates and collaborator (with the enemy) and untill our feet walk once again in the stolen land of Andalusia and our desecrated Jerusalem.

AQIM is thus aiming to serve as a hub for regional terrorist organisations and especially to become the unavoidable intermediary through which to send fighters to Iraq in exchange for Al-Qaeda's logistic support in the region.[79]

Until the winter of 2011, Muammar Qadhafi's Libya had been spared a civil war and escaped the fate of Saddam Hussein's Iraq. However, Al-Qaeda Islamists continue to view it as an enemy. In the words of Sheikh al Libi, an Al-Qaeda "commander" in Afghanistan who died in 2009, "Qadhafi is the tyranny of Libya. After long years, he has suddenly discovered that America is not an enemy and is turning Libya into another crusader base". Unlike in Iraq and Algeria, the Al-Qaeda rhetoric is not carried out in deed. Libya had never had a suicide attack on its territory. It seemed highly likely that the return of Libyan combatants from Iraq would have consequences for security in Libya, but at the time the Libyan regime was faced with forms of protest that seemed harmless in comparison to those in Algeria and Iraq. In September 2009, on Saif al Islam's initiative, the regime released fifty-six Libyan Islamic Fighting Group (LIFG) prisoners as a gesture of national reconciliation. To demonstrate its desire for reconciliation, the regime ordered the demolition of the Abu Salim prison, a symbol of repression against the Islamists in the 1990s.

This reconciliation policy was blown apart with the democratic uprising in February 2011. The population of Cyrenaica drove out those who represented the *Jamahiriyya*; a Libyan National Transition Council was formed and General Abdel Fatah Younis was appointed commander in chief of the revolutionary armed forces on 17 February 2011. The insurgents had the wild hope of liberating the country and marching on Tripoli to run out the Qadafhi clan. But once again, the Qadhafi regime demonstrated its remarkable survival capacity by sending its elite troops to retake the country. Although winter began with the hope of a Tunisian-style or Egyptian-style revolution, winter's end brought with it the insurgents' retreat, and bloody repression has fallen upon the population. Qadhafi's Libya has begun to look like Saddam Hussein's Iraq in 1991: a regime propped up only by the power of its paramilitary forces.

Conclusion

The return of financial abundance served to bolster the non-democratic regimes in Algeria and Libya. In Iraq, this unexpected financial windfall helped to support the costly installation of the new regime by the United States.[80] The following chapter will analyse the effect of European policy on governance in Algeria and in Libya. As El Houssain Abouchi points out, "Nearly forty years after the independence of the Maghreb states, the problem of democracy, beyond that of the quest and installation of a stable state and a political system that has the assent of all the political and sociological components, is on the agenda".[81] The hopes placed in the 1990s vanished to leave a lost decade: that of the civil war in Algeria and the international sanctions in Libya. The elections held during this period did not give rise to a foundational moment that inspired a democratisation process. The "institutional designs" built up by the regimes did not cause an unexpected and unpredictable but healthy "democratic derailment".[82] Likewise, as Kienle points out, economic liberalisation did not enable competing powers to emerge; it instead fostered the consolidation of authoritarian regimes.[83] The solidity of these regimes inspired a sense of powerlessness, making an evolution towards democracy seem impossible. The historical reasons for the impossibility of democracy are known; the factors explaining the "authoritarian syndrome" in the region have been rigorously demonstrated.[84]

And yet, from Tunis, a wind of revolt swept through the population. The people demanded political reform, the end of autocracy, the establishment of a constitutional state, respect for individuals and oversight over the wealth of their rulers. These demands, expressed by a youth that aspired to live under democratic regimes, provoked consternation in the EU, as they so severely shook the diplomatic framework that had been constructed with the countries on the Mediterranean's southern shore. Europe's Neighbourhood Policy until then had granted only a marginal place to instituting democracy, as the next chapter will show. Is the international agenda today more favourable to promoting and setting up democracies? Is it conceivable that the Euro-Mediterranean partnership and the European Neighbourhood Policy (ENP) will place greater emphasis on the installation of democracy in the region? Will the EU manage to export its norms and values at a lower cost and bring happiness to those disappointed in the oil wealth?

ALGERIA, LIBYA AND THE CHALLENGE OF
THE EUROPEAN NEIGHBOURHOOD POLICY

While in Iraq unprecedented but ambitious political experimentation is under way—an attempt to make a rentier economy function
under the aegis of the United States in an imposed democracy[1]—
Algeria and Libya are grappling with the European Neighbourhood
Policy. In May 2004 Chris Patten, then an EU Commissioner, pointed
out that "Over the past decade, the Union's most successful foreign
policy instrument has undeniably been the promise of EU membership. This is not sustainable. For the coming decade, we need to find
new ways to export the stability, security and prosperity we have
created within the enlarged EU. We should begin by agreeing on a
clearer vision for relations with our neighbours". The Commission
was launching its Neighbourhood Policy, which defined a new
framework for countries not eligible for integration into the EU. For
the southern Mediterranean countries (Algeria, Egypt, Israel, Jor-
dan, Lebanon, Libya, Morocco, Palestine, Syria and Tunisia),
exchanges with the EU henceforth take place in a framework produced and defined by the EU.[2] For interested Maghreb countries:

> Within the ENP the EU offers our neighbours a privileged relation-
> ship, building upon a mutual commitment to common values
> (democracy and human rights, rule of law, good governance, market
> economy principles and sustainable development). The ENP goes
> beyond existing relationships to offer a deeper political relationship
> and economic integration. The level of ambition of the relationship
> will depend on the extent to which these values are effectively

THE VIOLENCE OF PETRO-DOLLAR REGIMES

shared. The ENP remains distinct from the process of enlargement although it does not prejudge, for European neighbours, how their relationship with the EU may develop in future, in accordance with Treaty provisions.[3]

By encouraging bilateral relations, the ENP departs from the previous decade that worked towards building regional integration in the Maghreb:

> The central element of the European Neighbourhood Policy is the Bilateral Action Plans agreed between the EU and each partner. These set out an agenda of political and economic reforms with short and medium-term priorities. Implementation of the first seven ENP Action Plans (agreed in early 2005 with Israel, Jordan, Moldova, Morocco, the Palestinian Authority, Tunisia and Ukraine) is under-way and that of the latest to be agreed (with Armenia, Azerbaijan and Georgia) is about to begin. Lebanon will follow shortly and the EU-Egypt ENP Action Plan is nearly agreed. Implementation is jointly promoted and monitored through subcommittees.[4]

In the Maghreb, Libya and Algeria have not yet adopted Action Plans. Libya has not because it does not fulfil requirements: it has not signed the Euro-Mediterranean Partnership (EMP) and so has not entered into an Association Agreement with the EU. As for Algeria, after signing an EU Association Agreement in April 2002, with implementation to begin in 2005,[5] it at first refused to join the ENP in September 2007, but then in 2008 it showed interest in drawing up a plan. However, in 2009, Libya and Algeria were the only two countries in North Africa that were not involved in an Action Plan. Taking over from the ailing EMP (the expected virtuous circle did not materialise and the track record of the Barcelona Process was disappointing to say the least),[6] the ENP, because of its political and economic ambitions, aroused concern in Algiers and Tripoli. In fact, for these two countries, it institutionalised "a logic of hegemony"[7] in the framework of a bilateral relationship that can only be unfavourable, as it is likely to strip them of control of the agenda for economic and political reforms to be implemented. In 2002, Algeria had reluctantly signed a new EU Association Agreement; in 2009, it criticised the EU's lack of support for Algeria's integration in the WTO and the lack of investment outside hydrocarbons.[8] Through this criticism it expressed its disappointment in the EU and hence its refusal to rush into an Action Plan.

In fact, "resistance" to the European Neighbourhood Policy is a product of the oil wealth.[9] With Europe, Algeria and Libya are interested in the energy market and security cooperation but not by the political dimension of the ENP, even less by its intrusion into the agenda of economic reforms. For what reasons would they agree to such constraints? It is easy to understand why Morocco, Tunisia and Egypt play by Europe's rules. These countries expect a return on the investment of their participation in the neighbourhood policy, which could come in various forms of financial assistance. Moreover, depending on what develops with Turkey, they might accelerate political reforms or even halt them and settle for economic reforms alone if negotiations between the EU and Turkey end in a rejection of its accession; lack of "common values",[10] interest and expectations explains the acceptance of "hegemony". But for Algeria and Libya, with a fund endowed with approximately $140 billion and $100 billion in 2009, EU financial aid seems to be a tasteless carrot indeed compared with the progress to be made. And this even more since European "hegemony" could seriously shake up, if not bring down, the "coalitions that seek to exploit sources of revenue",[11] which, as shown in the previous chapters, have managed to survive against all odds. Thus the ideal relationship for Algeria and Libya would be to limit themselves to active participation in the EU's energy structure and integration into the regional security strategy. But in reaction to the EU's insistence on binding these two countries to the Neighbourhood Policy, Algeria and Libya take pleasure in pointing out that unlike other countries in the region, although they agree to discuss the ENP, they feel no need to be part of it. This calculated indifference is a strong asset in negotiations with the EU, as it forces the latter to considerably reduce its political ambitions and expectations, even to avoid broaching the fundamental problems of a lack of democracy and poor governance.

So as not to heighten Algeria's hostility to the ENP, a strategy paper on Algeria (2007–2013) pinpointed three areas in which change would lead to improvements: judicial reform; economic growth and employment; and improved access to basic public services.[12] The approach is a gradual one, as Rosa Rossi remarks: "A step-by-step or progressive approach towards EU neighbouring countries is also required in order to introduce a gradual engagement for each state depending on its willingness to progress with economic and political reform. The way to pursue this policy is not anymore political conditionality but rather benchmarks: clear and public definitions of the actions that the EU expects the partners to implement".[13] Contrary to the method employed by the United States in Iraq, the aim is to take the time needed to devise a policy that can stabilise the tools and instruments of the state in order to establish a modicum of trust between the public authorities and users.[14] Libya, although it was invited to join the EMP and benefit from the ENP,[15] did not rush in, either, although it began to measure its importance.[16] It however preferred to build trade and military relations with less cumbersome partners such as Italy and Russia. Theoretically, the ENP is concerned with implementing good governance, an ambition which, given the post-colonial trajectory of Algeria and Libya, seems fundamental. These countries have in fact demonstrated the limits of oil wealth when no democratic control is exercised; its use can only be poisonous to states and their societies as it results in corrupt practices, which present real obstacles to development.[17]

The EU's step-by-step approach in Algeria and Libya hinges on two aspects. The first is strategic: it involves building a common policy in order to address security concerns (terrorism, migration, border control) and energy concerns (securing supplies). The second is political: a concern not to achieve regime change but to foster the export of EU norms and values.[18] Articulating the two raises ethical problems: can Libya be made a strategic partner in migration policy, for instance? The lack of economic takeoff in the region contributes to the migration and security concerns that feed the ENP. Moreover, although the bilateral aspect fosters construction of an energy market and a common security policy, it prevents the construction of a horizontal Maghrebian space that would offer lasting advantages in terms of jobs and greater guarantees of stability than dependence on a rentier economy. One of the perverse effects of the ENP, in the absence of a perspective of "reinforced integration",[19] is likely to be to strengthen the energy sectors in Algeria and Libya—even while these countries are unable to satisfy the "ocean of needs"—to the detriment of economic diversification. Once integrated into the EU's supply networks, Algeria and Libya are bound to lose interest in integration in the Maghreb, despite the potential such a project would have to create jobs and wealth. Regional integration is thus more a demand stemming from countries with fewer natural resources, such as Morocco and Tunisia.[20] In that perspective, in addition to the historic disputes between Morocco and Algeria, the rentier economy is also a destructive force working against the "fathers of nationalism and the Maghreb liberation movement".[21]

The construction of an energy market: The EU, Algeria, Libya

On 27 April 2004, Muammar Qadhafi paid a historic visit to Brussels at the invitation of the European Commission. Since 1992, Muammar Qadhafi in fact could not enter a Western country owing to the various legal proceedings instituted against him. Nonetheless, as Romano Prodi, the then President of the European Commission, pointed out:

> The EU currently has no formal relations with Libya, and the Commission has no Delegation in Tripoli. However, Libya is a key country on the southern shore of the Mediterranean, while playing a major role on the continent of Africa. Libya has enjoyed observer status in the Barcelona Process since April 1999, after having been invited for the first time to the Euro-Med Conference in Stuttgart. Subsequently, it was invited to become a full partner of the Process. This requires a formal petition in which Libya accepts all the *acquis*, and which must be examined by the Council.[22]

Europe has long been eager to integrate Libya in the partnership. As soon as UN sanctions were suspended in April 1999, Prodi invited Muammar Qadhafi to Brussels. The objective was to involve him in discussions over membership of the Euro-Mediterranean Partnership. The invitation, however, prompted lively discussion involving Chris Patten, who was in charge of relations with the Mediterranean countries, and Javier Solana, head of external policy and common security. The two officials pointed out that Libya had not yet been cleared of the accusations levied against it. This attitude contributed to Muammar Qadhafi's critical stance on the prospect of association with Europe:

> The European experiment is of no value to us... The area known as North Africa must be Africanised. Either it is part of Africa, or it is an

Origin of European Union oil and natural gas imports (2008)

in billions of dollars

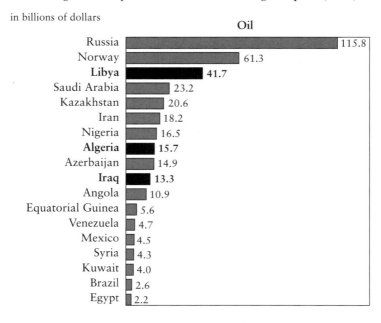

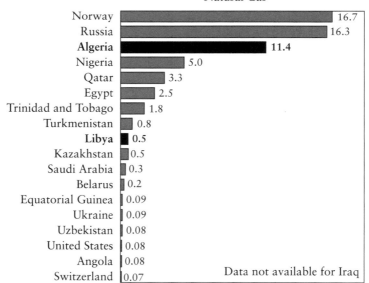

Sources: UN Comtrade, 2009.

Atelier de cartographie de Sciences Po, April 2010.

anomaly, and in that case it has no future. Being from this part of North Africa, I have always rejected the Barcelona Process. This is a conspiracy against African territorial integrity. […] They want to draw us in, to assist us through the Barcelona Process by dismembering the continent, stealing North Africa to annexe it to the European Union, now that is unacceptable.[23]

A few years later, the rejection of a political partnership with Europe led to a renewal of energy ties. The 7 October 2004 inauguration of the West Jamahiriyya Gas Project sealed Libya's bond to Europe, according to the Libyan press agency: "We declare before the world that Italy and Libya have decided to make the Mediterranean a sea of peace, a sea of trade and tourism, a sea under which oil and gas pipelines will pass through Libya and Italy to link Africa and Europe".[24] This energy convergence was enshrined in the Ministerial Declaration of the Euro-Med Energy Forum in May 2003, which underscored the need to complete the "Euro-Mediterranean gas ring" by strengthening support for the following projects in the 2003–2006 period:[25]

– a gas pipeline supplying Spain and France from Algeria;
– a gas pipeline supplying Italy and France from Algeria;
– a gas pipeline from Libya to supply Italy (via Malta);
– a gas interconnection between Egypt, Libya and Tunisia.

Algeria represents 10 per cent and Libya 2 per cent of gas imports to the EU, whose main supplier is Russia. The EU's dependence on natural gas imports is growing constantly: 62 per cent of its gas consumption was imported in 2006. Algeria has the sixth largest proven world reserves and is the world's fourth largest exporter of natural gas. Benefiting from the development of a gas market in Europe, Algeria has become the EU's third largest supplier, providing it with liquefied natural gas (LNG) and pipelines (Transmed, Maghreb Europe Gas Pipeline). Two projects are under way, GALSI to link Algeria and Italy via Sicily, and "MEDGAZ" linking Algeria and Spain.[26]

Libya was substantially behind in the exploitation of its natural gas. Algeria had initiated exploitation, production and sale of its own gas resources in the 1970s, whereas Libyan exploitation did not really get under way until 1990. Libya suffered from a serious

THE VIOLENCE OF PETRO-DOLLAR REGIMES

lack of gas production infrastructure compared to Algeria's. The Italian oil company Agip, however, worked to unify the gas sector across North Africa. Its objective, working through Agip North Africa and Middle East Ltd, was to bring about a convergence between Algerian and Libyan energy policies. Modelling its approach on French policy in Algeria, Italy aimed to become the "patron" of the new Libya. To achieve this, Italy had considerable advantages. Through the medium of Agip, it had maintained a privileged partnership with Libya for decades. With Europe's energy needs in mind, Italy attempted to coordinate both Algerian and Libyan gas suppliers in North Africa. Libya had an obvious interest in linking some of its gas fields to the Algerian transport network. The question remained whether or not it was in Algeria's interest for such synergy to develop. In the short term Algeria might well have been concerned to see a rival gas producer emerging in North Africa, but in the long term it could exploit its dominant position by becoming the real hub for exporting natural gas to Europe, via the Transmed pipeline. The construction of 1,385 kilometres of pipeline from Hassi R'Mel to Córdoba in Spain via Morocco showed that, despite the hostile relations between Morocco and Algeria, their convergence of interests had won out. Libya and Algeria also had a clear interest in aligning their positions in the international gas market.

On the strength of their experience in the oil industry, Sonatrach and the NOC worked together to consolidate and reinforce their positions. In the 1970s, Algeria and Libya had in fact joined forces in the petroleum sector. While Muammar Qadhafi's Arab nationalism showed the influence of President Nasser,[27] the model for building up its oil industry was Algeria. "Libya at the outset had no experience or industrial background. It would have been obliged to train a whole population from scratch at the highest technical and scientific level".[28] Cooperation between Algeria and Libya in the hydrocarbon sector began when Muammar Qadhafi took power. In the 1970s, the two countries planned to adopt a common position in dealing with foreign companies, intending to put up a common front to safeguard their positions and interests, while coordinating their efforts to develop their national economies. Cooperation was established between Sonatrach and

LIPTECO (which in 1970 became LINOCO and finally, in 1972, the NOC). The two companies exchanged information, technicians and experts, and formed joint companies for the exploration, production and transport of oil. In practice, the management of the NOC modelled itself on Sonatrach, turning the NOC into an instrument for the state to use to regain control over the country's natural resources. The NOC followed the same three phases that Sonatrach went through to free itself from foreign companies: increase investment, develop engineering skills to reduce dependence and require greater use of locally manufactured goods, and develop services. In 1971, nationalisation of gas fields and transport pipelines, together with the increase in its holding to 51 per cent, put Sonatrach in control of three-quarters of Algeria's oil production and all of its natural gas production.

In the 1980s, Sonatrach and the NOC signed cooperation agreements which on 11 November 1988 led to the establishment of two joint ventures: the Arab Libyan-Algerian Exploration and Production Company (ALEPCO), whose remit was oil exploration, and the Libyan-Algerian Geophysics Company (LAGC). The outcome of this cooperative enterprise was the discovery of an oil well at Oued Merabia in northwestern Algeria in 1994, in the Hassi Messaoud oilfield. In November 1999, Sonatrach and the NOC planned a further joint venture involving the exploration of blocks close to the two countries' common border.[29] Libya was also keen to develop its transport network, signing cooperation agreements with Algeria, Tunisia and Egypt. Additional joint companies were created, including the Arab Maghreb Company for Gas and Transportation, the Libyan Arab Algerian Company for Exploration and Production, the Algerian Libyan Company for Geophysics Inc., and the Arab Company for Engineering Consultancy. In the late 1980s, the patent failure of their economic models paradoxically encouraged them to compete to supply European gas-consuming countries. Forming a network with Algeria and Libya fitted in with a European concern to diversify its sources of supply. The fear of too great a dependence on Gazprom has increased interest in Libyan and Algerian reserves.

As soon as the sanctions were lifted in 2003, Libya appeared extremely attractive. Ahmed Abdulkarim, former chairman of the

NOC and current head of OilInvest, (the state-owned oil holding company), announced that the government was seeking to attract $10 billion in foreign investment in the hydrocarbon sector by 2010.[30] Only 25 per cent of the oil and gas reserves, currently estimated at 40 billion barrels, are in fact being exploited.[31] Moreover, Libya's production rate is about 1.5 million bpd, but the government aimed to increase its production capacity to 1.8 bpd in 2006 and to 3 million by 2020. This would restore production to the level it had reached prior to nationalisation in 1971.[32] Regarding natural gas, Libya hopes soon to export to Italy via the GALSI underground pipeline crossing the Mediterranean. Libya's gas reserves are estimated at 1500 billion m^3, or 1 per cent of world reserves, and in 1999 its production was 12,200 billion m^3/year.[33] To coordinate this revival, Libya established the Council for Oil and Gas Affairs, whose remit is to develop a strategy as effective as Algeria's.

It is obvious that Libya's slide into violence, at the time of writing in early 2011, seriously undermines implementation of these projects. Worse still, the confrontation between pro-Qadhafi forces and the rebels has damaged oil infrastructure and considerably reduced production. Only a swift return to stability would allow foreign oil company staff to return and hence restart Libyan oil production, providing that the United Nations Security Council does not vote to impose a ban on oil exports.

Building a security strategy

A prerequisite to connecting Algeria and Libya to the EU's supply system was regime stability and territorial security, two conditions that were lacking throughout the 1980s. As J. Percebois has pointed out: "Supply security is one of the most important preoccupations of the European Commission".[34] Even if long-term sales contracts ensured a continuity of supply, the pipelines had still to be safeguarded from sabotage. Stability returned with the strengthening of the regimes owing to the third oil crisis. Integration into the NATO-Mediterranean dialogue offers additional resources that should help to improve security in areas affected by the terrorist activity of organisations such as AQMI.[35]

Conscious of the advantages of their geographical position, the Algerian and Libyan regimes still had to prove that European fears concerning stability and security threats to the region were a thing of the past if they hoped fully to exploit this rapprochement between consumer and producer states. The Euro-Mediterranean gas ring had shown that the countries in the region were able to achieve a level of understanding sufficient to foster the transport of hydrocarbons to Europe in the best possible conditions. The gradual integration of the armed forces of the Maghreb countries in a regional defence structure (NATO-Mediterranean dialogue) has offered stronger security guarantees by warding off the spectre of a direct conflict. Growing United States involvement in the region,[36] in the wake of the 11 September attacks, has also fostered the construction of a regional anti-terrorist coalition. With the Middle East Partnership Initiative (MEPI) launched by President George W. Bush, the Maghreb suddenly became the focus of particular attention in three sectors; security, economy and energy. Donald Rumsfeld carried out a "Maghreb tour" in February 2006 in the framework of the war on terrorism and with a view to fostering a rapprochement between the Maghreb countries and NATO.[37] Since the "NATO-Mediterranean dialogue" was launched in March 2000, joint exercises have been organised continually between NATO, Algeria and Morocco for instance. In the economic sector, the free trade agreement signed between Morocco and the United States opened up new trade perspectives. Moreover, investment by American companies in Algeria and Libya has been constantly on the rise. The re-establishment of diplomatic ties with Libya and plans for a military base in the Sahel in Mauritania in the framework of the fight against terrorism further demonstrate the United States' new commitment to the region. The European Union's lack of involvement in the Western Sahara conflict, justified by the wish to avoid antagonising both Morocco and Algeria, has left the United States an opportunity to work in the Maghreb.

The 11 September 2001 attacks had a double impact on North Africa in so far as they legitimised the fight against terrorism, including violation of human rights in that cause, and facilitated the integration of the Maghreb into the global mechanism of the "War on Terror", undertaken by the Bush administration.

The 11 March 2004 Madrid attacks led to the creation of an EU common strategy to fight terrorism, following which Islamist armed groups from the Maghreb began to be seen as one of the main threats for Europe's southern countries. North African regimes thus found a favourable echo to their security policies both among the EU member states and in the US.[38] For the Bush administration the main threat in North Africa is in the Sahel. As underlined by the report of the "Maghreb roundtable" held at the Centre for Strategic and International Studies in February 2006, "The activities of terrorist networks that operate in ungoverned areas of North Africa and the Sahel are the primary threat in the Maghreb. Indigenous extremist groups and jihadi fighters fleeing Afghanistan have found safe havens near the Sahara where they are able to operate free from government interference".[39] From this perspective the building of a regional coalition was the best instrument in the fight against terrorism in the Maghreb region. These security initiatives are part of an effort to establish a climate of trust in an area where suspicion has reigned as much between the countries that constitute it as with respect to European security initiatives. The time is long since past when in the Maghreb Eurofor and Euromarfor were considered "a flagrant interference and a direct threat to the sovereignty of the southern Mediterranean and even a danger to peace and security".[40] The building of a "Euro-Mediterranean gas ring" in fact obliged producer, transit and consumer countries to reach a certain degree of understanding regarding a security strategy in the Mediterranean.

This strategic understanding (gas ring, fight against terrorism) is also reflected in the "fight against migrants". The aim is to curb the arrival of illegal migrants by military means. The SIVE,[41] the European Naval Forces and Frontex are used to counter migrants from the Maghreb and sub-Saharan Africa. This array of systems is enhanced by maritime operations such as the Neptune project, Operation Active Endeavour led by NATO, the Atlantis Project and more recently the EU-funded Sea Horse project, with Frontex actually coordinating joint operations along maritime borders (the Hera, Minerva, Nautilus, Poseidon operations). The ambition is no longer only to control international waters but territorial waters as well. The effects of this militarisation are twofold: they close off certain passage routes, yet have not stemmed the flow of migrants.[42] From an administrative standpoint, they enable illegal migrants who have slipped through the system in the last country of transit (10 per cent of migrants entering the EU are illegal) to be taken back. Given Europe's concerns regarding migration issues, Libya agreed to have "camps" installed on its soil. In February 2003, Tony Blair launched the idea of creating "regional protection areas" outside Europe, and his project was taken up in August 2004 by Otto Schily, Germany's Minister of the Interior, and his Italian counterpart Giuseppe Pisanu, who suggested the idea of creating "closed centres", actually camps where migrants' asylum applications would be examined.[43] Since the onset of these initiatives, a few "camps" have been set up in the Maghreb, and bilateral cooperation and readmission agreements have been signed with the EU.[44]

Has the Maghreb become "Europe's policeman"? The flow of illegal immigrants from sub-Saharan Africa on their way to Europe has made the Maghreb a transit area. All the more so since two of its countries, Algeria and Libya, which migrants avoided in the 1990s owing to the civil war and international sanctions, once again became attractive in the 2000s. The populations of poorer neighbouring countries migrate to their richer neighbours (from Mali, Niger and Chad to Libya, for instance). The first factor explaining the departure of migrants from Africa to the Maghreb is poverty, whereas unemployment is the primary factor explaining migration of Maghrebians to Europe. Structural causes explain the migratory phenomenon of conflicts in Sub-Saharan Africa and discrepancies in wealth that continue to grow between north and south. Having militarised its Mediterranean border, Libya, with Malta's backing, requested military assistance to enhance security along its coastal and land borders. In September 2007, Muammar Qadhafi even requested about ten billion euros in financial assistance from the EU to combat these flows. If not money, Libya hoped that Italy would give it help to build an efficient navy. Malta, the main EU member state concerned with the issue of illegal migration, requested that the EU provide Libya with concrete support: "if Libya had better patrols along its southern border, it could reduce the number of migrants that reach Malta and Italy", stressed Tonio Borg, Malta's Minister of Internal Affairs.

Economic failure and demographic pressure send young people on migratory routes in search of a brighter future. The economic gap between the Maghreb countries and the EU makes migration an attractive proposition despite the lack of legal access to the job market. The broad application of visa requirements by the EU countries in the Schengen space has led migrants to seek new access routes to Europe, particularly to migrate to Spain and Italy. Over the last decade, the Maghreb has become a place of transit for migrants originating from south of the Sahara. For the moment, Mehdi Lahlou explains:

> the migration of citizens of countries south of the Sahara is of little concern for Europe, because most of the sub-Saharan migrants settle for more or less long periods in the Maghreb, in Libya, in Algeria to a lesser extent, and more and more in Morocco. The number of people from sub-Saharan Africa currently living in Libya is thus estimated at over 2 million... Figures from various sources indicate that the number of sub-Saharan migrants entering the Maghreb is between 65,000 and 80,000 each year.[45]

Only 15 per cent of these African migrants seek to enter Europe directly.[46] This means that the Maghreb has become an area of immigration although its economy is incapable of creating the jobs required to support its active population. When the confrontation between Libyan insurgents and the regime began in early 2011, Saif al-Islam, one of Qadhafi's sons and considered as his potential successor, used blackmail on the EU, reminding it of the risk it would take if it sided with the rebels: "They have to support us... otherwise this country could become the Somalia of North Africa. You will see pirates in the Mediterranean Sea, in Crete, in Sicily, in Lampdusa. You will see millions of illegal immigrants, chaos will be at your door".[47]

Energy market and security strategy: What happens to regional integration?

Algeria and Libya's successful integration in the EU's supply system and regional security strategy does not meet the region's needs and concerns. Worse, it makes economic integration of the region seem more elusive, even when this appears to be one of the most effective responses for creating jobs and wealth. Growth of the active population in the Maghreb implies that "16 million jobs [will be] needed between 2000 and 2020 to provide for new entrants. And with unemployment in the Maghreb estimated at 20.4 per cent, to absorb the unemployed as well as new entrants, these countries will have to create nearly 22 million jobs in the next two decades".[48] In the space of a half-century, the population of the Maghreb multiplied by 3.4, from 25.7 million inhabitants in 1950 to 77.8 million inhabitants in 2001. Life expectancy went from 42 to 67 years, except for Mauritania where life expectancy does not exceed 50. This demographic revolution has resulted in an expansion of the 20–40 year age bracket, from 23 million to 28 million between 2000 and 2010. In 2010, it represented 36 per cent of the total population. As many observers point out, this age bracket corresponds to potential candidates for migration. Quite clearly, 9 million young people are threatened by serious economic hardship in the immediate future. The population in this age bracket will not shrink until 2030, at which time it will represent only 33 per cent of the total population. Oil revenues of the past and gas revenues to come will not amount to enough to meet such demands. In June 2005, Rodrigo de Rato, Managing Director of the International Monetary Fund, made the following critical observation:

> throughout the region, economic growth has remained below its potential, unemployment is still much too high, and poverty remains pervasive. This suggests that there are important constraints on the economies that need to be addressed. What are these and what can be done? (...) The Maghreb countries represent relatively small, fragmented markets, whose best chance for development lies in openness and integration. In practice their restrictive trade regimes and cumbersome investment regulations have discouraged domestic private investment and attracted only limited amounts of foreign direct investment, outside the hydrocarbon sector. (...) Greater regional economic integration would yield important benefits. It would create a regional market of more than 75 million consumers (...). It would bring efficiency gains and make the region more attractive for foreign investors. And, most important, the complementary economic structures of the Maghreb countries would create opportunities for mutually beneficial trade within the region.[49]

In 2003 intra-regional trade between the Maghreb countries (Algeria, Morocco and Tunisia) only reached 3 per cent. In contrast, "intra-zone trade represented 60.2 per cent of the EU exchanges, 22.3 per cent for the ASEAN, 10.6 per cent for the PECO and 19.9 per cent for the Mercosur countries".[50] The feeble trade rate can be explained by a structural reason: weak economic complementarity.[51] According to Mohamed Boussetta, one of the solutions to boost intra-regional trade is the dismantling of tariffs. Thus, for Algeria "a cut of 50 per cent or 100 per cent in taxes to farming imports from Morocco and Tunisia would lead to a progress of 20.9 per cent and 47.9 per cent, respectively in trade with these two countries (…) with regards to industrial trade it would amount to an increase in trade of 34.4 per cent and 84.9 per cent, respectively".[52] Such a weak level of integration leads to "the deprivation of 2 per cent to 3 per cent of the annual GDP of North African countries" and one cannot help wonder why this is the case.[53] Indeed, given their economic situation, North African countries do not seem to be in a position to afford to waste such opportunities. The "benefit for all" has so far been denied. When the North Africa Trade Forum was organised on 19–20 February 2007, the introductory memo bearing the subtitle "Trade for Growth and Job Creation" pointed out that "while the increase in economic growth rates didn't have a significant impact on unemployment reduction in particular and poverty alleviation in general, recent studies… show that with basic and adequate measures, intra-regional trade could be multiplied by 5 to 10". One of the Forum's objectives was to "explore the solutions to the issues that are preventing trade promotion in the region".[54] Could the rentier economies of Algeria and Libya be an obstacle to regional integration? In short, is it the assurance of being able to take advantage of the European market that released them from the political constraint of working towards regional integration?

Some observers hailed the March 2005 meeting between President Abdelaziz Bouteflika and the King of Morocco, Mohammed VI, as the beginning of a "thaw". The press reported rumours about the reopening of the Algerian-Moroccan border, an initial symbolic gesture in the renewed relations between the two countries. In the wake of this event Libya, which then held the chairmanship of the AMU (Arab Maghreb Union), announced the date of a summit of heads of state to be held in Tripoli on 25–26 May that same year. This enthusiasm proved to be short-lived. Mohamed VI announced that he would not take part in the meeting, which was subsequently cancelled. Remarks made by President Bouteflika a short time before regarding the Sahrawi people's right to self-determination were used as a pretext to call into question attempts at a reconciliation between Algeria and Morocco. In fact, Algeria's official stance on the Sahara had not changed. As Abdelkader Messahel indicated in March 2006, "the solution to the conflict lies in the Sahrawi's people exercise of its sacred right to self-determination (…) it's Algeria's final position (…) it is first of all up for the UN to move and take its responsibilities in order to solve the stalemate".[55] This view was reiterated by Mohammed Bedjaoui, Foreign Affairs Minister, in June 2006 in the daily newspaper *Liberté* (5 June 2006), laying emphasis on the Baker Plan and support for resolution 1675 (2006), which recalls the right to self-determination of the Sahrawi people. For Morocco, the return of financial abundance in Algeria explained its lack of economic interest in the region. In fact, the border closure cost Morocco more than it did Algeria. The risk of a direct conflict was ruled out, as James Baker pointed out, explaining, "Algeria and Morocco are working closely with the United States in its war on terror. It is therefore particularly difficult for Washington to favour one or the other because it wants to remain close to both of them… Algeria is very strong, Morocco won the war; Polisario, under the occupation, is weak. Armed conflict is not on the agenda. As long as Algeria tells Polisario not to fight, it won't".[56] However, with the Medgaz project, Algeria is trying to circumvent Morocco to reach Spain directly. This regional tension exasperates companies operating in the area. Economic actors have all the more interest in supporting a project for regional integration since the region's political leaders seem to be entering once again into a "cold war". Algeria, Morocco and Libya are engaged in a small-scale regional "arms race".[57]

The Western Sahara conflict constitutes the main impediment to the building of the AMU. It illustrates the inability of Algeria and Morocco since the 1963 "Sand War" to improve a relationship based on mistrust and sometime even hostility. The Western

Sahara conflict mainly represented a great political opportunity for the two countries to establish their authority. It enabled the Moroccan monarchy to harness nationalist sentiment, until then monopolised by Istiqlal, which placed the idea of a Greater Morocco at the core of its struggle for power. For the Algerian regime, it represented a means to justify the army's power and to keep nationalist feelings alive. Clear benefits were drawn from the Sahara conflict: it allowed both states to establish, under the cover of nationalist feelings, authoritarian political regimes. During the 1970s and 1980s, the conflict was a pretext to establish hostile relations. Once facing internal criticism over human rights violations, corruption, wealth concentration and lack of freedom, Algeria and Morocco relied on the Western Sahara conflict as an occasion to dispense prejudice and clichés about the "Other", using a compliant press to rally to their cause a population frustrated with the degradation of economic and social conditions.

At the end of the 1980s, the Maghreb countries rallied to the AMU, which was perceived as a means of forging closer ties with Europe. But only two years after its inception, the AMU was already raising doubts about whether regional integration would be achieved: "The political and practical uncertainties remain obvious. When and how will it become a stable institution? What is the main theme of the project? What is its driving force, at least in the initial stage? Official statements are either vague or contradictory. For an outside observer, the integration process is not really under way. The Maghrebian theme as used in domestic political speech seems to be intended for foreign ears".[58] From the start, the political ambition of the AMU seemed to be instrumental, aiming to meet Europe's expectations. Jacques Delors pointed out that "by building the AMU, the Maghreb countries considerably broaden perspectives for partnership on either side of the Mediterranean".[59] For the Maghreb countries, the AMU was an opportunity to develop privileged relations with Europe. The aim of building this new space was to move closer to the European Community, an objective that would be achieved in the framework of Association Agreements with the EU in the framework of the EMP. From this perspective, the development of regional integration was not the primary goal.

Today, along with the ENP, Algeria and Libya have shed the burden of regional integration. Morocco and Tunisia, although interested in it as it would enable them to increase exports, have formed ties in all directions to make up for the lack of a regional market (Morocco-United States Free Trade Area in 2006, Morocco-Turkey in 2006, the Agadir Treaty in 2004). The cost of disregarding the Maghreb regional possibilities exasperates companies working in the region, for whom national strategies are at odds with the needs of their societies. On 17 February 2007, heads of Maghreb employers' associations met in Marrakesh and announced the founding of the Maghreb Employers Union. The date was not chosen at random: the AMU was created on 17 February 1989. The AMU, originally a political undertaking, has become a major issue for business. As Hammad Kassal, vice president of the General Confederation of Moroccan Entrepreneurs and one of the founders of the Maghreb Employers Union, points out: "It is the economy that will break down the political barrier that exists today. We want to put pressure on our governments to improve their relations".[60]

By increasing its energy demand, the EU has heightened the ascendancy of the hydrocarbon sector over the Algerian and Libyan economies. It is virtually hegemonic; hydrocarbon exports already make up 98 per cent of external revenue. Furthermore, by guaranteeing the energy market and seeking to institutionalise bilateral relations, the EU has also liberated these two countries from pursuing regional integration in the Maghreb, the lack of which is more detrimental to Morocco and Tunisia. From a strategic standpoint, the EU has managed to integrate these countries into both its natural gas supply system and its policy of combating migrants. But on a political level, is it able to export its norms and values? In short, can it go beyond energy and security? It will have to, because Vladimir Putin's Russia has also offered Algeria and Libya a "strategic partnership".

The limits of the European policy

Given Algerian and Libyan resistance, the economic and security aspect of EU policy has very largely taken precedence over political reforms. Democracy is the poor relation of this policy, and yet, how can economic change come about if satisfaction of its citizens' needs is not at the heart of the political leaders' preoccupations?[61] Do the achievements made in building a natural gas market and in fighting terrorism and illegal immigration give the EU enough confidence capital to tackle political problems? The realist approach suggests that to neutralise Russian ambitions in Algeria and Libya, the EU should disregard political problems (democracy and good governance) in both countries in order to maximise its presence in the fields of energy and security. For the region's populations, this strategic choice explains the indifference, even complacency, with which the European Union member states regard corruption in the region. The monopolisation of public resources to private ends by "authoritarian coalitions" was already disregarded within the Euro-Mediterranean Partnership, which largely contributed to discrediting it in the eyes of public opinion. What will become of the new European policy if this problem is once again ignored? What can be done to increase confidence among foreign investors, thereby increasing FDI outside hydrocarbons, if national capital is invested elsewhere?[62] The ENP does not seem to be the most appropriate framework in which to tackle the problem of corruption and hence that of governance. And yet, the discourse of Islamist movements in southern Mediterranean societies feeds on these problems, contrasting regime corruption and the "virtues" of an Islamic regime.

In the recent past, one of the advantages of the oil rent was to make those who controlled it immune to any form of pressure or threat from the international community. Oil wealth had produced self-interested friendships with democratic countries, which freed the regimes from any worries about economic or diplomatic retaliation in the event of human rights violations. Oil was a diplomatic weapon during the period of sanctions in Libya (1992–99) and the civil war in Algeria (1991–99). The establishment of European oil companies in Libya under the embargo was used to considerable advantage to neutralise the conflictual relationship with the United States. The Clinton administration discussed the possibility of tightening the sanctions on Libya by including oil in their scope; in practice, a gamut of sanctions was put in place to punish foreign companies that invested in Libya. Italy and Germany made clear to the Clinton administration their opposition to an oil embargo on

Libya, because of the huge proportion of Libyan oil exports to these two countries. The development of an interdependent relationship with Europe was a considerable diplomatic advantage during the period of tension with the United States. The regime had achieved its foreign policy objective. Libya had established significant linkages in Europe to hold at bay the policy of sanctions promoted by the United States.[63] Moreover, unlike open authoritarian regimes such as those in Tunisia and Egypt that depend on tourist revenue and foreign investment, authoritarian rentier regimes can boldly suppress their populations or opponents because the tourism sector is in its infancy, and investors in the energy sector are fairly insensitive to the fate of local populations. In such cases, whereas an authoritarian regime like Tunisia strove to find sophisticated methods of repressing its opponents without appearing to do so, Algeria in 1995 waged a "total war" on Islamists without putting a damper on investment in the hydrocarbon sector.[64] Not long ago, Europe protected Libya from the American regime of sanctions. Today, would Russia protect Libya and Algeria from an ambitious European policy to export democratic norms and values? Up to now, Algeria and Libya are more often faced with delegations of representatives from major weapons manufacturers than with missions of democracy engineers.

The reality principle

On the verge of implosion ten years earlier, Algeria and Libya have accumulated reserve funds to regulate the huge sums raked in during the third oil crisis, which the economy cannot absorb. Cast out by the international community in the 1990s, these countries have become the object of considerable courtship owing to their renewed wealth. In addition to civil infrastructure that requires restoration after a decade of embargos and violence, major arms contracts, industrial projects, plans for new towns and so on have also made their return. Several foreign investors from the EU, Russia, the United States, China, etc. have turned their attention to the opportunity offered by this new financial windfall.

The lifting of the European Union ban on arms sales encountered some reluctance. During a debate at the Western European Union on 22 October 2004, a British representative, Lord Russell-Johnston, said, "No sooner does Libya begin to behave better than the first reaction of the European Union is to sell it arms... This is not the best solution". The question for Libya was how to persuade international opinion that it needed to resume its conventional armaments policy. The EU justification for lifting the ban on arms sales to Libya rested on the argument that Libya had to be supplied with the means to combat illegal migration.[65] In September 2004, one month before the EU decision, Italy gave a clear signal that it wished to assist the Libyan regime to acquire the range of military equipment it needed to control migratory flows, including new radar equipment, helicopters, optical surveillance equipment and patrol boats. On the grounds of an "invasion" of African immigrants arriving from Libya, which had already resulted in the illegal residence in Italy of some two million Africans, Italy managed to persuade its European partners to lift the ban on arms sales to Libya; in return, Libya would authorise the establishment on Libyan soil of "holding centres" for illegals.[66] The exploitation of the migration issue for military and commercial purposes had the desired effect. The argument held sway, and the EU lifted the ban on arms sales to Libya. After giving up its WMD programme, Libya's goal was to reconstruct its conventional military power. The arms industries in Russia, Britain, France, Germany, Italy and the United States were all in the running. EU sanctions were lifted in October 2004, and the United States ended its embargo in May 2006.

For the moment, the Libyan arms market involved the modernisation of the nine frigates in the Libyan navy, border control, and the refitting of Mirage fighter aircraft. From July 2006, the French CIEEMG (Interministerial Commission for Examination of War Material Exports) explored the possibility of selling Tiger combat helicopters to Libya. Libya still hoped to be a leading country in the region and on the continent. It sought to obtain the status of a "responsible power" and become a mediator between the EU and Africa. The convergence of interests between France and Libya, particularly as regards Africa, explains the rapprochement between the two countries.[67] On 21 October 2007, the Defence Ministry confirmed that a Libyan offer was being studied by the CIEEMG. The Libyan arms market has been highly coveted: the competition among European weapons manufacturers was stiff, all the more so since Russia has been aiming to become Algeria and Libya's primary arms supplier once again. Integration into the EU may be a guarantee of protection from Russia for the Central European countries, but for Algeria and Libya, Russia has been a useful safeguard against the eventuality that European policy might decide to raise its expectations regarding democracy and good governance.

In the framework of strategic partnerships with Algeria (2001) and Libya (1998), Russia in fact has offered these two countries strategic cooperation with no political strings attached. Unlike the EU, which couples energy and security strategy with political conditionalities (democracy and governance), Russia focuses solely on energy and security, thus offering these countries a flexible framework. Vladimir Putin on a visit to Algiers had declared, "Algeria is a key partner for Russia in the Mediterranean". For Russia, considering its importance in the EU gas supply system, Algeria has become a country to draw into Gazprom's strategy to heighten EU dependence and thereby increase the mutual benefits for the two countries.[68] So when Russia agreed to convert the military debt Algeria incurred in the 1960s-70s ($4.7 billion) for $3.5 billion in arms purchases, Putin wanted to make it contingent on Gazprom's acquiring a 15 per cent share in Sonatrach. President Abdelaziz Bouteflika rejected this condition, to the great relief of the European partners who feared that Gazprom would manage to turn Sonatrach into a subsidiary.[69] The Algerian army, considered pro-Russian (80 per cent of its equipment is Russian), was "defeated" by the Sonatrach energy specialists, considered pro-EU. Algeria was prepared to rearm in Russia but not deliver its natural gas there, because Algeria could now pick and choose between EU demands and those of Russia. Russia continues to be its main armaments supplier—it became the second largest importer of Russian arms in 2008[70]—and the EU is the main outlet for its gas.

Dismissed from Algeria's gas fields, Gazprom turned to Libya. As in Algeria, Russia aimed to recover the role of main arms supplier that it had held in the 1970s and 1980s. Moreover, it offered to purchase the natural gas produced by Libya, which it would integrate into its supply routes to Europe. In early 2007 the Gazprom management, led by its deputy chairman Alexander Medvedev, travelled to Tripoli to negotiate a Memorandum of Understanding with NOC. Their aim was to strike a deal with Libya similar to the one with Sonatrach on natural gas liquefaction, and agree on common calls for projects. All this made the Europeans nervous. The meeting in Tripoli between Yuri Safranik, chairman of the Russian Oil and Gas Union, and Muhammad Saleh Mansouri, president of the Libyan Business Council, was also attended by representatives of the big Russian industrial groups: Lukoil, Tafnet, SoyuzNefteGaz, Gazpromenet, Makhachkala Seaport, etc. Like Algeria, Libya was rearming in Russia but was not prepared to join the "gas cartel" under Gazprom's control. However, unlike Algeria, Libya did not rescind its Memorandum of Understanding with Gazprom. Freed from its shackles, the Qadhafi regime did a remarkable job of exploiting Europe's fear of Gazprom in negotiating its framework agreement with the EU.

The main obstacle to European policy in Algeria and Libya has thus been the Russian presence, which from a strategic standpoint offers perspectives in the energy and military domains that are just as attractive as those proposed by the EU but without the constraints of the ENP. In this trilogy, where strategic issues dominate, the countries' societies are largely disregarded. An analysis of the uses of the oil rent from 1970 to 2000 shows, as discussed in the previous chapters, that the oil rent has been incapable of creating jobs and improving the population's wellbeing in a lasting fashion, owing to the lack of democracy. The gas rent over the years 2005–2030 is thus likely to be just as ineffective if the political framework does not change. In an article published in *L'Expression*, Dr Chems Eddine Chitour expressed the general feeling about this third oil crisis:

> more than ever we need to review everything we're doing. To start with, the state has to stop living in a style of wealth that does not go along with the creation of wealth. We have to restore our know-how by counting on ourselves, not on the Chinese, the French, the Turks or the Koreans who treat Algeria as a bazaar where they can sell off any old junk amounting to $30 billion of instantly obsolete gadgets… A new programme is needed to manage Algeria, a programme based on training people. It starts at school.[71]

The oil rent has destroyed local know-how, generated consumer expectations, sustained the illusion of wealth and disregarded investment in human capital. The oil rent has produced the same effects as cannabis production. In the Rif area, in Morocco, farmers have come to prefer growing hashish, more lucrative although more harmful to their environment, and has generated *nouveaux riches* behaviour among traffickers.[72] Be it the oil economy or the drug economy, the illusions that have grown out of the effect of wealth vanish quickly with the emergence of violence and the spread of poverty. In short, the oil rent has not developed Algeria, Libya or Iraq any more than the drug economy has fostered development in Morocco, Burma or Afghanistan.[73] But as the world demand for oil and natural gas is greater than the demand for cocaine, opium and hashish, hydrocarbons generate far greater revenues than those accruing to narco-states.[74]

The "gas riots"

The return of the oil wealth occurred in a context of deep disenchantment and pessimism. Unlike the first oil crisis, which fostered a form of oil nationalism symbolised by the slogan "Arab oil for the Arabs",[75] the third crisis sparked no enthusiasm either among the elites or in the population at large. Between the two, it had become apparent that oil wealth was vain if no democratic authority could exercise control over the way it was used. Nothing has fundamentally changed in the exercise of power in these two countries. The French initiative of the Union for the Mediterranean project has provided an opportunity to re-discuss the place of political reform in the framework of Euro-Mediterranean relations. The very balance of European policy rests on the principle of non-interference and respect for sovereignty. So as not to offend the authoritarian regimes involved in relations with Europe, it is commonly agreed that problems touching on violations of human rights and freedoms are excluded from public exchanges and relegated to the private level where "firm but friendly" criticism is voiced. Coupled with this self-censorship is a method based on a step-by-step approach with authoritarian regimes. Rather than tackling the issue of a democratic deficit, the rigging of elections, violation of human rights and corruption, the ENP has "invested" in sectors with potential such as freedom and justice. The basic idea involves doing away with any form of conditionality, because of the unproductive effect it has on regimes. The problem is that since 11 September 2001, the EU's political ambition is hampered by fears regarding the security of the energy supply and the obsession with Islamist terrorism.[76]

The changes that occurred during the first decade of the new century have raised questions about the uses of the oil rent. While in Iraq regime change brought the issue of oil rent control and redistribution to the centre of transactions between the new political actors, in Algeria and Libya the oil rent still remains under the exclusive control of authoritarian coalitions. Forty years after the Arab nationalist slogan "Arab oil for the Arabs" was coined, local populations (Kurds and Shia Arabs in Iraq and Mozabites in Algeria) are now demanding a fair return of the wealth from oil-producing regions to the populations that live in them. These demands, long-standing in Iraq, new in Algeria and still beneath the surface in Libya, raise the question of democratic control over the oil rent. In 2004, the administered price of butane gas rose in Algeria from 170 DA to 300 DA. In January 2005, in the middle of winter, riots that the press labelled "gas riots" broke out in the *wilaya* of Djelfa and spread to central and western Algeria. Since then, uprisings have regularly occurred in southern Algeria, sparked by a feeling of injustice: why should the main source of external revenue, oil and gas, be controlled, managed and distributed by "foreign" elites (in Algiers) to the oil-rich areas? For the first time, the population claimed a right to control Algeria's main resources and demanded that the government account for its spending choices. Why is Algeria's richest area in terms of energy resources not better equipped with civil infrastructure? Disturbingly, the rioters concluded that the answer lay in their Berber identity. In May 2008, in the M'zab valley, the city of Berriane became the symbol of a clash between "Arabs" and "Berbers". In the city streets, conflicts broke out among people convinced that the amount of oil wealth distributed depended on their ethnic or racial belonging. After Islamist protest and violence, it seemed that the time had come for regional vengeance, from Kabylia to the M'zab Valley.

In March 2011, Libyan oil production dropped by 1.5 million bpd to 200,000 bpd, causing serious concern in Italy, the main importer of Libyan oil. Having neglected the needs and expectations of the populations in oil producing states on the southern shore, the EU is now faced with a major crisis in its neighbourhood. Will it be able to fully gauge the political changes occurring in the area? The strategic surprise that the democratic aspirations in North Africa and the Middle East represent for the EU is patent.[77] Its responses to the Libyan crisis will be indicators of its ability to take on board the changes underway.

Conclusion

The fear of an energy supply crisis probably explains Europe's weakness when tackling political problems in the Maghreb supplier countries. Its dependence on Russia obliges it to deal tactfully with Algeria and Libya. The choice of gas forces consumer and producer states to respect a minimum of common rules needed to build a secure network of pipelines. Diplomatic issues (the Western Sahara conflict) as well as political issues (democracy and governance) seem to breed conflict and dissension that should be kept separate from the energy structure taking shape. These problems are compounded by the fear of "the end of oil", making the natural gas supply all the more essential. Between the 11 September 2001 attacks and the world financial crisis, the rise in the per-barrel price of oil, which reached $147 in 2008, became a source of panic for consumer states, as illustrated by the publication of pessimistic essays announcing the end of a world based on a source of cheap and abundant energy that had been built up since the beginning of the twentieth century.[78] The third oil crisis (2003–08) caused the oil fear to resurface, a fear based on forecasts of per-barrel prices reaching $200. At its height, the price of oil was explained by the end of cheap oil due to a fall in production and rising demand owing to the energy needs of emerging countries. Yet after its collapse down to $40 in 2009, one of the factors explaining its prior surge, speculation on raw materials, seemed more convincing. But for the producer countries, this concern rooted in fear of the end of oil appeared irrational, as society had stopped giving any thought to the wastefulness of the major industrialised countries whose overconsumption of energy is explained by a desire to satisfy boundless needs. As Sheikh Yamani, former Saudi Arabian Oil Minister, pointed out wryly, "the Stone Age did not end due to a lack of stones". On the other hand, the end of oil should be placed more in perspective with a change in mentalities regarding the use of oil and gas. As with coal in the past, the threat for oil producing countries comes more from the negative image associated with this form of energy, particularly with respect to the environment, which could bring about the development of new forms of energy.[79] But while waiting for an energy revolution, the third oil crisis was beneficial for Abdelaziz Bouteflika's Algeria and Muammar Qadhafi's Libya. It encouraged a shift from an oil rent to a natural gas rent by linking them to European energy policy. But if the EU does not want to see a recurrence of disillusionment over the past uses of the oil rent in Algeria and Libya, it must implement a policy of exporting democratic norms and values. If not, it will expose itself not only to managing instability in the Maghreb, but also to facing problems of supply if the local populations decide to sabotage an energy structure that does not provide it with jobs or a civil infrastructure that meets their expectations. The 2004 "gas riots" in Algeria are there to remind us that the security of Europe's energy supply entails the wellbeing of the populations in the producer countries.

CONCLUSION

This research supports the hypothesis advanced by Benjamin Smith:[1] authoritarian rentier regimes have enough resources available to surmount the political crises that inevitably occur with oil counter-crises. Analysis of uses of the rent between 1970 and 2003 confirms that the Algerian, Iraqi and Libyan regimes managed to survive not only the 1986 collapse in oil prices, but also the ensuing conflicts and uprisings. The price of adapting to the new environment was the transformation of a rentier economy into an economy of plunder. A little-studied aspect in the trajectory of authoritarian rentier regimes, it is nevertheless a fundamental aspect of the survival of authoritarian coalitions in a time of resource scarcity. The present research also confirms the observations made by Kiren Aziz Chaudhry,[2] who notes that oil revenues destroyed the steering mechanisms of those in power. With the sudden and bountiful inflow of revenue, governments lost control over spending. This inability to manage unexpected wealth arose from the revolutionary context in which the wealth appeared. The legitimacy of the revolutionaries rested on their ability to redistribute a portion of the oil wealth to the population in the form of goods and services. The lack of democratic institutions through which to exercise control over spending brought about the collapse of these economies.

But far from being a curse, as advocates of this theory believe (projecting as they do a rational vision on uses of the oil rent in the economic sphere), for these regimes the windfall has in fact been the engine of an economy of waste and plunder that has ensured their longevity. Some theorists believe that all that is needed is good governance for the rent to raise national wealth and the wellbeing of all. But this reasoning, which holds true for a democratic country such as Norway, is not applicable to authoritarian rentier regimes insofar as the oil bonanza is not invested in achieving economic efficiency but in the mechanisms and structures that reinforce a system of patronage. In short, although the Algerian, Libyan and Iraqi economies have "failed", the regimes have "succeeded" in remaining in power despite meagre economic results, revolts and wars. Thus, in 2007, Libya held about 100 billion dollars in reserves but its economy depends almost exclusively on oil: 98 per cent of its export earnings come from hydrocarbons, which produce 80 per cent of budget receipts. The oil sector accounts for 74 per cent of GDP and 70 per cent of the active population is employed by the state. The unemployment rate is 30 per cent and 14 per cent of the population lives below the poverty threshold ($150 per month). From an economic standpoint, it is a failure, but politically speaking it is not, Muammar Qadhafi's regime, which rose from the 1969 coup d'état, celebrated its fortieth anniversary in power in September 2009. That same year, President Abdelaziz Bouteflika was elected by an overwhelming majority in a ballot that could scarcely be considered democratic, affording him the luxury of reliving the illusion of the Houari Boumediene era (1965–1978). Here again, 98 per cent of foreign revenue comes from hydrocarbon sales, which ensure 60 per cent of budget receipts. Since 1962, the ruling elites have all come from the FLN and ensure that the regime remains strong despite highly criticised economic and political choices that have been unable to provoke a regime change. Resource allocation has been used to foster the installation of this regime and consolidate it, but the price of this success has certainly been Algeria's economic failure. Lastly, Saddam Hussein's regime would probably still be intact if the Bush administration, in the wake of September 11, 2001, had not decided to unseat it. The Baath party would thus have celebrated its forty years in power in 2008, but in a battered and devastated Iraq.

As Isabelle Beaulieu rightly points out, "The rent is not in itself a curse or a blessing for a country's economy. Its impact varies according to the institutional forms of regulation of the said country that can use it to invest in capital formation and can behave in a fashion other than predatory".[3] Her analysis of Malaysia, a Muslim country, demonstrates the successful cohabitation of a rentier economy and an authoritarian political system. Rent allocation has enabled huge investments in human capital and the birth of an "industrialised rentier state". In short, Malaysia has become the country that the nationalist elites in Algeria, Libya and Iraq would have liked to achieve in the 1970s: a strong, industrialised state. Unlike Malaysia, these three countries made poor choices that led them to make ineffective use of the oil rent. The revolutionary framework in which the rent was deployed prompted leaders to establish an economy based on waste that has brought them to the brink of financial bankruptcy. By raising oil to the status of the nation's symbol, comparing it to the people's blood and using it as fuel for the revolution, these regimes have been blinded by the magic powers they attributed to this natural resource. This voluntary blindness only lasted because of a lack of regulatory institutions: the flow of oil wealth was pumped into clientelistic networks without any democratic oversight being exercised. Other means of regulation—security services during the period of abundance (1973–86) and mafia-like organisations during the period of shortage (1986–2000)—supplanted regulatory institutions by default. Under their influence, the regimes survived the many trials that punctuated their trajectory, but these default regulatory bodies were incapable of building a lasting and effective development strategy.

Owing to the third oil crisis (2003–08), these countries recovered unhoped-for financial abundance that enabled them to accumulate precious reserve funds in a period of financial crisis. But this new financial bonanza was cause for concern. Although it has been a windfall for the new regime in Iraq, in Algeria and Libya it has aroused contradictory expectations. For the rulers, this new manna arrived in an empty ideological context. There was no more revolution to finance, Arab socialism to maintain, or regional ambition to achieve. The wealth was there, and with it came the worry that it would be squandered. Given the lack of regulatory institutions, enormous waste was to be feared once again. At the World Economic Forum on Global Competitiveness in 2009, a dismal report was made on competitiveness in Algeria and Libya. Out of a list of 133 countries, Algeria ranked 83rd, ahead of Libya (88th) but far behind Tunisia (40th). With one of the most rigid labour markets in the world, a deplorable education system and a lack of transparency in state expenditure, Libya and Algeria are aware of the considerable progress to be made if they hope to come close to Malaysia, ranked 24th. For lack of adequate instruments to exploit the financial surplus, it is placed in reserve funds in the event of a possible collapse in oil prices, despite the huge needs to be addressed. The Algerian and Libyan economies are incapable of absorbing the billions of dollars that the third oil crisis generated. Under-industrialised and lacking the necessary human capital, major construction projects in Algeria and Libya are designed and completed by foreign companies. In a context of social and political violence, Abdelaziz Bouteflika and Muammar Qadhafi are in the grips of the paradox that make these heads of state rich leaders incapable of meeting social demands. Riots regularly break out in Algeria and the uprising in Libya helped bring Qadhafi's rule to an end, reminding such regimes how vulnerable their social cohesion is. Furthermore, as in Iraq, terrorist violence continues to prosper with or without the complicity of the security forces.[4] Such violence has its useful side: it veils the mechanisms of the government machine and sustains the illusion of an Islamist threat. Radical Islamists in the Maghreb have found in Al-Qaeda the armed organisation that was lacking in the area, and the regimes sustain the fear that this organisation arouses in Europe and elsewhere. This diplomatic rent thus enables governments to avert a critical gaze on the past and present uses of the oil rent.

Will Algeria and Libya be able to escape from the infernal spiral into which the oil rent has led them? The Iraqi experience—cohabitation of a rentier economy and a democracy—is likely to influence its two former cronies in the OPEC hardliner clan if it turns out to be conclusive.[5] The insurrection in Libya shows that the people aspire to live in states with democratic institutions able to exercise control over the oil wealth and capable of handling political demands in a peaceful manner. It remains to be seen whether the democratic wave sweeping through the Arab world will come up against the violence of the oil rent.

NOTES

INTRODUCTION

1. Iraq holds the fourth largest oil reserves in the world (115 billion barrels in stock, 1.5 million barrels per day); Libya, the ninth largest proven oil reserves in the world (41 billion barrels in stock, 1.6 mbd); Algeria, the fifteenth largest proven oil reserves (12 billion barrels in stock, 1.9 mbd), besides being the world's sixth largest producer of natural gas and fourth largest world exporter of natural gas. *Energy Information Administration*, 2007–08: P. Zelenko, C-A. Paillard and C. de Lestange, *Géopolitique du pétrole*, Paris, Edition Technip, 2005.

2. J.-M. Chevalier, *The New Energy Crisis: Climate, Economics and Geopolitics*, London, New York, Palgrave Macmillan, 2009.

3. *Business Monitor International*, 1 September 2008.

4. *Human Development Report 2005*, chapter 2, HDI, p. 33.

5. A. Mebtoul, "Pour l'amélioration du rapport de 2008 du Conseil Economique et social algérien sur l'IDH", *El Khabar*, 14 September 2009.

6. *Human Development Report 2006*, p. 332; Libya's GDP fell by 6.7 per cent between 1982 and 1992. The World Bank Group, http://www.worldbank.org/data/.

7. IMF, December 23, 2005, http://www.imf.org/external/np/sec/pr/2005/pr05307.htm.

8. National Economic and Social Council, http://www.unicef.org/specialsession/hox_country/edr_algeria_fr.PDF.

9. "L'Irak en danger", report by the France-Iraq friendship group in the Senate. Mission of 18 to 23 June 2001.

10. "Les effets de l'embargo sur les finances extérieures de la Libye", *Marchés Tropicaux*, 11 September 1998.

11. Speech by Muammar Qadhafi before the General People's Congress in January 2000.

12. L. Wantchekon, *Why do Resource Abundant Countries Have Authoritarian*

Governments?, Yale University, 15 October 2002; O. Listhaug, "Oil Wealth Dissatisfaction and Political Trust in Norway: A Resource Curse?", *West European Politics*, Vol. 28, No. 4, 2005, p. 835.

13. A. Rosser, "Escaping the Resource Curse: The Case of Indonesia", *Journal of Contemporary Asia*, Vol. 37, No. 1, February 2007, pp. 38–58.

14. P. Collier and A. Hoeffler, "Démocraties pétrolières", *Afrique Contemporaine*, No. 216, 2005.

15. For a critical digest of the research on this theme see L. Wantchekon, "Why Do Resource Dependent Countries Have Authoritarian Governments?" New Haven, Yale CIAS, November 1999; Y. Matsunaga, "L'Etat rentier est-il réfractaire à la démocratie?", *Critique Internationale*, No. 8, July 2000; M.L. Ross, "Does Oil Hinder Democracy?", *World Politics*, Vol. 53, No. 3, pp. 325–61, 2001.

16. T. Karl, *The Paradox of Plenty: Oil Booms and Petro-States*, Berkeley, University of California Press, 1997.

17. P. Collier, "Doing Well out of War: An Economic Perspective", in M. Berdal and D. Malone (eds), *Greed and Grievance: Economic Agendas in Civil Wars*, Boulder, Lynne Rienner, 2000; P. Collier and A. Hoeffer, "On the Incidence of Civil War in Africa", *Journal of Conflict Resolution*, Vol. 46, No. 1, 2002.

18. J. Di John, "Oil Abundance and Violent Political Conflict: A Critical Assessment", *Journal of Development Studies*, Vol. 43, No. 6, August 2007, pp. 961–86: M.L. Ross, "What Do We Know about Natural Resources and Civil War?", *Journal of Peace Research*, Vol. 41, No. 3, 2004.

19. M. Camau and V. Geisser, *Le syndrome autoritaire*, Paris, Presses de Sciences Po, 2003; P. Droz-Vincent, "Quel avenir pour l'autoritarisme dans le monde arabe", *RFSP*, Vol. 54, No. 6, December 2004.

20. P. Collier and A. Hoeffler, "Greed and Grievance in Civil War", *Oxford Economic Papers*, Vol. 56, No. 4, 2004, p. 588.

21. Di John, *op. cit.*, 2007, p. 80.

22. R. Marchal and C. Messiant, "De l'avidité des rebelles. L'analyse économique des conflits par Paul Collier", *Critique Internationale*, No. 16, June 2002.

23. M.L. Ross, "What Do We Know about Natural Resources and Civil War?", *Journal of Peace Research*, Vol. 41, No. 3, 2004, p. 342.

24. M.L. Ross, "A Closer Look at Oil, Diamonds, and Civil War", *Annual Review of Political Science*, No. 9, 2006, p. 288.

25. A. Oyefusi, "Oil and Probability of Rebel Participation among Youths in the Niger Delta of Nigeria", *Journal of Peace Research*, Vol. 45, No. 4, 2008; D.C. Bach, "Nigeria: paradoxes de l'abondance et démocratisation en trompe-l'œil", *Afrique Contemporaine*, No. 219, 2006, p. 121; P. Sébille-Lopez, "Les hydrocarbures au Nigeria et la redistribution de la rente pétrolière", *Afrique Contemporaine*, No. 216, 2005.

26. B. Smith, "Oil Wealth and Regime Survival in the Developing World, 1960–1999", *American Journal of Political Science*, Vol. 48, No. 2, April 2004, p. 232.

27. B. Smith, "The Wrong Kind of Crisis: Why Oil Booms and Busts Rarely Lead to Authoritarian Breakdown", *Studies in Comparative International Development*, Vol. 40, No. 4, Winter 2006, p. 55.

28. K. Morrison, "Oil, Nontax Revenue and the Redistributional Foundations of Regime Stability", *International Organization*, No. 63, 2009, p. 108.

29. M-A. Legrange and T. Vircoulon, "Zimbabwé: réflexions sur la dictature durable", *Politique Etrangère*, Vol. 3, 2008, pp. 653–66.

30. E. Bellin, "The Robustness of Authoritarianism in the Middle East: Exceptionalism in Comparative Perspective", *Comparative Politics*, Vol. 36, No. 2, 2004.

31. S. Heydemann, "D'Assad à Assad: la politique syrienne n'est pas un théâtre d'ombre", *Critique Internationale*, No. 9, October 2000: K. Eberhard, *Ba'th vs Ba'th*, London, Tauris, 1990.

32. J.D. Sachs, J.E. Stiglitz and M. Humphreys (eds), "What Is the Problem with Natural Resource Wealth", in *Escaping The Resource Curse*, New York, Columbia University Press, 2007.

33. M. Camau, "Globalisation démocratique et exception autoritaire arabe", *Critique Internationale*, No. 30, 1998, pp. 59–82.

34. Jean-Noël Ferrié, "Entering the 'Virtuous Circle': The Strength of Democratic Designs in Egypt and Morocco", in E. Kienle (ed.), *Economic Reform and the Reconstruction of Politics: The Arab World in a Period of Global Transformations*, London, Saqi, 2003.

35. J-N. Ferrié and J-Santucci (eds), *Dispositifs de démocratisation et dispositifs autoritaires en Afrique du Nord*, Paris, CNRS, 2005, p. 11.

36. E. Picard, "Syrie: la coalition autoritaire fait de la résistance", *Politique Etrangère*, 2005.

37. M.L. Ross, "The Political Economy of The Resource Curse", *World Politics*, Vol. 51, No. 2, 1999, p. 12.

38. D. Vandewalle points out that the Libyan monarchy fell because, unlike in Kuwait and Saudi Arabia, it failed to form the necessary alliances for its consolidation. Furthermore, the sale of oil, useful for building a system of patronage, began only after 1961, ten years following independence: *Libya since Independence. Oil and State Building*, Ithaca University Press, 1998, p. 59.

39. H. Bozarslan writes: "This monarchy (1930–58) attempted to set up a 'bourgeois democracy' which turned out to integrate 'dominated groups', however modestly into 'states, communities and dissident fringes in Iraq'", *Critique Internationale*, No. 34, 2007, p. 20.

40. L. Addi, *L'impasse du populisme*, Algiers, Enal, 1990.
41. K. Mofid, *The Economic Consequences of the Gulf War*, London, Routledge, 1990.
42. L. Martinez, *The Libyan Paradox*, London, Hurst, 2007.
43. A. El Kenz, *L'Algérie et la modernité*, Dakar, Codesria, 1989.
44. O. Le Cour Grandmaison, *Coloniser, exterminer: sur la guerre et l'Etat colonial*, Paris, Fayard, 2005.
45. P. Sluglett, *Britain in Iraq: Contriving King and Country*, London, Tauris, 2007.
46. A.A. Ahmida, *The Making of Modern Libya. State Formation, Colonization and Resistance, 1830–1932*, New York, SUNY, 1994; D. Vandewalle, *A History of Modern Libya*, Cambridge University Press, 2006.
47. *Révolution Africaine*, 28 September–4 October 1977, p. 13.

1. CAPTURING THE RENT

1. "If we were to analyse Algerian oil, we would realise that it contains the blood of our martyrs, because we came into possession of this wealth by paying with our blood". Speech at Skikda, 16 July 1970.
2. John Davis, *Libyan Politics*, Berkeley and Los Angeles, University of California Press, 1987, p. 251.
3. M. Farouk-Sluglett and P. Sluglett, *Iraq since 1958. From Revolution to Dictatorship*, London, Tauris, 2001, p. 171.
4. John Davis, *op. cit.*, p. 251.
5. Alain Rouquié points out that between 1962 and 1968, nine successful military coups were carried out, paving the way for "national revolutions" that installed new regimes (Peru, Bolivia) that either strove to "control foreign economic penetration, recover their natural wealth and carry out certain structural reforms to accelerate social progress" or, as in Brazil and Argentina, installed authoritarian, anti-communist, economically liberal regimes that were hence receptive to foreign interests. "Révolutions militaries et indépendance nationale en Amérique latine (1968–1971)", *Revue Française de Science Politique*, No. 21, 1971, p. 1047.
6. A.G. Samarbakhsh, *Socialisme en Irak et en Syrie*, Paris, Anthropos, 1978, p. 257 and p. 275.
7. Batna speech, 24 February 1968, quoted by M. Elhocine Benissad, *Economie du développement de l'Algérie (1962–78)*, Paris, Economica, 1979, p. 23.
8. Michel Chatelus, "Iraq and its Oil: Sixty-five Years of Ambition and Frustration", in D. Hopwood, H. Ishow and T. Koszinowski (eds), *Iraq: Power and Society*, Oxford, St Antony's College, 1993 p. 153.
9. R. Mabro, "The Oil Weapon: Can it Be Used Today?", *Harvard International Review*, Fall 2007.

10 *Al Thawra*, Baghdad, 2 December 1973, quoted by A.G. Samarbakhsh, *Socialisme en Irak et en Syrie*, Paris, Anthropos, 1978, p. 255.

11. J.C. Hurewitz, *Middle East Politics: The Military Dimension*, New York, Octagon Books, 1974, p. 233; E. Santarelli, G. Rochat, R. Rainero and L. Goglia, *Omar al-Mukhtar. The Italian Reconquest of Libya*, London, Darf Publishers, 1986.

12. Iraq was placed under British mandate by the League of Nations in 1920 and became independent in 1930, but a treaty bound it to an alliance with the British for twenty-five years: P-J. Luizard, *La question irakienne*, Fayard, Paris, 2004.

13. The price of a barrel of oil in 1965 was $2.35.

14. In 2008, hydrocarbon export receipts accounted for 99 per cent in Libya, 98 per cent in Algeria and 99 per cent in Iraq.

15. Cited in A. Sid-Ahmed, *L'économie arabe à l'heure des surplus pétroliers*, ISMEA, p. 288.

16. Aziz Alkazag. "The Distribution of National Income in Iraq, with Particular Reference to the Development of Policies Applied by the State", in *Iraq: Power and Society*, *op. cit.*, p. 202.

17. Nicole Grimaud, "Le conflit pétrolier franco-algérien", *Revue Française de Science Politique*, Vol. 22, No. 6, 1972, p. 1284.

18. Jean-Marie Chevalier, *Le nouvel enjeu pétrolier*, Paris, Calmann Lévy, 1973, p. 166.

19. R.B. St John, "Libya's Oil and Gas Industry: Blending Old and New", *Journal of North African Studies*, Vol. 12, No. 2, June 2007.

20. Stephen J. Kobrin, "Diffusion of an Explanation of Oil Nationalization: Or the Domino Effect Rides Again", *Journal of Conflict Resolution*, Vol. 29, No. 1, March 1985.

21. C. Tripp, *A History of Iraq*, Cambridge University Press, 2007, p. 57.

22. On 19 August 1953, the CIA and the British secret services overthrew Premier Mossadeq after he nationalised the hydrocarbon sector.

23. Michael E. Brown, "The Nationalization of the Iraqi Petroleum Company", *International Journal of Middle East Studies*, Vol. 10, No. 1, 1979, p. 109.

24. A. Sid Ahmed, *Développement sans croissance*, Paris, Publisud, 1983.

25. Philippe Rondot, *L'Irak*, Paris, PUF, 1979 ("Que sais-je?" series), p. 45.

26. Alain Guerreau and Anita Guerreau-Jalabert, *L'Irak: développement et contradictions*, Paris, Le Sycomore, 1978, p. 50.

27. Aziz Alkazaz, "The Distribution of National Income in Iraq, with Particular Reference to the Development of Policies Applied by the State", in *Iraq: Power and Society*, *op.cit.*, p. 221.

28. Aziz Alkazaz, *ibid.*, p. 212.

29. Georges Mutin, "Les hydrocarbures dans le monde arabe", in J.-F. Troin (ed.), *Maghreb Moyen-Orient. Mutations*, CEDES, 1995.
30. Benjamin Shwadran, *The Middle East, Oil and the Great Power*, Jerusalem, Israel University Press, 1973.
31. Michel Chatelus, "Iraq and Its Oil: Sixty-Five Years of Ambition and Frustration", in *Iraq: Power and Society, op. cit.*, p. 151.
32. Paul Stevens, "Iraqi Oil Policy 1961–1976", in Tim Niblock (ed.), *Iraq: The Contemporary State*, London, New York, Palgrave Macmillan, 1982, p. 170.
33. Aziz Alkazaz, *op. cit.*, p. 219.
34. *Ibid.*, p. 220.
35. Joe Stork, "State Power and Economic Structure", in *Iraq: Power and Society, op. cit.*, p. 181.
36. The NOC, http://www.noclibya.com/html.
37. S. Ghanem, *The Pricing of Libyan Crude Oil*, La Vallette, Adams Publishing, 1975.
38. Jean-Jacques Regnier and Larbi Talha, "Les problèmes de développement économique", in *La Libye nouvelle, op. cit.*, p. 225.
39. Judith Gurney, *Libya: the Political Economy of Energy*, Oxford University Press, 1996; John Anthony Allan (ed.), *Libya since Independence: Economic and Political Development*, London, Croom Helm, 1982.
40. François Burgat and André Laronde, *La Libye*, Paris, PUF, 1996 ("Que sais-je?" series).
41. Dirk Vandewalle, *Libya Since Independence. Oil and State-Building*, London, Cornell University Press, 1998.
42. Omar I. El Fathaly and Monte Palmer, *Political Development and Social Change in Libya*, Toronto, Lexington Books, 1980, p. 129.
43. *Ibid.*, p. 28.
44. "L'urbanisation en Méditerranée de 1950 à 1995", *Les Cahiers du Plan Bleu*, No. 1, 2001, p. 3.
45. Libya Higher Education Profile, http://www.bc.edu/bc.
46. Hervé Bleuchot, *op. cit.*, p. 90.
47. John Davis, *op. cit.*, p. 252.
48. M. O. El-Kikhia, *Libya's Qaddafi. The Politics of Contradiction*, University Press of Florida, 1997, p. 91.
49. Houari Boumediene, Discours APN, 23 April 1978, quoted by M. El. H. Bénissad, *Economie du développement de l'Algérie*, Paris, Economica, 1979, p. 23.
50. *Le Soir* (Brussels), 27 February 1973.
51. J-Luc Deheuvels, *Islam et pensée contemporaine en Algérie*, Paris, Edition CNRS, 1991, p. 228.
52. M. Bénissad, *op. cit.*, p. 22.
53. M. Bénissad, *op. cit.*, p. 49.

54. G. Destanne de Bernis, "Industries industrialisantes", *Economie Appliquée*, No. 3–4, 1966, pp. 415–73.

55. G. Destanne de Bernis, "Les industries industrialisantes et les options algériennes", *Tiers-Monde*, Vol. 12, No. 47, 1971, p. 550.

56. Ick-Jin Seo, *La Corée du Sud. Une analyse historique du processus de développement*, Paris, L'Harmattan, 2000, p. 165.

57. Houari Boumediene, Constantine speech, 1974.

58. Tahar Benhouria, *L'économie de l'Algérie*, Paris, Maspéro, 1980, p. 300.

59. Expression used by the PRI in Mexico, and employed, in Algeria to describe government representatives: "this family is not only metaphorical, it is indeed founded on kinship. Made up of former *mujahideen* or who claimed to be, it also includes 'the children of *shuhadâ*', and 'children of *mujahideen*', called 'legal claimants'. The progeny of the latter is already organising as 'children of legal claimants'. Government representatives believe that these descendants are the extension of their parents and should be appreciated and rewarded in this right": A. Moussaoui, "Algérie, la guerre rejouée", *La Pensée de Midi*, No. 3, 2000.

60. Marc Raffinot and Pierre Jacquemot, *Le capitalisme d'Etat algérien*, Paris, Maspéro, 1977, p. 1977.

61. P. Zelenko, C-A. Paillard, C. de Lestanges and F. Chalabi, *Géopolitique du pétrole*, Paris, Edition Technip, 2005.

62. B. Shwadran, *The Middle East, Oil and the Great Powers*, Jerusalem, Israel University Press, 1973.

63. B. Dillman, "Illicit Economies and Reconstruction", in L. Binder (ed.), *Rebuilding Devastated Economies in the Middle East*, New York, Palgrave Macmillan, 2007, p. 60.

64. F. Brié, "Irak: au pays des déportés", *Outre Terre*, No. 14, 2006, p. 193.

65. E. Kienle, *Ba'th v. Ba'th*, London, Tauris, 1990, p. 22.

66. Marion Farouk-Sluglett, "Rente pétrolière et concentration du pouvoir", *Maghreb-Machrek*, No. 131, January-March, 1991, p. 5.

67. P-J. Luizard, "L'impossible démocratie en Irak: le piège de l'Etat nation", *Egypte-Monde Arabe* (Cairo), Cedej, 1990, No. 4, p. 87.

68. Marion-Farouk Sluglett, *op. cit.*, p. 5.

69. "The Zuwara speech laid the groundwork for the Popular Revolution: suspension of all existing laws; elimination of all the 'sick' people opposed to the progress of the revolution; total freedom given to the masses and the people who would bear arms; administrative revolution. All passive civil servants were dismissed, a cultural revolution. All imported theories that contradicted Islam and the objective of September 1 would be eliminated". See Hervé Bleuchot, *Chroniques et documents libyens*, Paris, CNRS, 1983, p. 56.

169

70. Hanspetter Mattes, "The Rise and Fall of the Revolutionary Committees", in Dirk Vandewalle (ed.), *Qadhafi's Libya, 1969–1994*, New York, St. Martin's Press, 1995.

71. Henry F. Jackson, *The FLN in Algeria. Party Development in a Revolutionary Society*, London, Greenwood Press, 1977, p. 203.

72. A. Dahmani, *op. cit.*, p. 26.

73. M. Bennoune and Al Kenz, *Le hasard et l'histoire: Entretien avec B. Abdesselam*, 1990, *op. cit.*, p. 273.

74. Bruno Etienne, *L'Algérie cultures et révolution*, Paris, Seuil, 1977, p. 262.

75. B. Etienne, *op. cit.*, p. 304.

76. Abdelkader Yefsah, "L'Armée et le pouvoir en Algérie de 1962 à 1992", in Pierre Robert Baduel (ed.), *L'Algérie incertaine*, Aix-en-Provence, Edisud, 1994, p. 84.

77. M. Bennoune and Al Kenz, *op. cit.*, 1990, p. 200.

78. See Chapter 3: Oil Rent and Mafia Regimes.

79. John Galvani, "The Baathi Revolution in Iraq", *Merip Reports*, No. 12, September-October 1972, p. 17.

80. John F. Devlin, "The Baath Party: Rise and Metamorphosis", *The American Historical Review*, Vol. 96, No. 5, 1991, p. 1406.

81. Speech at the Islamic Summit Conference in Lahore, February 1974. See H. Sanson, "L'Islam de Houari Boumediene", *AAN*, Vol. 17, 1978, pp. 267–77.

82. R. Springborg, "Baathism in Practice: Agriculture, Politics and Political Culture in Syria and Iraq", *Middle Eastern Studies*, Vol. 17, No. 2, April 1981, p. 201.

83. Benjamin Shwadran writes: "The most outstanding characteristic of Iraq even by comparison with other major oil-producing Middle Eastern countries and which is a key to its entire history and development is its political and general instability", *The Middle East, Oil and the Great Powers*, Jerusalem, Israel University Press, 1973, p. 267.

84. Philippe Rondot, *op. cit.*, p. 60.

85. A. Baram, "Neo-Tribalism in Iraq: Saddam Hussein's Tribal Policies 1991–96", *International Journal of Middle East Studies*, Vol. 29, No. 1, 1997.

86. David Blundy and Andrew Lycett, *Qaddafi and the Libyan Revolution*, Boston, Brown & Co., 1987; Hanspetter Mattes, "The Rise and Fall of the Revolutionary Committees", in Dirk Vandewalle (ed.), *Qadhafi's Libya, 1969–1994*, *op. cit.*

87. Televised speech in May 1988, quoted by D. Vandewalle, *Libya Since Independence*, Ithaca, NY, Cornell University Press, 1998, p. 147.

88. Mohamed Harbi, "Processus de relégitimation du pouvoir en Algérie", in Michel Camau, *Changements politiques au Maghreb, op. cit.*, p. 134.

89. Marion Farouk-Sluglett and Peter Sluglett, "The Historiography of Modern Iraq", *The American Historical Review*, Vol. 96, No. 5, December 1991, p. 1412.

90. Ferhat Abbas, *L'indépendance confisquée*, Paris, Flammarion, 1984.

91. Marion Farouk-Sluglett, "Irak: rente pétrolière et concentration du pouvoir", *Maghreb-Machrek*, No. 131, January-March 1991, p. 6; H. Bozarslan explains, "Everything indicated that gradually the new Prince that came out of the Baath had come to consider the state as a *mulk*, a personalised end in itself that could finally only ensure its durability by being handed down to male heirs": "L'Irak en perspective", *Revue des Mondes Musulmans et de la Méditerranée*, No. 117–118, July 2007, p. 8.

2. THE ILLUSORY POWER OF OIL

1. Sol Pérez Schael, *Petroleo, cultura y poder en Venezuela*, Monte Avila, 1993, cited by F. Langue, "Machiavel et la démocratie au Vénézuéla", *Nuevo Mundo*, 2005, Nuevomundo.revues.org/index768.html, p. 5.

2. I. Skeet, *OPEC: Twenty-Five Years of Prices and Politics*, Cambridge University Press, 1991, p. 236.

3. J. Leca, "Social Structure and Political Stability: Comparative Evidence from the Algerian, Syrian and Iraqi Cases", in Adeed Dawisha and I. William Zartman (eds), *Beyond Coercion: The Durability of the Arab State*, London, Croom Helm, 1988, p. 173.

4. J. Leca and J.C. Vatin write, "…the Charters fulfil two functions. They describe the vision that the authorities have of the actual, empirically observable society, [and their] second function is to form a *doxa* and consequently outline orthodox behavior", in "Algérie: le système politique", *AAN*, Paris, CNRS, 1977, p. 16.

5. "Political, Economic and Social Bases of the Third Universal Theory. Muammar Qadhafi's Thought", Belgrade Colloquium, April 1982, World Center For Researches and Studies of "The Green Book", Tripoli.

6. H. Beblawi, "Yet the fact remains that even limited revenue from abroad dramatically improves the state's ability to buy legitimacy through allocation and increases regime stability. Iraq since the early seventies and Algeria almost since independence have had remarkably stable power structure": in G. Luciani (ed.), *The Arab State*, London, Routledge, 1990, p. 79.

7. Oystein Noreng, "Oil and Islam: Misuse of Money Causing Social and Political Tensions", *Oil and Islam. Social and Economics Issues*, Chichester, Wiley, 1997, p. 6.

8. W. Zartman and A. Buendia, "La politique étrangère libyenne", in G. Albergoni *et al.*, *La Libye nouvelle*, Paris, CNRS, p. 129.

9. Cited by E. Kienle, *Ba'th v. Ba'th*, *op. cit.*, p. 94.

10. R. Leveau, *Le Sabre et le turban*, Paris, F. Bourin, 1993, p. 225.

11. M.A. Heller, "Iraq's Army: Military Weakness, Political Utility", in A. Baram and B. Rubin (eds), *Iraq's Road to War*, New York, St Martin's Press, 1993.

12. See René Lemarchand for a detailed analysis of Libya's policy to destabilise regimes in Africa between 1976 and 1986: "Beyond the Mad Dog Syndrome", in Lemarchand (ed.), *The Green and The Black: Qadhafi's Policies in Africa*, Bloomington, Indiana University Press, 1988, p. 9.

13. http://www.global security.org/intell/world/libya/jso.htm.

14. Sandrine Santo, "L'ONU face au terrorisme", Groupe de Recherche et d'Information sur la Paix et la Sécurité, www.grip.org.

15. See Philippe Moreau Defarges; "'L'Etat voyou', un concept instrument", *Défense Nationale*, No. 2, February 1998.

16. Helmy Ibrahim, "La Libye ou l'institution politique du terrorisme", *Esprit*, No. 94–95, May-June 1983; Allan Dowes, "Qu'est-ce qu'un Etat terroriste?" *Les Cahiers de l'Orient*, No. 36, 1986; St John, Ronald Bruce, "Terrorism and Libyan Foreign Policy, 1981–1986", *World Today*, No. 42, 1986.

17. In August 2000, Mathaba organised a Congress attended by Presidents Sam Nujoma (Namibia), Robert Mugabe (Zimbabwe), Yoweri Museveni (Uganda) and Idris Deby (Chad), and by Shaffik Handal (FMLN, El Salvador), Daniel Ortega (FSLN, Nicaragua), Raul Reyes (FARC, Colombia), etc., http://globalsecurity.org/intell/world/libya/jso.htm.

18. "Between 1979 and 1983, Libyan imports of military hardware amounted to $12,095 million [...] Libya's 1970 to 1985 total expenditures on overseas purchases of military goods and services [were estimated] at some $29 billion". William J. Foltz, "Libya's Military Power", in René Lemarchand (ed.), *The Green and the Black, op. cit.*, p. 62; see also Anthony H. Cordesman, *A Tragedy of Arms: The Maghreb*, Westport, CT: Praeger, 2001, p. 60.

19. In a public confession broadcast on television on 4 February 2003, Abdul Qadeer Khan, the "father of Pakistan's atom bomb", revealed that he had supplied Libya with plans for building centrifuge equipment. The *New York Times* of 18 February 2003 describes the private networks that supplied Libya not only from Pakistan but also from Malaysia.

20. "The German firm Imhausen-Chemie AG played a central role in the construction of the Rabta facility": Joshua Sinai, "Libya's Pursuit of WMD", *The Nonproliferation Review*, Spring-Summer 1997, p. 93.

21. "Libya Has Trouble Building the Most Deadly Weapons", *The Risk Report*, Vol. 1, December 1995.

22. William J. Foltz, "Libya's Military Power", *op. cit.*, p. 53.

23. O.M. and Bettie Smolansky, *The USSR and Iraq: The Soviet Quest for Influence*, Durham (NC), Duke University Press, 1991.

24. Abdelkader Sid Ahmed, "L'économie arabe à l'heure des surplus pétroliers", *Cahiers de l'ISMEA*, series F, No. 26, 1975.

25. David Baran, "Saddam Hussein's Armourers", http://www.eurozine.com/articles/2003–09–30-baram-en.html, p. 3.

26. J.F. Luizard, *La question irakienne, op. cit.*, p. 139

27. "We estimated that the total economic cost of the war to Iran from 1980 to August 1988 (in current prices) was $644.3 billion and to Iraq $452.6 billion. These were the purely monetary costs of the war to both countries and did not include losses through inflation, the deaths of hundreds of thousands of the working population…" in K. Mofid, *The Economic Consequences of the Gulf War*, London, Routledge, 1990, p. 146.

28. F.W. Axelgard, *Iraq in Transition*, Boulder, Westview Press, 1986, p. 83.

29. Faleh Abdel al Jabbar, "Why the Uprising Failed", *Middle East Report*, No. 176, May-June, 1992, p. 4.

30. Cited by Faleh Abdel al Jabbar, *The Guardian*, 10 June 1991.

31. In 1991 James Baker had threatened to "knock Iraq back to the Middle Ages" if its leaders did not cooperate.

32. A. Francos and J-P. Séréni, *Un Algérien nommé Boumediène*, Paris, Stock, 1976, p. 336.

33. Bruno Etienne. *L'Algérie: Cultures et révolutions*, Paris, Seuil, 1977; J.P. Entelis, *Algeria: The Revolution Institutionalized*, London, Croom Helm, 1986.

34. Y. Zoubir, "In Search of Hegemony: The Western Sahara in Algerian-Moroccan relations", *Journal of Algerian Studies*, Vol. 2, 1997.

35. A. Blom, "The 'Multi-Vocal' State: The Policy of Pakistan on Kashmir", in Christophe Jaffrelot (ed.), *Pakistan: Nationalism without a Nation?* London, Zed Books, 2002, p. 284.

36. K. Kadri and J. Fontanel, "Les conséquences stratégico-économiques pour l'Algérie de ses relations politiques privilégiées avec l'URSS et la Russie (1962–1993)", *Les Cahiers de l'Espace*, No. 11, 1997, p. 11.

37. "Western Sahara: The Cost of the Conflict", *ICG*, No. 65, 2007.

38. G. Ducatenzeiler, "Ouverture politique, transition démocratique et classe ouvrière en Argentine", *Politique*, No. 12, 1987.

39. Ahmed Dahmani, *L'Algérie à l'épreuve: Economie politique des réformes (1980–1997)*, Paris, l'Harmattan, 1999.

40. Kiren Aziz Chaudhry, "On the Way to Market. Economic Liberalisation and Iraq's Invasion of Kuwait", *Middle East Report*, May-June 1991, p. 14.

41. Kiren Aziz Chaudhry, *op. cit.*, p. 20.

42. R. Springborg, "Iraqi Infitah", *Middle East Journal*, Vol. 40, No. 1, 1988, pp. 35–56.

43. K. Aziz Chaudhry, *op. cit.*, p. 18.

44. D. Vandewalle, "Qadhafi's Perestroika: Economic and Political Liberalization in Libya", *The Middle East Journal*, 45, 1991, No. 2; F. Burgat, "1989: L'ouverture entravée", *Annuaire de l'Afrique du Nord*, T. XXVII, 1989, Paris, CNRS, 1991; M.B. Altunisik, "A Rentier State's Response to Oil Crisis: Economic Reform Policies in Libya", *Arab Studies Quarterly*, September 2002.

45. Y. Benabdallah, "La réforme économique en Algerie: entre rente et production", *Maghreb-Machrek*, No. 166, Sept.-Oct. 1999, p. 17; G. Corm, "La réforme économique algérienne: une réforme mal aimée", *Maghreb-Machrek*, No. 139, January-March 1993.

46. Ghazi Hidouci, "L'Algérie peut-elle sortir de la crise?", *Maghreb-Machrek*, No. 149, July-Sept. 1995, p. 27.

47. Ahmed Dahmani, *L'Algérie à l'épreuve: Economie politique des réformes (1980–1997)*, Paris, l'Harmattan, 1999, p. 148.

48. Bradford Dillman, "The Political Economy of Structural Adjustment in Tunisia and Algeria", *Journal of North African Studies*, No. 3, 1998, pp. 1–24; M. Lowi and G. Okruhlik, "Rentier Wealth, Unruly Law, and the Rise of Opposition: The Political Economy of Oil States", *Comparative Politics*, Vol. 31, No. 3, 1999, pp. 295–315.

49. Tim Niblock, *Pariah States and Economic Sanctions in the Middle East: Iraq, Libya, Sudan*, Boulder, Lynne Rienner, 2001.

50. Pierre-Jean Luizard, *La question irakienne*, Paris, Fayard, 2002, p. 35.

51. Luis Martinez, *The Algerian Civil War*, trans. Jonathan Derrick, London, Hurst & Co., 2000.

52. J-L. Margolin, "Indonésie 1965: un massacre oublié", *Revue Internationale de Politique Comparée*, Vol. 8, No. 1, 2001.

53. J. Semelin, *Purify and Destroy*, trans. Cynthia Schoch, London, Hurst & Co., 2009.

54. Luis Martinez, *The Libyan Paradox*, trans. John King, London, Hurst, 2007, p. 41.

55. J. Shankleman. *Oil, Profits and Peace*, Washington, DC, United States Institute of Peace, 2006, p. 121.

56. J. Ejobowah Boye, "Oil Dependency and Civil Conflict in Nigeria", *Center for the Study of African Economies*, paper 268, 2, 2007.

57. J. Rone, "Sudan: Oil and War", *Review of African Political Economy*, Vol. 30, No. 97, 2003.

58. M. Humphreys, "Natural Resources Conflict and Conflict Resolution", *Journal of Conflict Resolution*, Vol. 49, No. 4, August 2005.

59. Faleh Abdel al Jabbar, "Why the Uprising Failed", *Middle East Report*, No. 176, May 1992, p. 13.

60. F. Burgat, *L'islamisme au Maghreb,* Paris, Payot, 2008.

61. General Touati, *El Watan,* 27 September 2001.

62. *Nida'ul Islam,* October-November 1996, p. 25, http://www.islam.org.

63. *Nida'ul Islam,* October-November 1996, http://www.islam.org.

64. On 22 July 1996, a communiqué from the Libyan Movement for Change and Reform condemned the regime's repression in that month of the mutiny at Abu Salim prison in Tripoli, which was said to have claimed hundreds of victims. *El Hayat,* 28 July 1996.

65. E. Picard, "Arab Military in Politics: From Revolutionary Plot to Authoritarian State", in Z. William and A. Dawisha (eds), *Beyond Coercion: The Durability of the Arab State,* London, Croom Helm, 1988, p. 130.

66. Kiren Aziz Chaudhry, *op. cit.,* p. 8.

67. J.F. Devlin, "The Baath Party: Rise and Metamorphosis", *American Historical Review,* Vol. 96, No. 5, December 1991, p. 1406.

68. P-J. Luizard writes, "the armed forces numbered 382,000 active troops and 500,000 men in reserves, including 100,000 in the Republican Guard, to which should be added 45,000 men in the Iraqi Security Force, 100,000 others in the Special Force and Fedayeen Saddam… These numbers mask the fact that the army is in a shambles": *La question irakienne, op. cit.,* p. 127–9.

69. "Much of this force is in storage or non-operational, combat readiness is exceptionally low, and modernization rates are very poor": Anthony H. Cordesman, "The North African Military Balance: Force Developments in the Maghreb", *CSIS,* 28 March 2005, p. 31.

70. Hans Peter Mattes points out that "Up until the present, the Revolutionary Leadership's deployment of the security organisations to protect the Revolution has been so efficient that any attempts to depose the regime or to change the political system by oppositional military or political groups have been doomed to failure": "Challenges to Security Sector Governance in the Middle East: The Libyan Case", article presented at the "Challenges of Security Sector Governance in the Middle East" workshop in Geneva, 12–13 July 2004.

71. "Most prominent among them are Ahmad Qathaf al Damm, Masoud Abdul-Fatih, Misbah Abdul Hafith, Khalifa Ihneish, Omar Ishkal, Al Barani Ishkal, Omran Atiatallah al Qaddafi, Imhamad Mahmoud Al Qaddafi, Khamis Masoud Al Qaddafi, Saad Masoud Al Qathaf, Hassan al Kabir Qaddafi. Until April 1995 the central sector (Sirte) was under the command of Khalifa Ihneish, the southern sector (Sebha) under Colonel Masoud Abdul Hafith, the Benghazi sector under Misbah Abdul Hafith and Tobrouk sector under Ahmad Qaddafi al Damm. A failed coup attempt in February 1995 prompted Colonel

Qaddafi to make changes that gave his cousins even more encompassing powers. Ahmad Qathaf al Damm's territory was expanded to include all of the Cyreanica. Khalifa Ihneish was appointed the commander of armaments and munitions, Masoud Abdoul Hafith was promoted to commanding officer of military security in Libya, and Al Barani Ishkal was assigned to command domestic military security": Mansour O. El-Kikhia, *Libya's Qaddafi*, University Press of Florida, 1997, p. 90.

72. *El Djeich*, March 1993.
73. *El Mounqidh*, September 1995, p. 46.
74. M. Sol Pérez Schael, *El Excremento del diablo. La democracia venezolana y sus protagonistas*, Caracas, Alfadil Ediciones, 1997.

3. OIL RENT AND MAFIA REGIMES

1. G. Favarel-Garrigues, "Mafia Violence and Political Power in Russia", in J-L. Briquet and G. Favarel-Garrigues (eds), *Organized Crime and States*, New York, Palgrave Macmillan, 2010, p. 148.
2. The Libyan regime displays the characteristics of a sultanistic regime more than those of Algeria and Iraq. Juan Linz and Houchang Chedhabi, *Sultanistic Regimes*, Baltimore, Johns Hopkins University Press, 1998.
3. Paolo Pezzino, "La mafia, Etat et société dans la Sicile contemporaine", *Politix*, No. 49, 2000, p. 17.
4. G. Salamé, *Quand l'Amérique refait le monde*, Paris, Fayard, 2005.
5. G. Favarel-Garrigues, "Mafia Violence and Political Power in Russia", in Jean-Louis Briquet and Gilles Favarel-Garrigues, *Organized Crime and States*, *op. cit.*, p. 148.
6. Eric Brousseau points out that "a coalition's effectiveness is linked to the distribution of ownership rights among its members", in "L'approche néo-institutionnelle de l'économie des coûts de transactions", *Revue Française d'Economie*, No. 4, 1989, p. 147.
7. Regarding traditional modes of domination, see J. Leca and Yves Schemeil, "Clientélisme et patrimonialisme dans le monde arabe", *International Political Science Review*, Vol. 4, No. 4, 1983; G. Salamé writes, "Perceptions of the state's strength and/weakness are substantially marked, in the Arab World, by a tradition of authoritarian rule, where the military ghalab (domination) has preceded and practically made possible a generally unrestrained plunder of the society's available resources", in G. Luciani (ed.), *The Arab State*, Routledge, London, 1990, p. 31.
8. In 2002, General Belkheir stated, "I regret nothing. I made the choice to spare Algeria the fate of Afghanistan": *Jeune Indépendant*, 4 May 2002.

9. "Why Japan", asked Charles Issawi in 1983. "Why not, for instance, Iraq, whose potential was, and still is, so great?" G. Salamé, in *The Arab State, op. cit.*, p. 62.

10. Thierry A. Brun, "Comment fabriquer un Etat fragile: réflexions sur l'exemple irakien", in *Etats et sociétés fragiles: entre conflits, reconstruction et développement*, Paris, Karthala, 2007, p. 107.

11. Between 1991 and 1996, the percentage of children below five years of age suffering from chronic malnutrition (rickets) went up from 18 per cent to 31 per cent; weight loss due to malnutrition went from 9 per cent to 26 per cent; acute malnutrition or stunting from 3 to 11 per cent; the under-five mortality rate reported by public hospitals amounted to 40,000 more deaths than in 1989 and 50,000 more deaths among those over five. Unicef, *Situation Analysis of Children and Women in Iraq*, 30 April 1998. On the accuracy of figures produced by the regime, see A. Baram, "The Effect of Iraqi Sanctions: Statistical Pitfalls and Responsibility", *Middle East Journal*, Vol. 54, No. 2, 2000.

12. Hosham Dawod, "Le pouvoir irakien, dix ans après la guerre", *Esprit*, No. 272/2, 2001.

13. Françoise Rigaud, "Irak: le temps suspendu de l'embargo", *Critique Internationale*, No. 11, 1998.

14. N. Alahmad, "The Politics of Oil and State Survival in Iraq (1991–2003): Beyond the Rentier Thesis", *Constellations*, Vol. 14, No. 4, 2007, p. 590.

15. David Baran, *Vivre la tyrannie et lui survivre: Irak en transition*, Paris, Mille et Une Nuits, 2004, p. 91; S. Graham-Brown, *Sanctioning Saddam: The Politics of Intervention in Iraq*, London, Tauris, 1999.

16. Officially 1 dinar was worth $3; on the black market $1 dollar was exchanged for 3 Libyan dinars. Consumer prices were aligned with the price of the dinar on the black market.

17. "The Impact of the UN Sanctions Against Libya", September 1996.

18. S. Naaoush, "Effets de l'embargo sur les finances extérieures de la Libye", *Marchés Tropicaux*, 11 September 1998, p. 1907.

19. In 1996, the *Jamahiriyya* took retaliatory measures against the development of informal trade. So-called purification committees made up of junior officers were charged with stamping out "corruption". In July 1996, a law defining the scope of the purification prescribed the death penalty for "all persons who carry out currency exchange operations in violation of Central Bank regulations or who export the national currency" and for those who practice "speculation in foodstuffs, clothing, housing and transportation". During that year, "purification committees" closed down 1,500 businesses, mainly in Cyrenaica. Muammar Qadhafi considered private business was "plundering the state",

declaring in 1996 "it is not acceptable for a kilo of imported cheese that costs one dinar at the official price to be sold for 18 times more in private shops". See Eric Gobe, "Chronique Libye", *Annuaire de l'Afrique du Nord*, 1998.

20. Emmanuel Grégoire, "Réseaux et espaces économiques trans-étatiques", Réunion du Groupe d'Orientation des Politiques, July 2003, p. 11.

21. Hassen Boubakri, "Echanges transfrontaliers et commerce parallèle aux frontières tuniso-libyennes", *Maghreb-Machrek*, No. 170, October 2000, p. 39.

22. H. Boubakri, "Echanges transfrontaliers et commerce parallèle aux frontières tuniso-libyennes", *op. cit.*

23. Moncef Ouannes, "Chronique politique Libye", *Annuaire de l'Afrique du Nord*, Vol. 37, 1998, Paris, CNRS.

24. L. Anderson, *The State and Social Transformation in Tunisia and Libya (1830–1980)*, Princeton University Press, 1986.

25. Nesroulah Yous, *Qui a tué à Bentalha?*, Paris, La Découverte, 2000, as well as Habib Souadia, *La sale guerre*, Paris, La Découverte, 2001.

26. The National People's Army (ANP) regarded this development as a genuine strategy of war being waged at it by "occult forces": "the third phase of the attack by the relentless enemies of our country targeted our military institution, the ANP", *El Djeich*, January 1998.

27. *L'Expression*, 19 August 2002.

28. CENEAP report, 2000.

29. *Liberté*, 7 December 2000.

30. A. Rebah, *Sonatrach. Une entreprise pas comme les autres*, Algiers, Edition Casbah, 2006, p. 223.

31. Omar Benderra, "Economie algérienne 1986–1988", in J. Cesari (ed.), *La Méditerranée des réseaux, Marchands, entrepreneurs et migrants entre l'Europe et le Maghreb*, Paris, Maisonneuve et Larose, Maison méditerranéenne des sciences de l'homme, 2002, pp. 231–67.

32. O. Benderra, *op. cit.*, p. 241.

33. P. Adams, "Iraq's Odious Debts", *Policy Analysis*, No. 526, 28 September 2004.

34. "The country's hard currency reserves, which had been some $37 billion before the outbreak of the war were $2 billion in 1987. After 1983 the government was forced to undertake debt conversion negotiations and to ask suppliers for credit. At the end of 1986 the Iraqi foreign debt was estimated to be about $50 billion. By the middle of 1989 it was $65 billion", P. Adams, *op. cit.*, p. 225.

35. G. Joffé, "La Libye et l'Europe", *Maghreb-Machrek*, No. 170, 2000.

36. *Marchés Tropicaux*, 11 September 1998.

37. Andrew Rosser explains how Indonesia on the other hand escaped the resource curse: "the political victory of counter-revolutionary social

forces over communist and radical populist social forces in the mid-1960s; the economic opportunities opened up by the country's geopolitical significance during the Cold War and its geographical proximity to Japan and the 'tiger' economies of East Asia. The first of these factors, I argue, laid the political foundations for the Indonesian government to reorient its economic policies away from the radical economic nationalism of the 1950s and early 1960s and towards an economic policy agenda more favourable to capitalist economic development in the 1970s and 1980s": A. Rosser, "Escaping the Resource Curse: the Case of Indonesia", *Journal of Contemporary Asia*, Vol. 37, No. 1, 2007, p. 43.

38. 2004 Report, Transparency International.
39. International Anti-corruption Conference, Durban, 10 October 1999.
40. D. Baran notes that in Iraq, the Saddam Hussein regime's Fedayeen were paid a salary of $25 per month, the officers in the "prestigious Special Security" organisation $500 and the Special Republican Guard between $1,000 and $1,500, *Vivre la tyrannie*, *op. cit.*, p. 271.
41. G. Duncan, "Les seigneurs de la guerre à la conquête des villes de Colombie", *Les Cahiers de la Sécurité*, Paris, IHES, 2005, pp. 63–85.
42. T. Shelley, *Oil: Politics, Poverty and the Planet*. London, Zed Books, 2005.
43. Mario Farouk-Sluglett, "Rente pétrolière et concentration du pouvoir", *op. cit.*, p. 7.
44. Ahmad Dahmani, *L'Algérie à l'épreuve*, Paris, L'Harmattan, 1999, p. 24.
45. Michel Chatelus, "Nouvelles orientations de la politique pétrolière algérienne", *Maghreb-Machrek*, October-December, 1999, p. 5.
46. M.O. El-Kikhia, *Libya's Qadhafi: The Politics of Contradiction*, Gainesville, University of Florida, 1997, p. 90.
47. Smail Goumeziane, *Le mal algérien, économie politique d'une transition inachevée*, Paris, Fayard, 1994.
48. *Arab Oil and Gas Directory*, 2000, p. 260.
49. *Middle East Economic Digest*, 18 August 2000.
50. Quoted in A. Rebah, *Sonatrach, une entreprise pas comme les autres*, Algiers, Edition Casbah, 2006, p. 225.
51. According to its champions, the pilot study addressed "the concern for coherence with the country's new orientation which is an orientation toward a market economy, i.e. toward competition, free trade, transparency and openness", quoted in A. Rebah, *Sonatrach, op. cit.*, p. 227.
52. M. Barah, *Irak: état des lieux, évolutions et perspectives en matière énergétique, op. cit.*, p. 70.
53. Kanan Makiya, "All Levels of the Iraqi Government Were Complicit", *Middle East Quarterly*, Spring 2005, pp. 81–7.
54. *Al-Hayat*, 2 June 2005.
55. Thierry A. Brun, "Comment fabriquer un État fragile", *op. cit.*, p. 115.

56. Report on the Management of the Oil-for-Food Programme. Independent Inquiry Committee into the United Nations Oil-for Food Programme", 7 September 2005, pp. 4 and 185–259.

57. *Maghreb Confidentiel*, No. 622, 30 October 2003. Regarding funds held by oil states, Thierry Coville has written, "Some years ago it was supposed that the creation of stabilisation oil funds was a solution. The idea was to place excess oil income—in other words oil income in excess of what had been budgeted for—in a fund that would be used to sustain the economy at times when oil prices fall. However, experience shows that such funds are not a solution when the principles of transparency and rigour are not applied to budgetary policy. On the contrary, such funds, in the present state of development of institutions in the Middle East, only serve to exacerbate patronage and corruption". Thierry Coville, "Des économies du Moyen-orient marquées par la malédiction de la rente pétrolière", www.strategics-international.com.

58. http://www.nfsl-libya.com/PressReleases/3013-e.htm

59. *Arabies*, February 2003, p. 21.

60. For example, between 2003 and 2008, the government envisaged the transfer of 360 units of production out of the public sector and into private ownership. *El Fajr al Jadid*, 18 December 2003.

61. Henry Clément Moore, "Algeria's Agonies: Oil Rent Effects in a Bunker State", *Journal of North African Studies*, Vol. 9, No. 2, 2004.

62. In 1991, the state monopoly of foreign trade was ended and in 1993 a new investment code was enacted "lifting the constraints on private, domestic and foreign investment".

63. Djilali Hadjadj, "Violence et corruption: cas de l'Algérie", *Le Bulletin de L'apad*, No. 25, June 2003.

64. Testimony given by A. Boutamine in *Le Matin*, 15 October 1998.

65. Fatiha Talahite, "Economie administrée, corruption et engrenage de la violence en Algérie", *Revue Tiers-Monde*, No. 161, 2000, p. 9.

66. *Challenges*, No. 135, April 1999, cited by Fatiha Talahite, *ibid.*, p. 21.

67. G. Hermet, *Les populismes dans le monde*, Paris, Fayard, 2001, p. 331.

68. C. McPherson and Stephen Mac Searraigh, "Corruption in the Petroleum Sector", in Edgardo Campos and Sanjay Pradham (eds), *The Many Faces of Corruption*, Washington, DC, World Bank, 2007.

69. O. Roy, *The Politics of Chaos in the Middle East*, trans. Ros Schwartz, London, Hurst, 2007.

4. THE UNFORESEEN RETURN OF FINANCIAL ABUNDANCE

1. Speech before the General People's Congress, January 2000.

2. *Jeune Afrique*, 22–28 June 2003, p. 72.

3. J. Peterson, "Qatar and the World", *Middle East Journal*, Vol. 60, Autumn 2006.

4. I. Beaulieu, *L'Etat rentier. Le cas de la Malaysie*, Ottawa, PUO, 2008, p. 191.

5. *Human Development Report*, 2004, UNDP, p. 185.

6. *Human Development Report*, 2006, UNDP, p. 332.

7. R. Bertrand, "La démocratie à l'indonésienne. Bilan critique d'une transition qui n'en finit pas de commencer", *Revue Internationale de Politique Comparée*, Vol. 8, No. 3, January 2001, pp. 435–60.

8. *Human Development Report*, 2004, p. 186.

9. K.A. Chaudhry, "The 'Uncanny' Writ Regional. New and Recurring Forms of Poverty and Inequality in the Arab World", in L. Binder (ed.), *Rebuilding Devastated Economies in the Middle East*, Basingstoke, Macmillan Palgrave, 2007, p. 48.

10. World Bank, 2003b, p. 257; IMF, 2003a, p. 22.

11. D. Brumberg and A. Ahram, "The National Iranian Oil Company in Iranian Politics", The James. E. Baker III Institute for Public Policy, Rice University, 2007.

12. D. Recondo, "Pétrodollars et politiques sociales", in O. Compagnon, J. Rebotier and S. Revet (eds), *Le Venezuela au-delà du mythe*, Paris, Edition Ouvrières, 2009, p. 52.

13. Frédérique Langue, "Pétrole et révolution dans les Amériques", *Hérodote*, No. 123, 2006.

14. On the elites in Algeria, see the volume by I. Werenfels, *Managing Instability in Algeria. Elites and Political Change since 1995*, London, Routledge, 2007.

15. J-Jacques Gabas and Bruno Losch, "Fabrications and Illusions of Emergence", in C. Jaffrelot (ed.), *Emerging States: The Wellspring of a New World Order*, trans. Cynthia Schoch, London, Hurst, 2008.

16. Quoted by A. Rebah, *Sonatrach, op. cit.*, p. 227.

17. M. Benachenhou, "10 arguments contre la privatisation de Sonatrach", *Le Jeune Indépendant*, 3 November 2001; A. Belaid, *Le Jeune Indépendant*, 24 February 2000, quoted by A. Rebah, *op. cit.*, p. 227.

18. The following chapter deals with the topic of EU energy supply and the role of Algeria and Libya in the EU system.

19. H. Bozarslan writes, "Turning a deaf ear to opposition in Baghdad, the Erbil government passed its own law on oil production on 6 August and negotiated large contracts with companies from as diverse countries as Korea, France, the U.S. and the Gulf": *Le conflit kurde: le brasier oublié*, Paris, Autrement, 2009, p. 91.

20. M.R. Lowi, "War-Torn or Systemically Distorted? Rebuilding the

Algerian Economy", in Leonard Binder (ed.), *Rebuilding Devastated Economies in the Middle East*, New York, Palgrave, 2007.

21. External debt was $30.47 billion, 63.2 per cent of GDP in 1998. In 2008, after early repayment, it was $4 billion and represented only 2.39 per cent of GDP: *Economist Intelligence Unit*, "Algeria Country Forecast", 1 July 2008.

22. Political Risk Services, *Algeria Databank*, 1 December 2008, p. 6.

23. Interview given on France's RFI radio, 17 July 1999.

24. L. Martinez, "Guerre et paix: les étapes de la réconciliation nationale", *AAN*, Vol. 37, CNRS Editions, 1998, pp. 105–123.

25. *Le Journal Indépendant*, 11 October 2001.

26. *Le Matin*, 18 July 2002.

27. The National Human Rights Commission of Algeria (CNCPPDH) claims to have received 4,753 files from families of the disappeared. The International League for Human Rights estimates that 10,000 persons actually disappeared.

28. *Echourouk El Yaoumi*, 3 November 2001.

29. *L'Intelligent/Jeune Afrique*, No. 2186, December 2002.

30. N.E. Hammouda, "Secteur et emploi informel en Algérie", in M.S. Musette and J. Charmes (eds), *Informalisation des économies maghrébines*, Algiers, Cread, 2006.

31. "Alger, Marché du travail et emploi en Algérie", International Labour Organisation report, October 2003, p. 43.

32. "Political Risk Services", *Algeria Country Forecast*, 1 July 2008, p. 13.

33. ICG, 2001, *Algeria's Economy*, http://www.crisisweb.org, p. 10.

34. The Khalifa scandal refers to the spectacular rise of the Rafik Khalifa banking and transport group during the 1990s. The group was accused of laundering the "generals'" money. Countering this hypothesis, A. Belkaid writes, "with considerable financial means, unwavering political support until at least 2002, and the support of Western business circles, Khalifa had the opportunity to build a powerful and credible group similar to the Russian oligarchs", *Un regard calme sur l'Algérie*, Paris, Seuil, 2005.

35. Chems Eddine Chitour, "Troisième contre-choc pétrolier. Que doit faire l'Algérie?", *L'Expression*, 24 November 2008.

36. *El Watan*, 20 May 2007.

37. *Le Quotidien d'Oran*, 19 May 2007.

38. M. Hachemaoui, "Permanences du jeu politique en Algérie", *Politique Etrangère*, 2009.

39. Interview, *Le Figaro*, 8 December 2007.

40. In 2008, B.R Barber, Hernando de Soto, R. Putnam, A. Giddens, F. Fukuyama, and J. Nye visited "The Guide", *Maghreb Confidentiel*, 23 December 2008.

41. The Libyan League for Human Rights, "A Judiciary Without Justice", Saturday, 15 January, 2005.

42. Speech before the General People's Congress, January 2000. In 1998, most of the ministers were transferred from Tripoli to the cities of Benghazi, Kufra and Sirte.

43. "Welfare in the Mediterranean Countries. Great Arab Popular Socialist Libyan Jamahiriyya", http://www.unpan.org/.

44. Zidan Mohamed, "Libye, la fin des illusions", *La Lettre du Cermam*, No. 9, December 2005.

45. Speech by Muammar Qadhafi, 2 September 2006, Libyan press agency, JANA.

46. Call for Reform in Libya, "A Vision of Libya's Future".

47. Only 25 per cent of natural gas and oil reserves are exploited. Interview with Tarek Hassan, director of planning at the Libyan NOC, *New York Times*, 23 July 2004.

48. On 15 July 2008, Hannibal Qadhafi, Qadhafi's fourth son, and his wife were arrested in Geneva following complaints filed by two servants who accused them of beating them. After paying bail, the couple was released. In retaliation, Libya cut off its supply of petroleum to Switzerland, curbed trade and took two Swiss citizens hostage. To wheedle its way out of a diplomatic crisis, the president of the Federal Council "apologised" and triggered a political crisis in Switzerland, because Libya had still not forgiven it and one of the two Swiss citizens remained captive.

49. Ibn Sheikh al Libi (Ali Mohamed Al Fakheri), arrested in 2001 on the border between Pakistan and Afghanistan, under torture in Egypt made false declarations concerning the ties between Saddam Hussein's regime and Al-Qaeda. He died on 10 May 2009 in Tripoli in an Internal Security facility.

50. Hans Blix, *Disarming Iraq*, New York, Random House, 2004.

51. B. Rougier, "Le Grand Moyen-Orient: un moment d'utopie internationale?" *Critique Internationale*, No. 26, January 2005.

52. T. Dodge, "The Cause of a US Failure", *Survival*, Vol. 49, No. 1, 2007.

53. "Iraq is a multinational, multilingual and multiconfessional state", wrote H. Hakim, "L'Irak: de la constitution intérimaire à la constitution permanente", *Cahiers d'Etudes sur la Méditerranée Orientale et le Monde Turco-iranien*, No. 38, 2004.

54. M. Benraad, "Irak, avancées et écueils d'une transition (2005–2006)", *Le Moyen Orient en crise*, Paris, Documentation Française, 2006–2007.

55. "Iraq and the Kurds: The Brewing Battle over Kirkuk", *ICG*, No. 56, 18 July 2006; M. Van Bruinessen, "Kurdish Challenges", *Chaillot Paper*, No. 79, July 2005.

56. "Where is Iraq Heading? Lessons from Basra", *ICG*, No. 67, 25 June 2007.
57. M. Benraad, "Du phénomène arabe sunnite irakien", *Hérodote*, No. 130, 2008, p. 65.
58. "Iraq's Civil War, the Sadrists and the Surge", *ICG*, No. 72, 7 February 2008.
59. B. Hoffman, "Insurgency and Counterinsurgency in Iraq", *Studies in Conflict and Terrorism*, Vol. 29, No. 2, 2006.
60. Bassam Youssif, "Coalition Economic Policies in Iraq", in Leonard Binder (ed.), *Rebuilding Devastated Economies in the Middle East*, New York, Palgrave Macmillan, 2007, p. 229.
61. David Baran, *Vivre la tyrannie, op. cit.*, p. 21.
62. Bilal A. Wahab, "How Iraqi Oil Smuggling Greases Violence", *Middle East Quarterly*, Fall 2006, p. 2.
63. *The Peninsula*, Doha, 27 May 2006.
64. *Ibid*.
65. "Iraq: Building a New Security Structure", *ICG*, No. 20, 2003; Donna Miles, "Iraqi Civil Defense Corps Grows in Number and Role", American Forces Press Service, http:www.defenselink.mil.
66. "Reconstructing Iraq", *ICG*, September 2004.
67. 54 per cent of members of Parliament voted for maintaining troops The US Status of Forces Agreement (SOFA) was backed by the Kurdish bloc, the Daawa party and other Shia parties in the government alliance as well as the Islamic Supreme Council of Iraq: fourteen members abstained and seventy-seven were absent at the time of the vote.
68. Iraq, Economist Intelligence Unit, December 2008, p. 10.
69. H.M. Mohammed, *Suicide Bombers in Iraq: The Strategy and Ideology of Martyrdom*, Washington, DC, US Institute of Peace Press, 2007.
70. M. Benraad, "De la tentative hégémonique au déclin de l'organisation d'Al-Qaida en Irak", *Maghreb-Machrek*, No. 197, 2008.
71. Interview in *Le Monde*, 17 June 2009.
72. Iraq, The Economist Intelligence Unit, December 2008, p. 14.
73. "Iraq's reconstruction and economic development will require hundreds of billions of dollars of infrastructure investment and Baghdad hopes that foreign partners will play a sizeable role", www.emergingmarketsmonitor.com.
74. P. Le Billon, "Corruption, Reconstruction and Oil Governance in Iraq", *Third World Quarterly*, Vol. 26, No. 4–5, 2005.
75. L. Bucaille, "Exiger des excuses de la France", *Raison Publique*, No. 10, 2009.
76. Voter turnout reached 51 per cent.
77. In September 2009, the government offered blocks up for auction to

increase production in the hopes of reaching the 4 million barrels per day it produced in the 1970s.

78. In an interview given to *Echourouk El Youmi* on 5 July 2009, Hassan Hattab, former chief of the Salafist Group for Preaching and Combat (GSPC), stated that his group, formally affiliated with that organisation, always refused to carry out suicide bombings, although claimed by Al-Qaeda as its followers. This statement revives the hypothesis that AQIM is manipulated by Algerian security services.

79. Richard A. Oppel, Jr., "Foreign Fighters in Iraq Are Tied to Allies of US", *New York Times*, 22 November 2007.

80. The Bilmes and Stiglitz study estimates that the cost of the war (2003–10) could reach $2,000 billion and asks, "Would they [the American people] have thought that there might be better ways of advancing the cause of democracy or even protecting themselves against an attack, that would cost but a fraction of these amounts": L. Bilmes and J. Stiglitz, "The Economic Costs of the Iraq War", Milken Institute, 4th Quarter, October 2006, p. 34.

81. "Démocratie et gouvernance de la politique électorale en Afrique du Nord", http://www.francophonie-durable.org.

82. Jean-Noel Ferrié, "Les limites d'une démocratisation par la société civile en Afrique du Nord", *Maghreb-Machrek*, No. 175, 2003.

83. E. Kienle, "Libéralisation économique et délibération politique: le nouveau visage de l'autoritarisme", in O. Dabène, V. Geisser and G. Massardier (eds), *Autoritarismes démocratiques et démocraties autoritaires au XXI siècle*, Paris, La Découverte, 2008.

84. M. Camau and V. Geisser, *Le syndrome autoritaire*, Paris, Presses de Sciences Po, 2003.

5. ALGERIA, LIBYA AND THE CHALLENGE OF THE EUROPEAN NEIGHBOURHOOD POLICY

1. R. Springborg (ed.), *Oil and Democracy in Iraq*, London, SOAS Middle East Issues, 2007.

2. M-F. Labouz, C. Philip and P. Soldatos (eds), *L'UE élargie aux nouvelles frontières et à la recherche d'une politique de voisinage*, Brussels, Bruytlant, 2006; Bernd Weber, *Europe's Neighbourhood between Conditionality, Network Governance and Bargaining*, http://www.ceri-sciences-po.org/themes/ue/articles/enp_weber.pdf.

3. See the ENP strategy paper, Brussels, 2004, http://ec.europa.eu/world/enp/pdf/strategy/strategy_paper_en.pdf.

4. http://ec.europa.eu/world/enp/policy_en.htm.

5. On 22 April 2002, Algeria signed an EU Association Agreement, to

be implemented on 1 September 2005. This agreement provides for reducing customs tariffs, encouraging the free circulation of capital for FDI in Algeria, encouraging political dialogue and respect for democratic principles and human rights, and working towards regional integration.

6. Jean Yves Moisseron, "Bilan mitigé des Accords de Barcelone", in *Le partenariat euro méditerranéen dix ans après Barcelone, Géoéconomie*, No. 35, 2005.

7. E. Barbé, "L'UE et son voisinage en Méditerranée", in J. Rupnik (ed.), *Les banlieues de l'Europe*, Paris, Presses de Sciences Po, 2007, p. 162.

8. "Le torchon brûle entre Alger et Bruxelles", *El Watan*, 23 May 2009.

9. H. Darbouche, "Decoding Algeria's ENP Policy", *Mediterranean Politics*, Vol. 13, No. 3, 2008, p. 11.

10. F. Bafoil, "Variété des processus d'européanisation en Europe centrale et orientale", in F. Bafoil and T. Belchelt (eds), *L'européanisation d'Ouest en Est*, Paris, L'Harmattan, 2008, p. 59.

11. G. Favarel-Garrigues, "Mafia Violence and Political Power in Russia", in *Organized Crime and States, op. cit.*, 2010, p. 148.

12. European Neighbourhood and Partnership Instrument: Algeria. Strategy Paper, 2007–2013, http://ec.europa.eu.

13. Rosa Rossi, "The European Neighbourhood Policy in Perspective", in Jean Monnet Centre (ed.), *"Euro-Med"*, Catania, 2004, p. 11.

14. In 2008, Transparency International ranked Algeria in 92nd place and Libya 134th.

15. "The long term objective of the EU policy relations with Libya is and remains Libya's full accession to the Barcelona Process and participation in the European Neighbourhood Policy. This would enhance the promising potential for joint co-operation in important international issues such as migrations and development in Africa".

16. There have been negotiations on a Libya-EU framework agreement in Brussels, not concluded.

17. Pranab Bardham, "Corruption and Development: A Review of Issues", *Journal of Economic Literature*, Vol. 35, No. 3, 3 September 1997.

18. Z. Laidi (ed.), *EU Foreign Policy in a Globalized World*, London, Routledge, 2008.

19. "Frontières de l'Europe", Les Carnets du CAP, Spring 2006, p. 83.

20. L. Martinez, "L'intégration régionale au Maroc et en Tunisie", *Euromesco*, January 2009, http//www.euromesco.net/images/paper78fra.pdf.

21. A. Abdou, "Le Maghreb en jachère", *Le Quotidien d'Oran*, 24 August 2006. The Tangiers Conference, 27–30 April 1958, with Neo-Destour, the Istiqlal and the FLN, stipulated that "conscious of the need to

express the unanimous will of the peoples of the Arab Maghreb to unite their fate in the strict solidarity of their interests, convinced that the moment has come to materialise this will to unite in the framework of common institutions, in order to allow them to secure the role it is entrusted with in the concert of nations, decided to work toward realisation of this union, considers that the federal form answers best to the realities of the participating countries".

22. *La Revue Parlementaire,* June 2005, p. 11.
23. Speech by Muammar Qadhafi in July 2001 in Lusaka upon the establishment of the African Union. *Géopolitique Africaine*, No. 4, November 2001.
24. *Jamahiriyya News Agency*, 7 October 2004
25. Euromed Report, 23 May 2003, http://europa.eu.int/comm/external_relations/euromed/publication.htm.
26. J. Percebois, "The Supply of Natural Gas in the European Union. Strategic Issues", *OPEC Energy Review*, March 2008, Vol. 32, p. 50; S. Boussena and J-P. Pauwels, *Le défi pétrolier*, Paris, Vuibert, 2006, p. 106.
27. Paul Balta, *Le Grand Maghreb: des indépendances à l'an 200*, Paris, La Découverte, 1990.
28. G. Destane de Bernis, "La Libye et l'Algérie: stratégies de développement comparées", *Annuaire de l'Afrique du Nord*, Paris, CNRS, 1971.
29. See "Algeria", in the *Arab Oil and Gas Directory*, 2000.
30. *Houston Business Journal*, 5 January 2004.
31. Interview with Tarek Hassan, NOC's director of planning, *New York Times*, 23 July 2004.
32. Yves Gazzo, *Pétrole et développement: le cas libyen*, Paris, Economica, 1980.
33. Energy Information Administration, July 1999, www.eia.doe.gov.
34. J. Percebois, "The Supply of Natural Gas in the European Union. Strategic Issues", *op. cit.*, p. 35
35. J.F. Coustillère, "Les rapports Europe-Maghreb en matière de sécurité et de défense", *Année du Maghreb*, Iremam, 2008; regarding AQIM see J-P. Filiu, "The Local and Global Jihad of al-Qa'ida in the Islamic Maghreb", *Middle East Journal*, Vol. 63, No. 2, Spring 2009.
36. A. Benantar (ed.), *Les Etats-Unis et le Maghreb: Regain d'intérêt?* Algiers, Cread, 2007.
37. "Le Maghreb stratégique", NATO Defense College, Research Branch, Rome, April 2006, http://www.ndc.nato.int.
38. L. Martinez, "La sécurité en Algérie et en Libye après le 11 September", *Euromesco Papers*, No. 22, May 2003.
39. CSI, Maghreb Roundtable, February 2006.
40. Eurofor (European Operational Rapid Force) and Euromarfor (Euro-

pean Maritime Force), staffed by France, Spain, Italy and Portugal, were formed during the 1990s with the aim of addressing security imperatives. *Le Dossier d'Athéna de l'IHEDN*, Paris, Documentation Française, 1997, second quarter.

41. SIVE (External Surveillance Integrated System) is an operational system used for surveillance of Spain's southern border. It has four functions: to detect, identify, follow and intercept any craft that attempts to enter EU territory illegally. *Revue Maritime*, no. 465, June 2003.

42. D. Lutterbek, "Policing Migrations in The Mediterranean", *Mediterranean Politics*, 2006, Vol. 11, No. 1.

43. Isabelle Saint-Saëns, "Des camps en Europe aux camps de l'Europe", *Multitudes 19*, Winter 2004.

44. J-P Cassarino, "Informalising Readmission Agreements in the EU Neighbourhood", *The International Spectator*, Vol. 24, No. 2, 2007. In 2004, the AENEAS programme was adopted. Endowed with 250 million euros for the 2004–2008 period, it provided technical and financial assistance "in the framework of a true partnership". http://europa.eu/legislation_summaries/development/general_development_framework/l14510_fr.htm.

45. Mehdi Lahlou, "Le Maghreb: lieux de transits", *La Pensée du Midi*, No. 10, 2003.

46. Mehdi Lahlou, "Plan d'action pour gérer les migrations irrégulières à partir de l'Afrique", *ILO*, Geneva, April 2003.

47. *Paris-Match*, 9 March 2011.

48. World Bank, Report by Paul Dyer, "Labor Supply, Unemployment and the Challenge of Job Creation in the Maghreb", p. 2. http://siteresources.worldbank.org/INTTUNISIA/Resources/Rapport+WB+Maghreb+EmploiANGLAIS.pdf.

49. Rodrigo de Rato, "Intégration économique au Maghreb: sur le chemin de la prospérité", *L'Economiste* (Morocco), 15 June 2005.

50. M. Boussetta, *Femise*, No. 13–21 August 2004, p. 59.

51. I. Bensidoun and A. Chevalier, "Europe-Méditerranée: le pari de l'ouverture", Paris, Economica, 1996.

52. M. Boussetta, *Femise*, No. 13–21 August 2004, p. 95.

53. "The North African development strategy is based on the 'Ras Lanuf programme' adopted in Libya in 1991. It lays out the three stages of regional integration, namely, a free trade area, a customs union and a common market": P. Botha and F. Aggad, "The Arab Maghreb Union as a Regional Economic and Political Grouping: a Case Study", *Politics*, 2004, No. 42, pp. 33–47.

54. North Africa Development Forum, http://www.northafricaforum.org/memo.html.

55. Abdelkader Messahel, Minister of North African and African Affairs, Algeria, *Algérie-UMA*, 26 March 2006.

56. *TelQel Magazine*, Morocco, August 2004.

57. In Algeria, a $3.5 billion arms contract (forty MiG 29 SMT fighter planes, twenty-eight Su-30Mk fighter planes, sixteen Yak-130, eight groups of S-300 PMU surface-to-air missiles and forty T-90 tanks), "Achat d'armes au Maghreb", *El Watan*, 11 March 2006; in 2007, Morocco purchased twenty-four F16 aircraft ($2.4 billion) and Dassault and Libya negotiated the sale of Rafale aircraft. In Morocco's *Hebdo International* (6–12 September 2002), in an article entitled "Alger prépare la guerre", the author expressed the feeling that Algeria's massive stockpiling of weapons was a serious threat to its neighbours' stability.

58. Robert Bistolfi, "La politique maghrébine de la communauté", *AAN*, Vol. 28, 1990, p. 23.

59. Quoted by Robert Bistolfi, "La politique maghrébine de la communauté", *op. cit.*, p. 25.

60. *Le Figaro*, 16 February 2007.

61. Richard Gillespie, "A Political Agenda for Region-Building? The EMP and Democracy Promotion in North Africa", Working Paper, Institute of European Studies, University of California, Berkeley, 30 May 2004.

62. Richard Youngs, "The EU and Democracy Promotion in the Mediterranean: A New or Disingenuous Strategy?", www.liv.ac.uk/ewc/docs/Archives/Youngs2002.doc.

63. D. Cortright and G.A. Lopez, *The Sanctions Decade: Assessing UN in the 1990s*, Boulder, Colorado, Lynne Rienner, 2000.

64. L. Martinez, *The Algerian Civil War, op. cit.*, 2000.

65. The Luxembourg declaration (General Affairs and External Relations Council) states, "It is well-known fact that one of the EU member states—and therefore all member states because of the open borders—is having considerable problems with illegal immigrants coming from Libya. The Ministers agreed today that cooperation with Libya on the topic of migration has become a pressing matter".

66. N. Ferré, "La Libye pour 'externaliser' le droit d'asile de l'UE", *Le Monde*, 20 July 2005.

67. L. Martinez, "La Libye et la guerre au Darfour", *Revue Outre Mer*, No. 20, 2007.

68. H. Darbouche, "Russian-Algerian Cooperation and the 'Gas OPEC': What's in the Pipeline", *CEPS, Policy Brief*, No. 123, March 2007.

69. A dispatch from the Russian International news agency entitled "Russia loses footing in Algeria", 13 December 2007, aptly summarises the issues at stake in Gazprom's presence in Algeria: "Due to their assets in natural resources, the two countries could have controlled about 40 per cent of natural gas deliveries to the EU. But by trying to neutralise the

increasing pressure from Gazprom, European natural gas consumers decided to bank on Algeria and Libya. The stubborn struggle the EU has undertaken to diversify its energy supply makes Gazprom's presence in these countries unacceptable to gas buyers", http://fr.rian.ru.

70. Algeria possesses "the largest war navy in the region. Even Egypt cannot rival with it. In the field of aviation, the accumulation of Su-27, Su-30 and MiG-29SMT will enable Algiers to have clear superior air power in the entire region", in "L'Algérie puissance régionale méditerranéenne incontournable?", *Défense et sécurité internationale*, No. 25, April 2007, p. 62.

71. *L'Expression*, 24 November 2008.

72. Kenza Afsahi, Morocco Cannabis Survey. December 2003, http://www.unodc.org.

73. P.A. Chouvy, *Les territoires de l'Opium: Conflits et trafics du Triangle d'Or et du Croissant d'Or*, Geneva, Edition Olizane, 2002.

74. The number of cocaine consumers is estimated at 6 million in the United States, the main consumer country, which requires production of 450 kg per year and represents a market of $30 to $50 billion.

75. See Chapter 1.

76. R. Gillespie, "The EMP and Democracy Promotion in North Africa", 30 May 2004, http://escholarship.org.

77. "The Arab Democratic Wave: How the EU can Seize the Moment",. Report No. 9, March 2011, Institute for Security Studies.

78. Y. Cochet, *Pétrole apocalypse*, Paris, Fayard, 2005.

79. J-L. Winger, *La vie après le pétrole: de la pénurie aux énergie nouvelles*, Paris, Autrement, 2005.

CONCLUSION

1. Benjamin Smith, "The Wrong Kind of Crisis: Why Oil Booms and Busts Rarely Lead to Authoritarian Breakdown", *Studies in Comparative International Development*, Winter 2006, No. 4, Vol. 40.

2. Kiren Aziz Chaudhry, "On the Way to Market. Economic Liberalisation and Iraq's Invasion of Kuwait", *Middle East Report*, May-June 1991.

3. I. Beaulieu, *L'Etat rentier: Le cas de la Malaysia*, Ottawa, PUO, 2009, p. 47.

4. For some observers, the establishment of Al-Qaeda in the Islamic Maghreb is a ploy of the Algerian security services to arouse fear in Europe and the United States for their interests in the region, forcing them to cooperate in security matters. F. Gèze and S. Mellah, "'Al-Qaida au Maghreb', ou la très étrange histoire du GSPC algérien", *Algeria-Watch*, 22 September 2007.

5. P. Collier and A. Hoeffer, "Démocraties pétrolières", *Afrique Contemporaine*, No. 4, 2005.

BIBLIOGRAPHY

Books

ADDI Lahouari, *L'impasse du populisme*, Algiers, Enal, 1990.

AHMIDA Ali Abdullatif, *The Making of Modern Libya: State Formation, Colonization and Resistance, 1830–1932*, Albany, State University of New York Press, 1994.

ALLAN John Anthony, (ed.), *Libya since Independence: Economic and Political Development*, London, Croom Helm, 1982.

ALLAN John Anthony, *Libya: The experience of Oil*, London, Croom Helm, 1981.

ANDERSON Lisa, *The State and Social Transformation in Tunisia and Libya (1830–1980)*, Princeton, Princeton University Press, 1986.

AXELGARD Frederick W., *Iraq in Transition*, Boulder, Colorado, Westview Press, 1986.

BARAN David, *Vive la tyrannie et lui survivre. L'Irak en transition*, Paris, Mille et Une Nuits, 2004.

BAYART Jean-François, Stephen ELLIS and Béatrice HIBOU, *La criminalisation de l'Etat en Afrique*, Brussels, Complexe, 1997.

BEAULIEU Isabelle, *L'Etat rentier. Le cas de la Malaysia*, Ottawa, PUO, 2008.

BEBLAWI Hazem and Giacomo LUCIANI (eds), *The Rentier State*, London, Croom Helm, 1987.

BENANTAR Abdennour (ed.), *Les Etats Unis et le Maghreb: Regain d'intérêt?* Algiers, Cread, 2007.

BENHOURIA Tahar, *L'économie de l'Algérie*, Paris, Maspero, 1980.

BENISSAD Mohamed Elhocine. *Economie du développement de l'Algérie (1962–78)*, Paris, Economica, 1979.

BLEUCHOT Hervé, *Chroniques et documents libyens, 1969–1980*, Paris, CNRS, 1983.

BOZARSLAN Hamit, *Le conflit Kurde: le brasier oublié*. Paris, Autrement, 2009.

191

BIBLIOGRAPHY

CAMAU Michel and Vincent GEISSER, *Le syndrome autoritaire. Politique en Tunisie de Bourguiba à Ben Ali*, Paris, Presses de Sciences Po, 2003.

CHEVALIER Jean-Marie, *The New Energy Crisis: Climate, Economics and Geopolitics*, London, New York, Palgrave Macmillan, 2009.

CHEVALIER Jean-Marie, *Le nouvel enjeu pétrolier*, Paris, Calmann Lévy, 1973.

COLONOMOS Ariel, *La morale dans les relations internationales*, Paris, Odile Jacob, 2005.

DAHMANI Ahmed, *L'Algérie à l'épreuve. Economie politique des réformes (1980–1997)*, Paris, L'Harmattan, 1999.

DABÈNE Olivier, Vincent GEISSER and Gilles MASSARDIER (eds), *Autoritarismes démocratiques et démocraties autoritaires au XXI siècle*, Paris, La Découverte, 2008.

DAVIS John, *Libyan Politics*, Berkeley and Los Angeles, University of California Press, 1987.

DILLMAN Bradford, *State and Private Sector in Algeria. The Politics of Rent-Seeking and Failed Development*, Boulder, Colorado, Westview Press, 2000.

DODGE Toby, *Inventing Iraq. The Failure of Nation Building and a History Denied*, London, Hurst, 2003.

KIENLE Eberhard, *Ba'th vs Ba'th*, London, Taurus, 1990.

KIENLE Eberhard (ed.), *Economic Reform and the Reconstruction of Politics: The Arab World in a Period of Global Transformations*, London, Saqi, 2003.

ENTELIS John, Algeria. *The Revolution Institutionalized*, Boulder, Colorado, Westview Press, 1986.

ETIENNE Bruno, *L'Algérie cultures et révolution*, Paris, Seuil, 1977.

FAROUK-SLUGLETT Marion and Peter SLUGLETT, *Iraq since 1958. From Revolution to Dictatorship*. London, Taurus, 2001.

FERRIÉ Jean-Noël and Jean-Claude SANTUCCI (eds). *Dispositifs de démocratisation et dispositifs autoritaires en Afrique du Nord*, Paris, CNRS, 2005.

GOUMEZIANE Smail, *Le mal algérien, économie politique d'une transition inachevée*, Paris, Fayard, 1994.

GUERREAU Alain and Anita GUERREAU-JALABERT, *L'Irak: développement et contradictions*, Paris, Le Sycomore, 1978.

GURNEY Judith, *Libya: The Political Economy of Energy*, Oxford, Oxford University Press, 1996.

HERMET Guy, *Les populismes dans le monde*, Paris, Fayard, 2001.

HIBOU Béatrice, *La force de l'obéissance: économie politique de la répression en Tunisie*, Paris, La Découverte, 2006.

JACKSON Henry F., *The FLN in Algeria. Party Development in a Revolutionary Society*. London, Greenwood Press, 1977.

EL-KENZ Ali, *L'Algérie et la modernité*, Dakar, Codesria, 1989.

192

HIDOUCI Ghazi, Algérie, *La Libération inachevée*, Paris, La Découverte, 1995.

JOFFÉ George and S. McLACHLAN (eds), *Social and Economic Development of Libya*, Wisbech, Menas Press, 1982.

KARL, Terry Lynn, *The Paradox of Plenty: Oil Booms and Petro-States*, Berkeley, University of California Press, 1997.

EL-KIKHIA Mansour O., *Libya's Qadhafi. The Politics of Contradiction*, Gainsville, University of Florida, 1997.

LAIDI Zaki (ed.), *EU Foreign Policy in a Globalized World*, London, Routledge, 2008.

LECA Jean and Jean-Claude VATIN, *L'Algérie politique. Institutions et régime*, Paris, Presses de la Fondation nationale des sciences politiques, 1975.

LE COUR GRANDMAISON Olivier, *Coloniser. Exterminer: sur la guerre et l'Etat colonial*, Paris, Fayard, 2005.

LEMARCHAND René (ed), *The Green and The Black: Qadhafi's Policies in Africa*, Bloomington, Indiana University Press, 1988.

LEVEAU Rémy, *Le Sabre et le Turban*, Paris, F. Bourin, 1993.

LINZ Juan, *Totalitarian and Authoritarian Regimes*, Boulder, Colorado, Lynne Rienner, 2000.

LUIZARD Pierre-Jean, *La question irakienne*, Paris, Fayard, 2002.

MABRO Robert, *Oil in the Twentieth Century*, Oxford, Oxford University Press, 2006.

MARTINEZ Luis, *The Libyan Paradox*, trans. John King, London, Hurst, 2007.

MARTINEZ Luis. *The Algerian Civil War*, trans. Jonathan Derrick, London, Hurst & Co., 2000.

MOFID Kamran, *The Economic Consequences of the Gulf War*, London, Routledge, 1990.

NIBLOCK Tim, *Pariah States and Economic Sanctions in the Middle East: Iraq, Libya, Sudan*, Boulder, Colorado, Lynne Rienner, 2001.

QUANDT William B., *Revolution and Political Leadership. Algeria, 1954–1968*, Cambridge, (MA), MIT Press, 1969.

QUANDT William B., *Between Ballots and Bullets. Algeria's transition from Authoritarianism*, Washington D.C, The Brookings Institution Press, 1998.

REBAH Abdelatif, Sonatrach, *Une entreprise pas comme les autres*, Algiers, Ed. Casbah, 2006.

RONDOT Philippe, *L'Irak*, PUF, 1979 (Que sais-je?).

ROY Olivier, *The Politics of Chaos in The Middle East*, trans. Ros Schwartz, London, Hurst, 2007.

SALAMÉ Ghassan, *Democracy Without Democrats? The Renewal of Politics in The Muslim World*, London, Taurus, 1994.

SALAMÉ Ghassan, *Quand l'Amérique refait le monde*, Paris, Fayard, 2005.

SAMARBAKHSH A.G, *Socialisme en Irak et en Syrie*. Paris, Anthropos, 1980.

SEMELIN Jacques, *Purify and Destroy*, trans. Cynthia Schoch, London, Hurst & Co., 2009.

SHELLEY Toby, *Oil. Politics, Poverty and the Planet*, London, Zed Books Ltd, 2005.

SID AHMED Abdelkader, *Développement sans croissance*. Paris, Publisud, 1983.

SHWADRAN Benjamin, *The Middle East, Oil and the Great Power*, Jerusalem, Israel University Press, 1973.

SKEET Ian, *OPEC: Twenty-Five Years of Prices and Politics*. Cambridge, Cambridge University Press, 1991.

SLUGLETT Peter, *Britain in Iraq. Contriving King and Country*, London, Taurus, 2007.

SMOLANSKY Oles and Bettie, *The USSR and Iraq. The Soviet Quest for Influence*, Durham (N.C.), Duke University Press, 1991.

SPRINGBORG Robert (ed), *Oil and Democracy in Iraq*, London, SOAS— Middle East Issues, 2007.

TLEMCANI Rachid, *Etat, bazar et globalisation*, Algiers, El-Hikma, 1999.

TRIPP Charles, *A History of Iraq*, Cambridge, Cambridge University Press, 2007.

VANDEWALLE Dirk, *A History of Modern Libya*, Cambridge, Cambridge University Press, 2006.

WADDAMS Frank C., *The Libyan Oil Industry*, Baltimore, The Johns Hopkins University Press, 1980.

WERENFELS Isabelle, *Elites and Political Change Since 1995*, London, Routledge, 2007.

YERGIN Daniek, *Les hommes du pétrole. Les fondateurs 1859–1945*, Paris, Stock, 1991.

ZELENKO Pierre, Christophe Alexandre PAILLARD and Cédric de LESTANGE, *Géopolitique du pétrole*, Paris, Ed Technip, 2005.

Articles

ADAMS Patricia, "Iraq's Odious Debts", *Policy Analysis*, no. 526, September 28, 2004.

ALAHMAD Nida, "The Politics of Oil and State Survival in Iraq (1991–2003): Beyond the Rentier Thesis", *Constellations* 14 (4), 2007.

ALKAZAZ Aziz, "The Distribution of National Income in Iraq, with Particular Reference to the Development of Policies Applied by the State" in D. Hopwood, H. Ishow and Y. Koszinowsk (ed.), *Iraq: Power and Society*, Oxford, St' Anthony's College, 1993.

ALTUNISIK M. B., "A Rentier State's Response to Oil Crisis: Economic Reform Policies in Libya", *Arab Studies Quarterly*, September 2002.

AOUDIA Myriam Aït, "La naissance du FIS: une politisation conflictuelle, 1988–89", *Critique Internationale*, no. 30, January-March, 2006.

BACH Daniel C., "Nigeria: paradoxes de l'abondance et démocratisation en trompe-l'œil". *Afrique contemporaine*, no. 219, 2006/3.

BAFOIL François, "Variété des processus d'européanisation en Europe centrale et orientale" in F. Bafoil and T. Bechelt (eds), *L'européanisation d'Ouest en Est*, Paris, L'Harmattan, 2008.

BARAM Amatzia, "Neo-Tribalism in Iraq: Saddam Hussein's Tribal Policies 1991–96", *International Journal of Middle East Studies* 29 (1), 1997.

Amatzia BARAM, "The Effect of Iraqi Sanctions: Statistical Pitfalls and Responsibility", *Middle East Journal* 54 (2), 2000.

BARBÉ Esther, "L'UE et son voisinage en Méditerranée" in J. Rupnik (ed.), *Les banlieues de l'Europe,* Paris, Presses de Sciences Po, 2007.

BELLIN Eva, "The Robustness of Authoritarianism in The Middle East: Exceptionalism in Comparative Perspective", *Comparative Politics* 36, 2, 2004.

BENDERRA Omar, "Les réseaux au pouvoir. Effondrement de l'état de prédation", *Confluences Méditerranée*, no. 45, 2003.

BENRAAD Miriam, "Irak, avancées et écueils d'une transition (2005–2006)" in *Le Moyen Orient en crise*, Paris, Documentation française, 2006–2007.

BENRAAD Miriam, "Du phénomène arabe Sunnite irakien", *Hérodote*, no. 130, 2008/3.

BENRAAD Miriam, "De la tentative hégémonique au déclin de l'organisation d'Al-Qaïda en Irak". *Maghreb-Machrek*, no. 197, 2008.

BERTRAND Romain, "La démocratie à l'indonésienne. Bilan critique d'une transition qui n'en finit pas de commencer", *Revue internationale de politique comparée* 8 (3), January 2001.

BLOM Amélie, "The 'Multi-Vocal' State: The Policy of Pakistan on Kashmir", in Christophe Jaffrelot ed., *Pakistan. Nationalism without a Nation?* London, Zed Books, 2002.

BOZARSLAN Hamit, "Etats, communautés et marges dissidentes en Irak", *Critique Internationale*, no. 34, 2007/1.

BROWN Michael E., "The Nationalization of The Iraqi Petroleum Company" in *International Journal of Middle East Studies* 10 (1), 1979.

BRUN Thierry A., "Comment fabriquer un Etat fragile: réflexions sur l'exemple irakien", in *Etats et sociétés fragiles: entre conflits, reconstruction et développement*, Paris, Karthala, 2007.

BUCAILLE Laetitia, "Exiger des excuses de la France", *Raison Publique*, no. 10, 2009.

BURGAT François, "1989: L'ouverture entravée", *Annuaire de l'Afrique du Nord*, Tome XXVII, 1989, Paris, CNRS, 1991.

CAMAU Michel, "Globalisation démocratique et syndrome autoritaire. Remarques sur 'l'exception' arabe", *Critique Internationale*, no. 30, January-March, 2006.

CHATELUS Michel, "Iraq and its Oil: Sixty-five Years of Ambition and Frustration" in D. Hopwood, H. Ishow, T.Koszinauski (eds), *Iraq: Power and Society*, Oxford, St Anthony's College, p. 993.

CHATELUS Michel, "Nouvelles orientations de la politique pétrolière algérienne", *Maghreb-Machrek*, October-December 1999.

CHAUDHRY Kiren Aziz, "On The Way to Market. Economic Liberalisation and Iraq's Invasion of Kuwait", *Middle East Report*, May-June, 1991.

CHAUDHRY Kiren Azizi., "The 'Uncanny 'Writ Regional. New and Recurring Forms of Poverty and Inequality in the Ararb World" in L. Binder (ed), *Rebuilding Devastated Economies in the Middle East*, Palgrave, 2007.

COLLIER Paul and Anke HOEFFLER, "Démocraties pétrolières", *Afrique contemporaine*, no. 216, 2005.

COLLIER Paul and Anke HOEFFER, "On the Incidence of Civil War in Africa", *Journal Of Conflict Resolution*, 46 (1), 2002.

COLLIER Paul, "Doing Well out of War: An Economic Perspective" in M. Berdal and D. Malone (eds) *Greed and Grievance: Economic Agendas in Civil Wars*. Boulder, Colorado, Lynne Rienner, 2000.

COLLIER Paul and Anke HOEFFER, "Greed and Grievance in Civil War", *Oxford Economic Papers*, 56 (4) 2004.

CORM G., "La réforme économique algérienne: une réforme mal aimée", *Maghreb-Machrek*, no. 139, January-March 1993.

DARBOUCHE Hakim, "Russian-Algerian cooperation and the 'gas OPEC': What's in the pipeline", *CEPS, Policy Brief*, no. 123, March 2007.

DAWOD Hosham, "Le pouvoir irakien, dix ans après la guerre", *Esprit*, no. 2, 2001.

DESTANNE DE BERNIS Gérard, "Industries industrialisantes", *Economie appliquée*, no. 3–4, 1966.

DESTANNE DE BERNIS Gérard, "Les industries industrialisantes et les options algériennes", *Tiers-Monde*, vol. 12, no. 47, 1971.

DEVLIN John F., "The Baath party. Rise and Metamorphosis", *The American Historical Review* 96 (5), 1991.

DI JOHN Jonathan, "Oil Abundance and Violent Political Conflict: A Critical Assessment". *Journal Of Development Studies* 43 (6), August 2007.

DILLMAN Bradford, "Illicit Economies and Reconstruction", in L. Binder (ed), *Rebuilding Devastated Economies in the Middle East*, New York, Palgrave Macmillan, 2007.

DILLMAN Bradford, "The Political Economy of Structural Adjustment in Tunisia and Algeria." *Journal of North African Studies*, no. 3, 1998.

DROZ-VINCENT Philippe, "Quel avenir pour l'autoritarisme dans le monde arabe", *Revue française de science politique*, 54, 6, December 2004.

DODGE Toby, "The cause of a US failure", *Survival* 49 (1), 2007.

FAROUK-SLUGLETT Marion, "Rente pétrolière et concentration du pouvoir", *Maghreb-Machrek*, no. 131, January-March, 1991.

FAROUK-SLUGLETT Marion and Peter SLUGLETT, "The Historiography of Modern Iraq". *The American Historical Review* 96 (5), December 1991.

FERRIÉ Jean-Noël, "Entering the 'Virtuous Circle': The Strength of Democratic Designs in Egypt and Morocco", in E. Kienle (ed.), *Economic Reform and the Reconstruction of Politics: The Arab World in a Period of Global Transformations*, London, Saqi, 2003.

FERRIÉ Jean-Noel, "Les limites d'une démocratisation par la société civile en Afrique du Nord", *Maghreb-Machrek*, no. 175, 2003.

GALVANI John, "The Baathi Revolution in Iraq", *Merip Reports*, no. 12, September-October, 1972.

FAVAREL-GARRIGUES Gilles, "Mafia Violence and Political Power in Russia," in Jean-Louis Briquet and Gilles Favarel-Garrigues, *Organized Crime and States*, New York, Palgrave Macmillan, 2010.

GRIMAUD Nicole, "Le conflit pétrolier franco-algérien", *Revue française de science politique* 22 (6), 1972.

HACHEMAOUI Mohamed, "Permanences du jeu politique en Algérie", *Politique étrangère*, 2009/02.

HARBI Mohamed, "Processus de relégitimation du pouvoir en Algérie" in Michel Camau (ed.), *Changements politiques au Maghreb*, Paris, CNRS, 1991.

HADJADJ Djilali, "Violence et corruption: cas de l'Algérie", *Le bulletin de l'APAD*, no. 25, June 2003.

HELLER M. A., "Iraq's Army: Military Weakness, Political Utility" in *Iraq's Road to War* (eds) by A. Baram and B. Rubin. NewYork, St Martin's Press, 1993.

HEYDEMANN Steven, "D'Assad à Assad: la politique syrienne n'est pas un théâtre d'ombre", *Critique Internationale*, no. 9, October 2000.

HOFFMAN Bruce, "Insurgency and counterinsurgency in Iraq", *Studies in Conflict and Terrorism* 29 (2), 2006.

HUMPHREYS Macartan, "Natural Resources Conflict and Conflict Resolution", *The Journal of Conflict Resolution*, no. 49, August 2005.

al-JABBAR Faleh Abdel, "Why the Uprising Failed", *Middle East Report*, no. 176, May-June, 1992.

JOFFE George, "La Libye et l'Europe" in *Maghreb-Machrek*, no. 170, 2000.

JOFFE George, The Role of Violence within the Algerian Economy", *Journal of North African Studies* 7 (1), 2002.

KIENLE Eberhard, "Libéralisation économique et délibération politique: le nouveau visage de l'autoritarisme" in O. Dabène, V. Geisser, M. Camau (eds), *Autoritarismes démocratiques et démocraties autoritaires au XXI siècle*, Paris, La Découverte, 2008.

KOBRIN Stephen J., "Diffusion of an Explanation of Oil Nationalization: Or the Domino Effect Rides Again", *The Journal of Conflict Resolution*, no. 29 (1), March 1985.

LISTHAUG Ola, "Oil Wealth Dissatisfaction and Political Trust in Norway: A Resource Curse?" *West European Politics* 28 (4), 2005.

LE BILLON P., "Corruption, reconstruction and Oil Governance in Iraq" in *Third World Quaterly* 26 (4–5), 2005.

LECA Jean and Jean-Claude VATIN, "Le système politique algérien (1967–1978). Idéologie, Institutions et changement social", *Annuaire de l'Afrique du Nord*, vol. XVI, 1977.

LECA Jean, "Etat et société en Algérie", in Basma Kodmani-Darwish, *Les années de transition*, Paris, Masson, 1990.

LECA Jean, "Paradoxes de la démocratisation. L'Algérie au chevet de la science-politique", *Pouvoirs*, no. 86, 1998.

LECA Jean, "Social Structure and Political Stability: Comparative Evidence from the Algerian, Syrian and Iraqi Cases" in Adeed Dawisha and I. William. Zartman (eds), *Beyond Coercion: The Durability of the Arab State*. London, Croom Helm, 1988.

LECA Jean and Yves SCHEMEIL, "Clientélisme et patrimonialisme dans le monde arabe". *International Political Science Review* 4 (4), 1983.

LEGRANGE Marc André and Thierry VIRCOULON, "Zimbabwe: réflexions sur la dictature durable", *Politique étrangère*, Vol 3, Autumn 2008.

LOWI Miriam, "Oil Rents and Political Breakdown in Patrimonial States: Algeria in Comparative Perspective", *Journal of North African Studies* 9 (3), 2004.

LOWI Miriam and G. OKRUHLIK, "Rentier Wealth, Unruly Law, and the Rise of Opposition: The political Economy of Oil States", *Comparative politics* 31 (3), 1999.

LUIZARD Pierre-Jean, "L'impossible démocratie en Irak: le piège de l'Etat nation" in *Egypte Monde arabe*, Le Caire, Cedej, no. 4,1990.

MABRO Robert, "The Oil Weapon. Can it Be Used Today?" *Harvard International Review*, Fall 2007.

MAHDAVY Hossein, "The Patterns and Problems of Economic Development in Rentier States: The Case of Iran", in M.A. Cook (ed) *Studies in Economic History of the Middle East*, Oxford, Oxford University Press, 1970.

al-MARASHI Ibrahim, "Iraq's Security and Intelligence Network: A Guide and Analysis", *MERIA* 6 (3), September 2002.

MARCHAL Roland and Christine MESSIANT, "De l'avidité des rebelles. L'analyse économique des conflits par Paul Collier", *Critique Internationale*, no. 16, June 2002.

MATTES Hanspetter, "The Rise and Fall of the Revolutionary Committees" in Dirk Vandewalle (ed.), *Qadahfi's Libya, 1969–1994*, New York, St Martin's Press, 1995.

MATSUNAGA Yasuyuki, "L'Etat rentier est-il réfractaire à la démocratie?"*Critique Internationale*, no. 8, July 2000.

MOORE Henry Clement, "Algeria's Agonies: Oil Rent Effects in a Bunker State", *Journal Of North African Studies* 9 (2), 2004.

MORRISON Kevin M., "Oil, Non tax Revenue and the Redistributional Foundations of Regime Stability", *International Organization*, no. 63, 2009.

MUTIN George, "Les hydrocarbures dans le monde arabe", in J-F. Troin (ed.), *Maghreb Moyent-Orient. Mutations*, CEDES 1995.

OYEFUSI Aderoju, "Oil and Probability of Rebel Participation among Youths in the Niger Delta of Nigeria", *Journal of Peace Research* 45 (4), 2008.

PERCEBOIS Jacques, "The supply of natural gas in the European Union. Strategic Issues", *OPEC Energy Review*, March 2008, Vol. 32.

PICARD Elisabeth, "Syrie: la coalition autoritaire fait de la résistance", *Politique Etrangère*, 2005/4.

PETERSON J., "Qatar and the World: Branding for a Micro-State" in *Middle East Journal*, Vol. 60, Autumn, 2006.

PEZZINO Paolo, "La mafia, Etat et société dans la Sicile contemporaine", *Politix*, no. 49, 2000.

RIGAUD Françoise, "Irak: le temps suspendu de l'embargo", *Critique internationale*, no. 11, 1998.

RECONDO David, "Pétrodollars et politiques sociales" in O. Compagnon, J. Rebotier and S. Revet (eds), *Le Venezuela au-delà du mythe*, Paris, Ed. Ouvrières, 2009.

RONE Jemera, "Sudan: Oil and War", *Review of African Political Economy* 30 (97), 2003.

ROUGIER Bernard, "Le Grand Moyen-Orient: un moment d'utopie internationale?" in *Critique Internationale*, no. 26, January 2005.

ROSS Michael-L., "Does Oil Hinder Democracy?" *World Politics* 53 (3), 2001.

ROSS Michael-L., "What Do We Know about Natural Resources and Civil War?" *Journal of Peace Research*, 41, 3, 2004.

ROSS Michael-L., "A Closer Look at Oil, Diamonds, and Civil War" *Annual Review of Political Science*, no. 9, 2006.

ROSSER Andrew, "Escaping the Resource Curse: The Case of Indonesia", *Journal of Contemporary Asia* 37 (1), February 2007.

SACHS Jeffrey D., J. E. STIGLITZ, M. HUMPHREYS (eds), "What is the Problem with Natural Resource Wealth" in *Escaping The Resource Curse*, New York: Columbia University Press, 2007.

SÉBILLE-LOPEZ Philippe, "Les hydrocarbures au Nigeria et la redistribution de la rente pétrolière". *Afrique contemporaine*, no. 216, 2005/4.

SMITH Benjamin, "Oil Wealth and Regime Survival in the Developing World, 1960–1999". *American Journal of Political Science* 48 (2), April 2004.

SMITH Benjamin, "The Wrong Kind of Crisis: Why Oil Booms and Busts Rarely Lead to Authoritarian Breakdown". *Studies in Comparative International Development* 40 (4), Winter 2006.

SPRINGBORG Robert, "Baathism in Practice: Agriculture, Politics and Political Culture in Syria and Irak", *Middle Eastern Studies* 17 (2), April 1981.

SPRINGBORG Robert, "Iraqi infitah", *Middle East Journal* 40 (1), 1988.

ST JOHN Ronald Bruce, "Libya's Oil and Gas Industry: Blending Old and New", *The Journal Of North African Studies* 12 (2), June 2007.

TALAHITE Fatiha, "Economie administrée, corruption et engrenage de la violence en Algérie", *Revue Tiers-Monde* 161 (1), 2000.

WANTCHEKON Leonard, "Why do Resource Abundant Countries Have Authoritarian Governments? Yale University, October 15, 2002.

VANDEWALLE Dirk, "Qadhafi's Perestroika: Economic and Political Liberalization in Libya," *The Middle East Journal* 45 (2), 1991.

WAHAB Bilal A., "How Iraqi Oil Smuggling Greases Violence", *Middle East Quarterly*, Fall 2006.

ZOUBIR Yahyia, "In Search of Hegemony: The Western Sahara in Algerian-Moroccan Relations", *Journal of Algerian Studies*, Vol. 2, 1997.

INDEX